DATE DUE

A CENTURY OF CHINESE REVOLUTION

A Century of
Chinese Revolution
1851-1949

WOLFGANG FRANKE

6689

University of South Carolina Press
Columbia, South Carolina

Translated by STANLEY RUDMAN from
Das Jahrhundert der Chinesischen Revolution, 1851–1949
by permission of R. Oldenbourg Verlag, Munich

Published 1970 in Great Britain by
BASIL BLACKWELL & MOTT, LTD.
49 Broad Street, Oxford

and in the United States of America by the
UNIVERSITY OF SOUTH CAROLINA PRESS
Columbia, S.C.   29208

Standard Book Number: 87249–145–5
Library of Congress Catalog Card Number: 72–113808
Manufactured in Great Britain

Contents

Preface to the English Edition

More than a decade has passed since the original German version of this book was written and published. In the meantime much additional research in the field of modern and contemporary Chinese history has been done and the results published in numerous books and articles. In order to incorporate the results of all these researches perhaps an entirely new book should have been written. The present writer, however, holds the opinion that notwithstanding all new researches his approach still has its points. Therefore only a few evident mistakes or statements superseded by recent events or otherwise have been eliminated or modified. To this purpose use has been made of the criticism expressed in some reviews of the original German version and of remarks made privately by several friends. I am indebted in particular to Dr Josef Fass of Prague, who was kind enough to draw the author's attention to a number of questionable statements. The title has been modified purposely from 'Das Jahrhundert' to 'A Century' which seems to be more appropriate.

The greatest changes have been made in the Select Bibliography. In the original version particular consideration was given to titles in German. These are for the most part omitted in the present edition. Only the titles of those German books and articles which provided important information and/or particular points of view to the author are still listed. A number of new works in English published after the original version of this book are added, in order to draw the reader's attention to important recent publications from which he can get additional information. The bibliography, however, is selective and therefore necessarily incomplete and subjective.

WOLFGANG FRANKE

June, 1969

Preface to the German Edition

The present book grew out of an article, 'The Stages of the Revolution in China', suggested by Professor Dr Werner Conze when I gave a lecture on the Chinese revolution and its underlying causes at the University of Münster in May, 1952. The idea of looking at the Chinese revolution as a series of stages proved a useful working hypothesis, which made it possible to trace the extremely complex development of China over the last hundred years and enclose it within a framework that could be taken in at a glance. Since the book is not intended simply to give a history of China over the last hundred years but rather the stages in the development of the revolution in China, this governed the selection of material. Only what was of direct importance to the theme could be taken into consideration; everything else had to be omitted. Thus, for instance, the frequent fighting between the different war-lords in the 1920s is not discussed because it is of only minor importance for the development of the revolution.

The present book is not intended primarily for specialists in the study of modern Chinese history, since the historical facts underlying the present study will be known to them. The author is chiefly concerned to make the results of modern scholarship in this field available to a wider circle of readers, so that they may understand the development of the Chinese revolution. That is also the reason for avoiding detailed reference to sources in the text. Works which have been used are cited in the bibliography at the end. No less important than such written works, however, are the personal experiences of the author during his thirteen-year stay in China from 1937 to 1950, when he was in constant touch with all sections of the population and particularly with Chinese intellectuals. In fact, this book could never have been written in its present form without the constant exchange of ideas on all the questions considered here with Chün-yin Franke-Hu, an exchange which began when we first met in Peking in 1939. She herself belongs to that generation of Chinese students and intellectuals who had such a considerable influence on the revolution in the twenties, thirties and forties.

Well-known Chinese names and expressions are given in their familiar romanized form. In all other cases the Wade–Giles international system is used.

Hamburg, July, 1957

1

Introduction:
Revolutions in Chinese History

THE IMPORTANCE OF THE IDEA OF
REVOLUTION IN THE PAST

The usual Chinese expression for revolution is *ko-ming*. This expression consists of two Chinese characters, the first of which means 'skin' (of an animal), and then as a verb, 'to cast the skin, change, renew'. In this case the character is used as a verb. The second character means 'order, instruction, mandate'. Hence *ko-ming* means 'change of mandate'. The expression was not introduced in the 19th or 20th centuries, but is found in the oldest Chinese literature, as, for example, in the *I-ching*, the 'Canonical Book of Changes', or in the *Shu-ching*, the 'Canonical Book of Documents'. The present texts of these works come from the time about the birth of Christ, but they go back to sources which are centuries older. The expression *ko-ming* has been current in Chinese literature from that time right up to the present. Its content today unites traditional concepts from the earliest period with modern Western ideas and the Western concept of 'revolution'. Thus, the expression *ko-ming* is an excellent reflection of the character of the Chinese revolution. It combines, like the actual events, traditional native ideas and characteristics with modern imported Western ones, and this combination gives the Chinese revolution of the 19th and 20th centuries its distinctive character. In what follows special attention will be paid to the differentiation of these native and foreign elements.

In order to clarify the traditional significance of the expression *ko-ming*, it is necessary to refer briefly to the classical Chinese form and view of the state, in so far as they are relevant. The passing of the feudal state, which was already complete in the pre-Christian era, and the subsequent development towards the centralized, bureaucratic state, which was basically concluded by the 7th century A.D., can be omitted here. It is important, however, to recognize the position of the central ruler, the emperor, which, in theory at any rate, remained substantially the same from the first millennium B.C. to the end of the last dynasty in 1911. Such a theory, of course, did not prevent the real power of the emperor changing considerably in the course of history.

According to the universalistic world-view of classical China the state on earth should be organized like the arrangement of the stars in heaven. Just as in heaven the pole-star is set firmly in the centre, and all other stars circle round it, so on earth the central ruler, as the son of heaven, should be the fixed pole round which mankind revolves. The central ruler is commissioned by heaven and is the connecting link between heaven and earth, between heaven and men. It is this mandate, in Chinese *ming*, that is referred to in the expression *ko-ming*. Heaven bestows its mandate on the worthiest of men. But heaven is free to recall this mandate at any time, if need be, and to give it to someone else more worthy. In this respect heaven corresponds to the wishes of the people:

'Heaven sees as my people see; Heaven hears as my people hear,' according to the 'Canonical Book of Documents'.[1] The legendary rulers of antiquity are said to have succeeded one another on the throne purely on the grounds of personal worth and not because of any dynastic principle. The establishment of an hereditary dynasty already counted as a deviation from the ideal path. On the other hand, in accordance with the empirical situation, the idea of the mandate from heaven was attached more to the whole ruling house of a family, i.e. a dynasty, than to the individual monarch. Thus, every ruler had to reckon with the possibility of losing the mandate of heaven not only for himself but also for his dynasty, if he proved unworthy of his position.

At the same time the oldest, pre-Christian writing contains the teaching of the 'five elements', fire, water, earth, wood and metal, each of which rules in turn, until replaced by the succeeding element. This succession of the 'five elements' was also linked with the

1. Legge, *The Chinese Classics*, III, Pt. II, p. 292.

succession of dynasties. Each dynasty represented one of the five elements, and like its element had to submit to being replaced by its successor. About the time of Christ's birth the idea also developed that heaven revealed its will regarding a new ruler or new dynasty by special signs. Such portents, it was thought, must unmistakably have directed the eyes of men in olden times to the successor chosen by heaven. At a later date particularly zealous founders of dynasties and their followers sometimes regarded it as their own responsibility to arrange such signs.

In order to accomplish such a change of its mandate, *ko-ming*, heaven made use of the people and the officials as its instruments. The result of this view of the position of the emperor was that the overthrow, by force if necessary, of a ruler or dynasty that had lost the mandate of heaven, could be regarded as legitimate according to the Chinese theory of the state. This view can be supported by certain passages in the Canonical Writings, which were regarded as absolutely authoritative in classical China. The importance of the people in relation to the ruler also has a bearing on this. Thus, Mencius, a particnlarly important author for the Confucian view of the state, who lived in the 4th century B.C., says:

The people are the most important element in a nation; the spirits of the land and grain (i.e. the state in all essentials) are the next; the sovereign is the least.

Or in another passage:

If the prince has great faults, the chief ministers who are noble and relatives of the prince ought to remonstrate with him; and if he does not listen to them after they have done so again and again, they ought to dethrone him.[1]

Mencius also quotes the passage from the 'Book of Documents' to which we have referred. He regards the murder of a wicked ruler, such as the tyrant Chou, for instance, the last ruler of the Yin-dynasty towards the end of the second millennium B.C., as justified. The passage reads as follows:

May a minister put his sovereign to death? He who outrages the

1. Legge, *The Chinese Classics*, II, pp. 359 and 268.

benevolence proper to his nature, is called a robber; he who outrages righteousness, is called a ruffian. The robber and ruffian we call a mere fellow. I have heard of the cutting off of the fellow Chou, but I have not heard of the putting a sovereign to death in his case.[1]

The removal of the ruler Chou, therefore, is not regicide, but the legitimate punishment of a criminal. And in the same sense Mencius advises his liege-lord to get rid of the unworthy, contemporary ruler of a degenerate dynasty:

King Wu (the first ruler of the Chou dynasty), by one display of his anger, gave repose to all the people of the empire (by overthrowing the Yin dynasty). Now let your Majesty also, in one burst of anger, give repose to all the people of the empire (i.e. by the overthrow of the ruling dynasty).[2]

The same ideas and often the same quotations or references to the texts of the Canonical Writings recur regularly whenever a new dynasty officially assumes power, irrespective of whether it had really been commissioned by heaven and could establish itself permanently, or whether it had only usurped heaven's mandate and could not maintain itself for more than a few years in a limited part of the empire. The idea of legitimacy plays an important role in Chinese political history. The official imperial history makes the last ruler of the Han dynasty in A.D. 220 hand over power to the first emperor of the new dynasty in the following words:

O thou, King of Wei! In ancient time the Emperor Yao relinquished the throne of his own free will in favour of Shun from Yü; and Shun gave the mandate to Yü.[3] Heaven's mandate is not permanent; it is given only to the virtuous. The rule of Han has expired; the world has lost its order. Thus, the trouble has reached me. Serious disturbances are creating confusion; all sorts of disaster are erupting unbridled; revolution rules the world.

Then he praises the King of Wei as the one who is to succeed him on the ground of his outstanding qualities:

1. Ibid., p. 43.
2. Ibid., p. 33.
3. The name of Shun's birthplace and the name of his successor sound the same, but they have nothing to do with each other; their written characters are quite different.

Heaven's mandate rests in thy person; preserve the empire uprightly and thou shalt possess the gifts of heaven eternally.[1]

A further example of this sort is worth noting. In the year A.D. 557 the northern Wei dynasty was overthrown by the House of the northern Chou. The last Wei ruler surrendered his power to the Chou in an edict, which says among other things:

I have heard that the mandate of the majestic heaven is not permanent and is bestowed only on the virtuous. As Yao gave the rule to Shun, and Shun gave the rule to Yü, it is now time to do likewise. Heaven abhors my land of Wei and has revealed this by bringing about a rebellion. This is well known to you. Even if I am ignorant, how could I dare not to surrender the mandate of heaven with due respect, so that it might be given to the virtuous! Now I follow the ancient rule of the T'ang (Yao) and Yü (Shun) and abdicate the throne of my own free will in favour of Chou.[2]

Such declarations on the part of the overthrown emperor could hardly have been made on his own initiative; they must have been due to a greater or lesser degree to the coercion of his victorious opponent. But the significant fact is that the victor and the historians of later times lay weight on such declarations.

A particularly authoritarian ruler, the first emperor of the Ming dynasty at the end of the 14th century, thought the passages just quoted and similar texts must constitute a danger to the stability of his own and his dynasty's rule. Accordingly he had the *Book of Mencius* summarily removed from the official Canon and also from the syllabus and examination for the civil service. Subsequently, however, because of the force of opinion among the officials and his closer associates the emperor had to agree to a compromise, with the result that only certain particularly offensive passages of the *Book of Mencius*, such as those quoted above, were omitted and a shorter text was introduced for official use.

Whereas Mencius lived at a time when there was nothing more to expect from the Chou dynasty and the only hope was the establishment of a new ruling house, Confucius, who lived about two hundred years earlier—at the turn of the 6th–5th century B.C.—

1. *San kuo chih*, ed. Wu-chou t'ung-wen, 2, 4b–5a. Cf. Otto Franke, *Geschichte des Chinesischen Reiches*, II, 4–5.

2. *Chou shu*, 3, 16b. Cf. Otto Franke, op. cit., II, 235.

regarded the strengthening of the Chou dynasty as the best way
to recovery from the troubles of the time. And yet about the time
of the birth of Christ there was a very influential school that based
itself on Confucius and sought to interpret him as a revolutionary,
who had set out in his works, especially in the 'Spring and Autumn
Annals' (Ch'un-ch'iu), which was looked upon as a textbook of
the principles of government, the right lines and basic rules for a
new dynasty. This new dynasty, of which Confucius was designated
the uncrowned king, was to succeed that of the Chou. The Reform
Movement of 1898, which we shall discuss later (pp. 39 ff.), was
based largely on this Confucian school.

THE COURSE OF REVOLUTIONS IN THE PAST

So far we have been dealing with the theory of revolution, *ko-ming*,
in the Chinese conception of the state. But in order to understand
its development in the 19th and 20th centuries it is important also
to see how revolutions in China took place at an earlier period.
The era that was coming to an end in the last centuries of the first
millennium B.C., an era that was very similar to the age of feudalism
in Europe, was succeeded in China not by a bourgeois society as in
the West but by a bureaucratic society, which is often referred to
in modern works as 'gentry' society. By virtue of the fact that
they combined ownership of land, education and official status the
gentry were, in fact, the ruling class. They were already establishing themselves as such in the first century A.D.; the power of the
feudal lords was over. The power of the gentry depended on their
social position. Theoretically any peasant, worker or merchant
could become one of the gentry. In many periods such social
climbing—and likewise decline—was comparatively frequent. At
other times it was rare or virtually impossible. The Chinese
emperor could usually not rely on his own power, but was very
largely dependent—in different degrees at different times, of
course—on the gentry. With certain exceptions he could even be
described as their champion. Changes of ruling dynasty, which were
fairly frequent in the first millennium A.D., apart from the almost
300-year rule of the T'ang dynasty, could occur in three different
ways:

1. As a result of the invasion of foreign peoples, whose leader became the Chinese emperor, as for example in the case of the Mongols in the 13th century or the Manchus in the 17th century.
2. As a result of a rival gentry group coming to power.
3. As a result of peasant revolts.

In all three cases, as a rule, peasant revolts would already have contributed substantially to the weakening of the ruling dynasty, even if other forces usually took the final step in overthrowing the old and setting up a new ruling house. Only infrequently were peasant leaders able to assert themselves and found a new dynasty. These cases are of particular interest in studying the course of past revolutions.

Throughout its history China has always been a land of farmers. The peasant class consisted for the most part of small farmers or tenant farmers. Outside of Manchuria, which has only recently been opened up as colonial territory, there were no large agricultural enterprises. The peasants either owned or rented the land they farmed: or they may have combined the two—owning part and renting part. Sometimes they farmed either totally or partially rented land and let their own land for hire. The larger landowners— primarily gentry families—did not farm their own land but lived on the incoming dues, sometimes in the country, sometimes in the towns. They not only collected rent for their own property but were often employed by the government to collect the taxes due to the state from the independent farmers of their area. Officials and other gentry families were excused from all public duties or from the taxes which took the place of such public service and in addition they not infrequently used their privileged social position to evade in various ways the taxes they should legally have paid. Thus eventually all taxes and duties had to be paid very largely by the non-privileged section of the population, i.e. primarily the peasants. Even in times of orderly government and stable economic relationships the peasants faced heavy demands from the state in the form of taxes and state-duties. Frugal means and an extremely strong, passive power of resistance on the part of the Chinese peasants together with the possible last resort of flight usually set certain limits to the caprice and encroachment of the officials and landowners and thus contributed towards a tolerable *modus vivendi*.

In times of political and economic decline, however, the pressure on the peasants increased until it finally became intolerable for many of them. If the harvest failed or other natural disasters also supervened many peasants could no longer pay the required taxes and were compelled to sell their land or surrender it. Land prices sank and rich gentry families accumulated more and more land. Ruined peasants had to leave their homes and took to roaming the countryside as bandits. In the distress and uncertainty in which they found themselves they quickly banded together. They were ready for anything, for they had nothing to lose. Such a peasant revolt could quickly seize whole districts and provinces, for secret societies and sects were scattered everywhere, smouldering like embers. In times of trouble, sparked off by natural catastrophe or human folly, they could suddenly blaze up into the bright flame of rebellion, in which social and religious elements were united. Wolfram Eberhard, after examining numerous peasant revolts, which showed consistently similar characteristics on a large scale, mapped out the following pattern of development in four stages:

First stage: for a variety of reasons which cannot be discussed in detail here, the economic position of the peasants over a fairly large area became intolerable. Groups of peasants had to leave their homes and banded together and fled into the mountains or other remote regions. They became robbers and lived by attacking travellers and rich landowners. Usually they maintained contact with their native villages in such a way that the bands in the mountains received a regular tribute from the nearest well-to-do landowner and provisions etc. from the villagers. In return they protected the village in question against attacks by other bands.

Second stage: the band grows, extends its radius of action and thus comes into conflict with other bands. The result is a struggle in which the superior band with the most capable leader absorbs the remainder of the defeated group and establishes sole control over an even larger area.

Third stage: as a result of this extension of power the band's initial link with the home village or villages has to cease. Protection against other bands is no longer necessary, since the band in question is now in control of the whole region. The landowners begin to resist the increasing demands of the band and refuse to pay. In order to cut off support from the landowners and to cover their own needs the band feels compelled to attack the nearest unwalled town, usually the administrative centre for the area. The local government had previously been warned by the gentry and had made preparations for defence. The attack on the town may have been doomed to failure from the start. Then the large band often split up once more into smaller groups and the same performance began afresh. Alternatively, a siege might be undertaken. In this case it sometimes happened that the government troops who were stationed there had no desire to fight for the government and were in sympathy with the rebels. In such a situation the officials and gentry had to decide either to fight to the bitter end and risk losing their lives or to surrender, in the hope of saving their lives. But in the latter event they were regarded as allies of the bandits by the government and they had to throw in their lot with the rebels.

Fourth stage: in order to satisfy their increased need for provisions and equipment, after conquering a town the bandits felt compelled to subdue other towns and to defend themselves against the now alerted government and its troops. As a rule the leaders of the bands lacked the necessary experience and they sought advice from the educated and more experienced members of the gentry who had come over to their side. These members of the gentry usually persuaded the robber-leaders to recognize or adopt the mode of life and point of view of the gentry. The leader of the band became a general or prince or even emperor, who could no longer do without the collaboration and support of the gentry; in fact, without them he felt helpless. Thus a revolutionary often became an upholder of traditional ideas.

This was Eberhard's way of reducing Chinese revolutions to general terms. In fact, ever since the beginning of the Christian era up to the 19th and 20th centuries rebellions and revolutions have taken this basic form. In spite of poor weapons, equipment, and organization the rebels often proved superior to the government troops. The rebels were poor and had nothing to lose apart

from their lives, which they normally had to surrender without
demur in case of defeat. Every victory, however, and every conquest of a new town could bring an improvement in their position,
even if only small at times, in the form of food, clothing and
equipment. In contrast, the government troops were as a rule well
provided with these necessities, they tended to be unused to
fighting and were addicted to a dissolute life. Few had volunteered
to become soldiers and they were far from their homes and families.
If they abandoned a town and fled before the enemy to more secure
regions their pattern of life was hardly altered at all. If they joined
the insurgents they were generally sure of a good reception. Many
were 'converted', so to speak, by the rebels, and were induced to
join them and fight on their side. If, on the other hand, they did
resist the rebels, they would be risking their lives for nothing. But
why should they do that for a worthless dynasty, a corrupt
government and a profiteering gentry? Only individual able and
brave commanders, who had themselves set their subordinates a
good example, succeeded in suppressing rebellions in times when a
dynasty was already at the stage of inner collapse. In fact, in the
last two thousand years of Chinese history only a few decades have
been entirely free from such rebellions. There were usually disturbances of some sort somewhere in the large empire. In bad times
the flames of rebellion flared up everywhere and soon became a
great conflagration which not infrequently brought the ruling
dynasty to the brink of disaster. Often in such cases it was saved
not by its own power but by the internecine strife of the different
revolutionary leaders and groups. Sometimes, too, the Chinese
dynasty invoked foreign aid in the fight against the rebels in return
for certain concessions in foreign policy. Time after time, Turks,
Uigurs, Tibetans and other steppe-peoples saved the ruling Chinese
dynasty from complete destruction. In the 17th century the
Ming dynasty, which was already on the verge of collapse as a
result of internal revolution, tried to prevent their fate by calling
in the Manchus, but on this occasion the approved method did not
help. The Manchus did, in fact, succeed in becoming masters of the
Chinese rebellion: but at the same time they also dealt the final
blow to the Ming dynasty. They founded their own dynasty in
China and ruled until 1911.

So far we have only discussed the social element in popular uprisings. In most cases, however, there was also a religious element. Alongside the official Confucian doctrine, on which state, society and family in China were based since the beginning of the Christian era, the teachings of Buddhism and Taoism, which were ultimately essentially hostile to the state and society, played no small role. Whereas Confucianism, which was unreservedly life-affirming, provided the standard and guide line for public and family life, Buddhist and Taoist teachings pointed the way to resignation and rejection of the world, as well as to the struggle against the existing order of state and society. Apart from the generally recognized forms of Buddhism and Taoism there were innumerable sects throughout the land, combining the most heterogeneous doctrines, and having a strong superstitious belief in signs and wonders from heaven, in prophets, in the approach of a new world-order and in the invulnerability of the sectarians, etc. These sectarian religious elements, when joined to an insurrectionary movement of oppressed peasants, often produced the sort of religious fanaticism which gave the revolutionary movement its real power and thrust.

Revolutionaries of the sort described could often maintain their independence alongside the official government for years and sometimes even decades in certain areas. On occasion they even styled themselves 'emperor' and had a court and ceremonial such as the official doctrine of the state prescribed. Only on three occasions in Chinese history, however, did a bandit-leader of the most humble origin succeed in founding a legitimate dynasty officially recognized as such by posterity. The first was the founder of the Han dynasty at the end of the 3rd century B.C. This is a special case because it occurred towards the end of the feudal era and the social factors at that time were substantially different from those obtaining later in the society of the gentry. The second case was the Later Liang dynasty. In 907 their founder took the place of the T'ang dynasty, which had ruled for 300 years: it was under the first rulers of this dynasty that China had reached its highest cultural and political peak. The Later Liang dynasty, however, was unable to survive more than two decades. Their two rulers did not succeed—obviously they also lacked the requisite personal qualities—in consolidating their rule and establishing themselves throughout China. Even if later Chinese historians recognized this dynasty as legitimate, this cannot be accepted as an unimpeachable criterion. The Later Liang dynasty achieved *de facto* recognition of their rule in only one part of the empire (i.e. central and east China on both sides of the Yellow River), even if it was a significant part: they had many similarities with the innumerable 'illegitimate' dynasties which were founded by revolutionaries in various regions, which existed independently alongside the official 'legitimate' dynasty for as long as ten years and sometimes even longer. They were in no position, however, to overthrow the dynasty and finally they themselves perished. In the case of the Later Liang dynasty, however, it was not the previous legitimate dynasty, which had already been overthrown, that brought their rule to an end but a foreign people, the Turkish Sha-t'o, who replaced the Later Liang dynasty with their own (Later T'ang). It is significant, however, that the founder of the Later Liang dynasty, a revolutionary leader who was the product of a peasant revolt, was ultimately unable to establish himself throughout the empire in the way that was possible earlier in the case of the Han dynasty, which ruled for about 400 years, or later in the case of the Ming dynasty, which was able to hold out for nearly 300 years. The Ming dynasty is the third and most characteristic instance of a revolutionary from the lowest class of the poorest peasants establishing a legitimate dynasty. It offers a number of parallels to the events of recent decades and for that reason deserves to be discussed a little more fully.

THE REVOLUTION AT THE END OF THE MONGOL PERIOD AND THE FOUNDING OF THE MING DYNASTY

The Mongols ruled large parts of China from the beginning of the 13th century. In the second half of the century they destroyed the remaining survivors of the native Sung dynasty and extended their sway over the whole of China and even beyond. The Mongol Khan became Emperor of China. By transferring his residence and the Mongolian centre of power from the steppes to China the Mongolian ruling house, which was rude and warlike in origin, and the Mongolian nobility were uprooted. The Mongols succumbed to the

influence of the refined Chinese culture, which counteracted their
warlike ways, and made them receptive to the pleasures of a higher
civilization. Signs of decadence and decline soon began to show
themselves. At the same time the social and economic position of
the country soon became intolerable. The Mongolian steppe-
dwellers had little understanding of the needs of the land-tilling
peasants and of their hard struggle for existence. The peasants
were disregarded and cruelly exploited, until they were soon
unable to carry the burdens placed on them. They had to provide
food not only for the Chinese gentry, as at other times, but also for
a great number of foreign government officials and merchants,
whom the Mongols had brought into the country. In addition, the
members of a vast number of entirely tax-free monasteries belonging to different religious groups lived on the work and produce of
the peasants. This state of affairs could not last for ever. Moreover,
under cover of the monastic exemption from taxes many private
businessmen and landowners tried to conceal what they owned in
order to avoid paying taxes. A constant deficit at the Treasury led
to the issue of paper money, which was not covered by solid reser-
ves, and hence to inflation. Thus, large areas of China that had
once been prosperous became poor. On top of this there was the
demoralization caused by Mongolian regulations, sometimes particularly discriminatory against the Chinese. For example, no Chinese
person could own weapons, military equipment or horses; no
Chinese person could hold important offices in the government—
these were reserved exclusively for Mongols and other foreigners;
the Chinese were forbidden to learn either the Mongol script or the
Arabic script which was used by the numerous Muslims who were
employed by the Mongols. Even if it was impracticable to see that
all these and numerous other prohibitions were carried out, so that
they had to be repealed in part for longer or shorter periods, they
nevertheless served to increase the hatred of the Chinese for their
foreign oppressors.

   In addition to such predominantly political abuses, there was a
series of serious natural catastrophes: there were drought and
floods (especially between 1333 and 1348) and in A.D. 1351 the
Yellow River of south Shantung and north Kiangsu changed its
course. If such natural catastrophes occur in times of stability a

certain measure of relief is perhaps possible; but in times of trouble they have a devastating effect and are regarded by the people as a sign from heaven that the existing dynasty has had its mandate withdrawn. In fact, there was often a close connection between natural catastrophes and decline in the political order: irrigation works and dikes were neglected, the transport system did not function, agricultural land was allowed to lie fallow by the peasants because of their impossible burdens, the granaries were empty. Thus, irregularities in the weather, which in more settled times could have been dealt with by taking precautions, easily developed into catastrophes. Thus, in the middle of the 14th century peasant revolts broke out everywhere and escalated in the way we have just described.

These revolts were also connected to a large extent with the 'Sect of the White Lotus', a popular cult derived from Buddhism and Taoism but with elements of magic and superstition and of other religions, particularly Manichæism. Its origin goes back to the 4th century A.D. At the turn of the 18th and 19th centuries it inspired a serious rebellion and after 1950 sects that stemmed from it[1] provoked strong military reprisals on the part of the Communist government. Whether they succeeded in rooting it out completely and permanently remains to be seen. In the middle of the 14th century the 'Sect of the White Lotus' awoke to new life in many quarters of China. With the slogan 'The world-empire is in rebellion, Buddha-Maitreya is born again, an enlightened ruler will appear', the prophets of the sect attracted a large following among the wretched peasants, especially in the provinces of Honan, north Anhui and north Kiangsu. One of these prophets claimed to be a descendant of the Sung ruling house and declared that the Mongol dynasty was deposed. Even at this stage the combination of religious and political elements is noticeable. The prophet and his followers tied a red piece of cloth round their heads for a badge. Thus they became known in history as the 'Rebels of the Red Turban'. The movement grew rapidly. Numerous subordinate officers formed *de facto* independent groups and roamed through the land plundering with their followers, who numbered up to

1. For example, the 'all-embracing doctrine', *I-kuan tao*.

100,000 men and more. Another centre of rebellion was the border territory of Hupei and Anhui, north of the Yangtze. Here a former draper together with a Buddhist priest, who was also wearing the badge of the 'Red Turban', had assumed leadership of the rebels and extended their sway over large parts of Hupei and Kiangsi. Subordinate officers, who soon made themselves independent, conducted their raids as far as Anhui-Kiangsu and Chekiang in the East: one of them marched in a westerly direction as far as Szechwan and there established his own kingdom, which lasted more than ten years. Szechwan is one of the most fertile and richly endowed parts of China. Natural boundaries separate it on all sides from neighbouring territories, so that it has always led a markedly independent life and has had periods of complete or substantial independence even until recently. In Kiangsu and Chekiang the salt-carrying boatmen had formed a large band independent of the 'Red Turbans'. At first their insurrection was directed only against the local gentry, with whom they had come into conflict; but it rapidly assumed greater proportions. The coast of Chekiang was under the control of a powerful pirate chief and his band. Numerous smaller rebel-groups formed in other parts of the kingdom. Thus about the middle of the 14th century the whole country was in turmoil. Even if they were not conscious of it, all the rebels had essentially the same goal—war against the rich gentry, against foreign oppressors and their native underlings, who today in communist terminology would be called the 'running dogs' of the foreigners. In spite of their common aims the separate groups, even different groups of the 'Red Turbans', had so strong a desire for independence that they campaigned against each other with extreme ferocity. But the government forces were also corrupt and divided as well, to such an extent that they too fought among themselves. Individual successes of the government troops against the rebels could not be fully exploited and followed up in the way that suppression of the rebels required. Everyone was fighting each other and the government had to look on almost powerlessly.

In the year 1352 one of the leaders of the 'Red Turbans' was joined by Chu Yüan-chang, a poor, orphaned son of a peasant, who, lacking any other means of making a living, had wandered about the country for several years as a mendicant friar. He now joined the rebel-army as a simple soldier, distinguished himself by bravery and prudence and thus quickly became the leader of a small company. As such he persuaded several hundred young people from his home-town, mostly sons of impoverished peasants like himself, to join the 'Red Turbans'. A number of these fellow-countrymen became his closest companions. After the death of the leader of the 'Red Turbans' whose troops he had joined, Chu made himself practically independent, even though he continued to profess allegiance to the 'Sect of the White Lotus' and its leader. By prudence and cunning and the loyal support of his fellows Chu gradually succeeded in deposing successive leaders of the 'Red Turbans' or in bringing them under his sway. He trained and disciplined his own troops so well that they were superior to all opponents in battle. Moreover, he took great pains to ensure that his own troops treated the peasants well, and did not plunder or steal from them. Thus he gained the support of most of the poor over a wide area. Soon Chu Yüan-chang had built up a considerable dominion in Anhui and Kiangsu with Nanking as the centre. But it was hardly feasible to consolidate his power by the methods of the sectarian peasant revolution he had used so far and with the help of illiterate confederates from the lowest classes. Despite his unpromising position Chu had the cleverness and critical insight to recognize his weakness. His opportunity came when in 1360 several highly educated scholars from the rich and powerful gentry of Chekiang joined him. They recognized Chu's prospects and were prepared to back him. These scholars now became his most important advisers in all non-military matters.

There followed further struggles and clashes with the government troops of the Mongol dynasty and with other powerful leaders of the strong rebel groups. Some of these latter had already been proclaimed king or emperor in their own territory and had thus staked a claim to the succession of the dying Mongol dynasty. Yet Chu Yüan-chang finally proved stronger than the Mongols as well as his rivals. In 1367 he founded the new Chinese Ming dynasty in Nanking, the 'Southern Capital', and in the following year his troops captured Peking, the capital of the Mongols. The last Mongol ruler fled homewards, to the steppe-country of Mongolia. In the following years Chu Yüan-chang succeeded in pacifying the whole kingdom, in reintroducing stable economic conditions and in securing the throne for himself and his descendants.

In considering the significance of revolution in Chinese history it is important to pick out briefly the characteristic elements of the revolution in the 14th century. Chu Yüan-chang was a poor, uneducated peasant, later a mendicant friar. As such he had traversed wide areas in north Anhui and east Honan, gaining experience of social conditions, and becoming acquainted with the 'Sect of the White Lotus'. As a convinced follower of this sect he had entered the army of the 'Red Turbans'. His closest circle of followers, who also formed the kernel of his troops, consisted of fellow-townsmen and blood relatives. He extended the number of blood relatives by means of the so-called 'adoptive sons' (*i-êrh*). For this purpose he selected the most able of his soldiers in order to attach them especially to himself. In doing this he successfully revived an old Chinese custom. Altogether he had more than twenty such adopted sons of whom several fell in battle. Soon after his official accession to the throne Chu Yüan-chang forbade this practice in view of his own experiences.

Initially Chu Yüan-chang was a sincere follower of the 'Sect of the White Lotus'. The rebellions of this and other sects were at first of a purely social nature, but steeped in religious superstition. They were directed at first with no clear aim against rich land-owners, merchants, etc., both Chinese and foreign. Almost all the leaders of the different insurrectionary movements came from the poorest and lowest strata of society. On the other hand, the surviving Chinese gentry at first ranged themselves on the side of the Mongol dynasty. The local militia which they organized began by playing an important part, together with the government troops, in resisting the rebellions, even if they later went over to the side of the rebels in ever greater numbers. The nationalistic element which had found its most obvious expression in the alleged restoration of the Sung dynasty was at first quite subordinate, but gained increasing importance with the rise of Chu Yüan-chang and finally became the most important factor in the revolution. At first the revolution relied entirely on the poor peasants, but now all China rallied together in the fight against the foreigner. In contrast to the cruel outrages perpetrated everywhere by the government troops some of the revolutionaries had practised discipline from an early stage, especially in their treatment of the poor. Under Chu Yüan-chang's leadership this discipline was visibly improved and generally made effective. The gentry joined the rebels of their own free will, as soon as they felt that the rebels had abandoned their purely social-revolutionary platform and were, furthermore, in a position to restore law and order. A change in Chu Yüan-chang's position from proletarian revolutionary to upholder of traditional order in state and society gradually followed through the influence of his gentry-advisers. They explained to him the importance of Confucian doctrines about the state, and made it clear that only on the basis of these could he really unite and control the empire. The result justified their advice. The traditional order of society with the gentry as the ruling class was continued by the new dynasty after it came to power. A number of the old gentry families, especially those which had joined Chu Yüan-chang at an early date, survived and to a large extent retained their possessions. Others were annihilated or disappeared completely. Their place was taken by rising new families, Chu Yüan-chang's companions and helpers in the revolutionary struggle, men mostly from the lowest class of society. The lot of the poor peasants and tenant-farmers improved somewhat as a result of a partial redistribution of land and reduction of taxes and rent-interest. There was also an overall improvement as a result of the creation of stable political and economic conditions. Fundamentally, however, the agrarian situation remained the same, with gentry-landowners and the few peasants who had large or medium-sized farms on the one side, and the large number of small farmers and leaseholders on the other side. This revolution, then, brought no change in the existing order of society, in spite of great changes within the ruling gentry-class.

2   Precursors of the 20th Century Revolutionary Movement

THE TAIPING REVOLUTION (1851–64)

Introduction

The Taiping revolution was one of the greatest revolutionary movements not only in China but in the whole history of the world. It affected the whole of central China as well as large parts of the North and South, altogether an area with more than a hundred million inhabitants. Approximately twenty million people are reputed to have lost their lives during the fifteen-year struggle.

The Taiping revolution reveals in essence the traditional character of Chinese peasant revolutions, as sketched briefly in the previous chapter. Like the great revolution at the end of the Mongol period it unites social, religious and nationalistic elements. Alongside the traditional ingredients, however, there occur for the first time elements which go back directly or indirectly to Western influences. This in itself is sufficient justification for regarding the Taiping revolution as a precursor of the revolutionary movement of the 20th century; in addition, the events of the 1850s and 1860s played a large part in setting the scene for the great upheavals of the 20th century. The new, foreign elements—as the following pages will show—are found firstly in the events leading up to the Taiping revolution, secondly and chiefly in the religious and social ideology of the revolutionaries, and finally also in its suppression, when the attitude of foreign powers—especially England and France—played a not unimportant role.

Well into the 20th century it was customary in China to describe and assess the Taiping revolution from the standpoint of the Manchu dynasty, which was still recognized as legitimate, as if it were nothing more than a 'rebellion'. Consequently it is known in the West as the 'Taiping rebellion' or the 'Taiping uprising'. But with the beginning of the anti-Manchu, revolutionary movement of Sun Yat-sen and even more after the downfall of the dynasty of 1911, a revaluation gradually took place. In the last thirty years, apart from close associates of Chiang Kai-shek or other outspoken conservative circles, the Taiping revolution has been regarded in China as a first stage of the modern revolution—with different nuances, of course, depending on the standpoint of the observer. This view is to be found not only among authors who sympathize with the Kuomintang or the Communists but also among politically independent personalities. Since there is no reason for us to judge events from the viewpoint of the last Chinese dynasty, we shall refer to it as the Taiping revolution. Even among the contemporaries of the Taiping revolution there were some who clearly recognized its significance at the time. In 1852 Dr Hobson, Bishop of Hong Kong, wrote as follows about the revolution which had just begun:

This movement is the most important epoch in the modern history of China, and these occurrences are but ushering in events of almost unparalleled magnitude, and on an almost unexampled scale, for the political, social, moral and religious emancipation of China.[1]

Dr Hobson's premonitions about future developments proved correct.

The Underlying Causes of the Taiping Revolution

In the first half of the 17th century the Manchus had forced their way into China from the northeast and had raised their own ruling house to the throne of China as the Ch'ing dynasty. The second ruler of the dynasty, best known by the name he took as emperor, K'ang Hsi (1662–1722), was one of the greatest and most important rulers China has ever had. Under his successors the dynasty was already past its peak, and after the end of the 18th century decline quickly set in. As at other times, signs of decadence at court and in the central government led to mismanagement in the provinces. There was extensive corruption and greed among officials. In order

1. Quoted from Ssu-yü Teng, *New Light on the History of the Taiping Rebellion*, Harvard University Press, 1950, p. 37.

to cover the financial needs of the government the sale of official positions assumed increasingly greater proportions. The purchaser of such a position often had to borrow the necessary money, which then had to be recovered as quickly as possible by means of his official position. In fact, one of the reasons for buying office was the desire to make a large personal profit. Taxes, which nominally were not too high, were arbitrarily doubled, trebled or even more heavily increased by the local officials and the landlords who also acted as tax-collectors. Thus, economic failure followed hard on the heels of political decline. The great majority of peasants had no protection against the exploitation of officials and gentry; land ownership was concentrated more and more in the hands of those who were not themselves active farmers, and the condition of most of the rural population was pitiable. Of course, even then many of these landlords possessed only a few acres of land. Large *latifundia*, which we sometimes associate with the term 'landlord' in Europe, were almost unknown in China.

On top of these abuses, which also caused popular uprisings at other times, the middle of the 19th century brought an additional special factor, namely the extraordinarily swift and unexpected increase in population. After the restoration of stable conditions under the new dynasty towards the end of the 17th century the population of China had grown enormously. Even if the entries in the official registers are only approximately correct, the population had more than doubled by the middle of the 19th century. Thus, within a century, from 1751 to 1851, the total population of China had risen from over 180 million to over 430 million.[1] The area of cultivated land, however, had not increased in anything like the same proportion. There was no industry to absorb the surplus population, no territory to which it might migrate. Manchuria, the home of the ruling dynasty, which later became an important area for colonization, was still barred to Chinese settlers. The only alternative, therefore, was further division and more intensive cultivation of land that was already being used; poverty and the lowering of living standards were the inevitable consequence for the great majority.

1. *Kao-tsung shih-lu*, 405, 19b; *Wen-tsung shih-lu*, 50, 33b.

The position was aggravated by a further factor: the impact of Western imperialism now being felt for the first time. Whereas the balance of trade had previously been in China's favour, since the beginning of the 19th century the import of goods from abroad, especially opium, had risen steeply compared with exports. As a result large quantities of silver had been exported from China to other countries and inflation had been the result. Before the beginning of the 19th century an ounce of silver was worth one thousand copper coins; in 1835 the rate of exchange was one ounce to two thousand. The great majority of the population usually used copper coins to pay for goods. Prices for agricultural products were reckoned in copper. But taxes had to be paid in silver. Thus, for the peasant, taxes were doubled simply by the alteration in the rate of exchange, since he was paid for his work in copper as before. A series of natural disasters between 1826 and 1850 had the usual effect of preparing the ground for a revolutionary uprising in many parts of the kingdom.

The political and economic position as a whole at that time is vividly summed up in the petition of a high-ranking imperial official at the beginning of the year 1852. Its author, Tseng Kuo-fan—not a Manchu, but Chinese—was the leading figure in the later successful suppression of the revolt. In his petition we read:

... The virtuous will of the sage emperor is not reaching the people, and the tribulations of the people cannot appeal to the emperor. Your minister takes the liberty of enumerating them.

Firstly, the price of silver is too high, and it is difficult to pay the taxes. . . . Previously an ounce of silver was worth a thousand copper coins, so that for a picul (= 133 lb.) of rice one received three ounces of silver. Today an ounce of silver is worth two thousand copper coins, so that for a picul of rice one receives only one and a half ounces of silver. Previously the sale of three pecks (1 peck = 13 lb.) of rice was equivalent to the land-tax on one *mou* (about one-sixth of an acre), with a margin to spare. Today the sale of six pecks of rice is not enough to pay the land-tax on one *mou*. The imperial government naturally adheres to the regular amount of the annual tax, but the poor people have to pay twice as much in taxes, although this is not made explicit. Moreover, taxes on household land or burial ground, which have to be paid in proportion to silver, are also double what they used to be.

Those who earn so little that they are unable to pay or have to be forced to pay because of the harvest-assessment are too numerous to count. The county and district prefects spend their entire strength in pressing for the payment of taxes. Because they are afraid they will not be paid, they frequently order employees to assist them and they dispatch subordinates and government runners everywhere. Day and night they harry and oppress the dilatory taxpayers with whippings and floggings. In every law-court the flesh and blood of those who are on trial for failing to pay their taxes is brutally and hastily spattered on the floor. Are such notions confined to cruel officials? No! For if they do not act in this way, they have the fear of being impeached if less than 70 per cent (of the required amount) has been collected when it's time to check their achievement; in this case they are responsible for what is missing, which might cost them tens of thousands, and thus store up trouble for their sons and heirs.

Before 1835 in Kiangsu the full amount of tax was paid. Since 1836 up to the present a poor harvest has been recorded every year, and every year taxes have to be remitted altogether or postponed. . . . Hence the method of 'cutting the money-string'.[1] This means that the autumn-tax is collected along with the previous spring-tax, and that the string of money for the following year is cut in this year (to pay the autumn-tax). If the poor people do not respond, then the tax is reduced a little, in order to induce them to come. If one cuts off too much in advance, then there is too much missing at the end, and when there is a change of official there is nothing left for his successor to collect. If a law-abiding official has no possibility of preserving his integrity, how much more pretext a greedy official has for treating the people as his fish and meat. By trickery and chicanery they get rid of those whose possessions they are after; they make unlawful and extortionate demands boldly and unscrupulously.

In Kiangsi, Hunan, and Hupei the level of taxation was lighter, but since the increase of the price of silver the payment of taxes has become increasingly difficult for the people and the threats and demands of the officials increasingly cruel. Sometimes if the family in question cannot pay, more prosperous members of the same tribe are arrested and made responsible for the payment instead of them. It has even gone so far that sometimes their relatives are arrested and their neighbours imprisoned. The people hate the officials who do this and resist them. This provokes

1. Chinese copper coins at that time had a hole in the centre and were threaded on a string in fixed amounts.

serious incidents, as at Lei-yang and Ch'ung-yang in Hunan and Hupei or at Kuei-hsi and Fu-chou in Kiangsi. Although the population was not free from refractoriness in these four incidents, they had some excuse in the doubling of the price of silver, in the excessive demands of the officials and the illegal punishments meted out by the government runners and servants. It really is true that people can no longer earn a living from one day to the next. That is the first thing your minister means by the needs of the people. Secondly, thieves and robbers are too numerous and it is difficult for honest people to live in peace. . . . It is reported recently that the disorder caused by bandits is increasing. They rob and plunder in broad daylight and they capture people and hold them to ransom. The people cannot avoid appealing to the officials, therefore. If the officials march out to arrest the bandits, they issue a public statement of their intentions beforehand, and when they reach the place the person on duty at the local centre of self-government has no hesitation in saying that the bandits have fled. In order to demonstrate their power the officials have the houses in the vicinity burnt down and then march off. The runners and servants exact money and property from the host who is paying the bill (i.e. the man who was robbed by the bandits and who appealed to the officials) and return home fully laden with the spoils. In fact, however, the bandits had not fled. Sometimes it is said—falsely—that a bandit has met his death. If the case (of the robbery by the bandits) cannot be cleared up, neither can the lost property be recovered and the family of the host who is footing the bill goes bankrupt. He can only swallow hard and drink his tears, with no power left to complain. But supposing he does complain and he is lucky enough to get soldiers sent out to resist the bandits and arrest them, the soldiers and officials are usually in league with the bandits and at a set time in return for a bribe they release the bandits in such a way that all traces of them completely disappear. Sometimes, on the other hand, they use the bandits as an excuse to intimidate the unintelligent villagers and to demand from them the payment of heavy bribes, or else they will brand them as abettors of the bandits. Then they burn their houses and arrest them. . . . Today there are law-breaking soldiers and greedy officials everywhere, who encourage the bandits and indulge them. Whenever one thinks of it, one's heart goes cold. . . . This is the second thing your minister means by distress among the people.

Thirdly, unjustified imprisonments are too numerous. . . . If a family has a court-case that remains undecided for any length of time, ten families are made bankrupt by it. If a person is falsely accused, a hundred people are compelled to suffer with him. Often a small, unimportant case remains undecided for years. Right and wrong are turned upside down and the accused grow old and die in prison. It makes one's hair stand on end to hear of it. This is yet another case of what your minister means by distress among the people.[1]

Indirectly the revolution was also assisted by China's defeat in the Opium War against England (1840–2). This not only weakened the prestige of the dynasty considerably, but it also contributed a great deal to the general demoralization of the Chinese government troops, accurately described by Tseng Kuo-fan again in an entry of 1851:

The soldiers have professional connections with the bandits. Moreover, they sit and smoke opium together in gaming dens. This is true of all the provinces, and in general, if nothing happens, they idle about with an arrogant air. When something does occur, they hire some tramps to take their place. If they catch sight of the bandits they look to the wind, take flight and scatter. If the bandits are elsewhere the soldiers kill a few people in order to pretend they have got results.[2]

Before the opium war foreign trade was limited to Canton. A great number of porters was regularly employed in transporting goods backwards and forwards by land between Canton and the Yangtze provinces; this was their livelihood. After the war the victorious English demanded that other ports situated in the North and having quicker and better communications with the hinterland should be opened to trade; this took away a great deal of trade from Canton and consequently a large number of porters lost their means of making a living. They regarded the victors of the opium war as responsible for their distress and hence a nationalistic attitude, hostile to foreigners, spread quickly amongst them. Attacks and outcries against foreigners in the environs of Canton were the result. Of course the English did not regard these outcries very seriously at first and took no countermeasures to avoid further incidents. This was interpreted as weakness by the populace, however, and there arose a proverb: 'The people fear the

1. *Tseng Wen-cheng kung tsou-kao*, 1, 36b–40a (ed. Ch'uan-chung shu-chü, 1876). Cf. also Ssu-yü Teng, op. cit., pp. 44–6.
2. *Tseng Wen-cheng kung tsou-kao*, 1, 24a.

officials, the officials fear the foreign devils, and the foreign devils fear the people'. If the people could frighten those who frightened the officials, how powerful the people must be! Thus, Karl Marx came to the conclusion that the Taiping revolution was caused by British cannons and that the opium war stirred the Chinese people into life.[1] Even if this conclusion is exaggerated, it is impossible to deny that the opium war had some influence on the outbreak of the Taiping revolution.

Although the economic and social conditions were of fundamental importance in creating the underlying causes for the outbreak of the Taiping revolution they were not the only factors. As in the revolts at the end of Mongol rule (see p. 13 above), the nationalistic element also played an important role. Oppression and discrimination against the Chinese were certainly not as widespread under the Manchus as they were under the Mongols. In fact, the Manchus were increasingly and visibly assimilated and naturalized by the Chinese. They had retained for themselves, however, significant privileges over the Chinese, and thereby ensured that consciousness of foreign overlordship did not die out among the Chinese. Followers of the Ming dynasty, which was deposed by the Manchus, had prepared a literary battle against foreign rulers at the end of the 17th century. A massive literary inquisition on the part of the government in the course of the 18th century could not counteract the influence of this literature entirely, and writings of this sort influenced the leaders of the Taiping revolution and other uprisings in their nationalistic emphasis. In particular it was a heterodox, secret society that stemmed from loyal supporters of the Ming dynasty, the Heaven and Earth Society (*T'ien-ti hui*) or the Triad Society (*San-ho hui* or *Hung-mên hui*), that made the phrase 'Overthrow the Ch'ing and restore the Ming' one of their slogans. Even today, in fact, the southern Chinese from Kwangtung and Kwangsi are extremely nationalistic; and at that time they found it difficult to get used to the rule of the Manchus. It was not entirely accidental, therefore, that the Taiping revolution began in the South, near the borders between the two provinces.

1. *New York Daily Tribune*, 14th June, 1853.

The Course of the Taiping Revolution

The leader of the Taiping revolution, Hung Hsiu-ch'üan, born on 1st January, 1814, was the son of a peasant, a member of a poor Hakka family in the South Chinese province of Kwangtung. The Hakka, or guest settlers, came originally from northern China and had entered Kwangtung and Kwangsi since the 4th century A.D. They there formed a separate ethnic group, whose number today— including those who later emigrated to South-East Asia—is estimated at approximately 20 million. The Hakka spoke a special dialect and had different practices and customs from the native population, with whom they had to wage a harsh struggle for existence. The Hakka were regarded as daring and tough, with a strongly nationalistic spirit directed against the Manchu dynasty. It was hardly accidental, therefore, that Hung Hsiu-ch'üan and many other Taiping leaders belonged to this ethnic group. Hung Hsiu-ch'üan showed himself a very gifted child. At great financial sacrifice his family sent him to school, although only up to his fourteenth year. He continued his studies independently as far as possible and was subsequently active chiefly as a village school-teacher till 1843. He applied several times for the lowest state examination. The passing of this was a pre-condition for entering an official career and the only chance of social advancement. He was unsuccessful, however. In 1837, while he was in Canton, a pamphlet of the Protestant Christian mission, written in Chinese, accidentally fell into his hands. He must have examined it cursorily, but did not give it further thought. In the following year he made another attempt at the state examination, but again without success. Bitterly disappointed and soured by his repeated failure he fell into a morbid trance, which is said to have lasted exactly forty days. He lost consciousness and had visions in which an old man appeared as his father and the man's son was his elder brother; they commissioned him to destroy the demons in the world. On his recovery he read the Christian pamphlet more closely and came to believe that the figures who had appeared to him were God and Jesus Christ, who had chosen him for a special mission on earth. These visions of Hung Hsiu-ch'üan were extraordinarily important for the revolutionary movement from beginning to end.

The suspicion that they were invented at a later date for expressly political purposes can by no means be ruled out. On the other hand, the visions are described in different, independent sources from a fairly early date, so that there is a great deal in favour of their reliability; moreover, they fit well with the psychopathic traits of Hung's character. The question whether Hung Hsiu-ch'üan really had the vision or not is of only minor importance for the development of the Chinese revolution. What is important and beyond all doubt is the fact that non-Chinese, Christian ideas, spread in China by Western missionaries, are involved.

The brief missionary pamphlet which Hung Hsiu-ch'üan had been given to read could of course only give him a superficial idea of the Christian religion; and even a two-month course of Christian instruction which he received in 1847 from an American missionary in Canton could hardly provide him with a deeper understanding. Thus, Christianity for him consisted chiefly in the worship of one god and in the rejection of other deities, including the ancestor cult which had been prevalent throughout China from the earliest times. He knew the Ten Commandments and believed that Jesus Christ could forgive wrongdoing and sin and help a person to be good, in order that he might enter paradise after his death. It was chiefly the ideas of the Old Testament that Hung took over. The deeper ideas of the New Testament and of genuine Christian ethics remained foreign to him. The effect of the religion on Hung and his followers was to make them destroy the idols of other religions, including the Confucian ancestor-tablets. They used to write God's name on a piece of paper, kneel before it, burn incense, light candles, pour a libation of wine and make sacrificial offerings. As a result of the visions Hung Hsiu-ch'üan regarded himself as the younger brother of Jesus Christ and God's son, called by God to destroy demons on earth and to establish a kingdom of God on earth. In practice this meant planning to destroy the Manchu dynasty and the existing political system and creating a new social order. The idea of the kingdom of God had been completely secularized.

The course of the revolution can only be traced here quite briefly. In 1847 Hung Hsiu-ch'üan and his helpers had gathered thousands of followers round them. They were mostly impoverished peasants from the Hakka or from the non-Chinese tribes of Miao and Yao. The centre of the movement was the 'Thistle-mountains' (Tzŭ-chin shan), north of Kuei-p'ing in the eastern part of the province of Kwangsi. Other groups of bandits also operated in the same region. Open hostilities between them and the followers of Hung Hsiu-ch'üan usually ended in favour of the latter, so that many of these other groups came to attach themselves to the movement of the 'God-worshippers', as the followers of Hung called themselves. Among them were members of several secret societies that were directed against the Manchu dynasty, such as the Heaven and Earth Society or the Triad Society, etc. Thus, the combination of religious, nationalistic and social elements, seen in the pseudo-Christian ideas of Hung Hsiu-ch'üan, the anti-Manchu aims of the movement, and the open revolt of landless, destitute peasants, formed the starting-point for the beginning of the Taiping revolution.

Open insurrection, the beginning of the revolution proper, began in the summer of 1850. All 'God-worshippers' were told to offer armed resistance to the government troops. In order to secure the firm loyalty of followers of the movement to their leaders, their houses were burnt down. Movable possessions were brought together and regarded as common property. As a result of this principle of primitive communism the movement gained most ground precisely among the Hakka who were living in great poverty and in a very short time it numbered about 10,000 men. Hung Hsiu-ch'üan was regarded as the leader appointed by God. In the autumn of the following year, after the influence of the movement had spread, Hung Hsiu-ch'üan was unanimously acclaimed 'Heavenly King' (t'ien-wang) in the 'Heavenly Kingdom of Peace' (t'ai-p'ing t'ien-kuo) by the 'God-worshippers'. Hence the name Taiping revolution. 1851 was the first year of the new dynasty, which was to take the place of the Manchu ruling house. All followers of the movement had cut off their pigtails, which had been forcibly introduced into China by the Manchus, and had taken to wearing the hair-style and clothing of the period before the Manchu invasion. Because they let their hair grow on the front part of the head, normally smoothly shaven according to Manchu custom, they were usually described in the documents of the imperial government as 'long-haired rebels' (*ch'ang-fa tsei*). With the authority of the 'Heavenly King', Hung Hsiu-ch'üan, five other leaders were also given the title 'king' (*wang*). Of these one was a charcoal-burner (Yang Hsiu-ch'ing), another a village school-teacher and healer like Hung himself (Fêng Yün-shan), the third was an impoverished small-farmer (Hsiao Ch'ao-kuei), the fourth a trader (Wei Ch'ang-hui), and the fifth a large farmer (Shih Ta-k'ai). Although the last two came from families of good position and although, with the exception of the charcoal-burner, all had obtained a certain degree of education, none of them belonged to the actual gentry-class. Their first followers consisted of several thousand Hakka peasants, mostly poor, several hundred charcoal burners, about a thousand miners and a number of former pirates, who had been driven from the seas by foreign warships. In addition there were a few traders, well-to-do peasants and educated people amongst them, as well as deserters from the government forces, and porters from Canton, who had lost their work as a result of the opium war.

The power of the Taiping revolutionaries grew quickly. In the summer of 1852 they left their original base in Kwangsi and marched northwards to Hunan, where they were joined by large numbers of impoverished peasants and adherents of other revolutionary movements. From Hunan the main force moved through Hupei down the Yangtze and after a short siege of eleven days captured Nanking, the 'Southern Capital' of the Ming dynasty, in the spring of 1853. Here the 'Heavenly King' established his court. An army was dispatched northwards with the aim of capturing Peking. The scene there was one of the utmost confusion. Preparations were made to move the capital northwards to Jehol, the summer residence of the Manchu rulers, and it seemed that before long the Taiping would occupy the whole of China. But because the military preparations had been inadequate the revolutionary army only penetrated as far as the region south of Tientsin. The lines of communication to the rear did not function, there was no cavalry, and the soldiers who came from the south were not used to the rough northern food and the cold winter climate, so that the thrust to the north came to nothing. A second army pressed westwards to gain control of Kiangsi, Anhui, Hupei and

Hunan. It was here that the first opponent able to prevent the further spread of the revolution appeared on the scene in the person of Tseng Kuo-fan; and he ultimately played a decisive part in suppressing it. Tseng Kuo-fan was a strict Confucian and he sought to train his troops, recruited in Hunan, in the spirit of traditional Confucianism. Thus it became a conflict of two ideologies, traditional Chinese–Confucian in conflict with imported, foreign, pseudo-Christian teaching.

Internally and externally the revolution could not for long maintain its full vigour and impetus. In 1856 in Nanking there was a serious internal conflict resulting in bloodshed, in which some of the most important leaders of the revolution, along with their followers, altogether about twenty or thirty thousand men, met their deaths. This brought the revolutionary offensive to an end and its continuance in the following years was purely defensive. In spite of increasing corruption and disintegration at the court of the 'Heavenly King' in Nanking, some of the able military leaders still gained many successes in battle and even up to 1864 were able to hold their own against the enemy who were pressing ever more strongly against Nanking. With the fall of the city in the summer of 1864, however, the fate of the revolution was sealed. The honour of defeating the revolution belonged chiefly to Tseng Kuo-fan and his army.

Tseng was a Chinese scholar and originally a civil official. He was an upright figure and as such he succeeded, in spite of the corruption of the Manchu dynasty and the government in Peking, in developing a first-rate battle-spirit in his troops. Ultimately, although he suffered heavy reverses, he was victorious in the struggle against the revolution. His efforts to restore order in the traditional sense are well known by the name of 'The T'ung-chih Restoration' (after the Emperor T'ung-chih who came to power in 1862). Later they were of particular influence as a model for Chiang Kai-shek (see below pp. 164f.). In recent years Tseng Kuo-fan has been much censured because he used his power to rescue an alien, reactionary, failing dynasty, instead of taking the side of the Chinese people against their native and foreign oppressors. Certainly Tseng represented the interests of the land-owning gentry of Hunan, who resisted the revolutionary programme of the

Taiping; and without their material and moral support he would not have been able to form and support his army. But over and above this the question for Tseng was rather different than for his modern critics: for him his fight against the Taiping was a defence of traditional Chinese culture and Confucianism against alien Christianity, imported from the West, and its political and social implications. Besides Tseng Kuo-fan there were other leaders of anti-revolutionary troops, especially Li Hung-chang and Tso Tsung-t'ang, both Chinese like Tseng and not Manchus, who deserve credit for the defeat of the revolution. Finally, a not unimportant factor was the 'Ever Victorious Army', a voluntary corps consisting of Chinese and Europeans or Americans under foreign leadership, which was ultimately vested in the famous Englishman, Charles George Gordon. The foreign powers—at that time represented chiefly by England and France—had at first adopted a sympathetic attitude to the Taiping, but they later revised this in favour of the Manchu dynasty and gave the dynasty extensive support, not least by the 'Ever Victorious Army', which admittedly was officially under the command of Li Hung-chang. The reason for the change in the attitude of the foreign powers, it was freely suggested, was disappointment with the Christian aims of the revolution. In fact, however, motives of imperialism rather than morality were probably decisive. England and France feared that if the revolution succeeded they would lose the concessions and preferences obtained from the Manchu dynasty after new armed interventions in 1858 by the Treaty of Tientsin, and by the Peking Convention of 1860, especially the important war-indemnity and the substantial profits from the opium trade. Moreover, the Taiping pursued a much more nationalistic course, and displayed a much more determined attitude to foreigners than the weak dynasty. The privileged position of the foreign powers in China, a position which they had only recently gained by force of arms, was closely linked with the fate of the Manchus.

The Revolutionary Measures of the Taiping

In the principles advanced by the Taiping revolution and the measures carried through by it there was much that denoted a direct break with ancient Chinese tradition, and many of the principles of the Taiping revolution served as an inspiration and model for Sun Yat-sen and the Kuomintang as well as the 'May 4th Movement' (see below) and the Communists. The Taiping took over from Christianity the idea of the equality of all men. This idea combined with certain ancient and utopian Chinese conceptions explains some of the particularly revolutionary points of the social programme. Traditional Chinese patterns were applied to the administrative organization, which, including the names for officials, was largely derived from the 'Rites of Chou' (*Chou li*), a work from the 3rd or 4th century B.C., describing the state organization of the kingdom of the Chou dynasty (*c.* 1050–255 B.C.). In the matter of the primitive communism of the Taiping it is difficult to decide whether Christian ideas, or descriptions of the original state of mankind in early Chinese, Taoistic writings, had the stronger influence. The most important points of the revolutionary programme of the Taiping may be briefly sketched as follows:

1. Common property: there were no private possessions, only a common treasury and a common granary, from which provision was made for individual weddings, births, funerals, etc.

2. Land reform programme: all land was divided into nine categories according to its quality and was allocated for the use of the population not as freehold private property but in accordance with the size of the population and the quality of the land. Men and women were regarded as equal in the allocation of land. Children under sixteen years of age received half-quantities. At harvest time it was permissible to retain only what was necessary for one's own subsistence. All the rest went into the common granary. Agricultural and handicraft products were divided in the same way. There are no reliable records, however, of this system having been put into effect in any region. Such a thorough revolution of the whole agricultural system in such a short time could hardly have been implemented on any large scale, and the new system can only have been implemented in a very limited area, if at all. It is well known, on the other hand, from various regions, especially from Chekiang and Kiangsu, that the existing agricultural and tax system was largely retained, although the taxes raised by the Taiping were lower than those demanded by the imperial

government and the burdens of the peasants were substantially reduced in consequence. If the agrarian reforms had been carried through, however, taxes would have ceased to be necessary. As a countermeasure during the struggles in the Yangtze valley the imperial government also tried to keep taxes as low as possible in order to win over the population to its side.

3. The position of women: apart from possible matriarchal relationships at a very early period, the position of the woman in traditional Chinese society was subordinate in every respect to that of the man. Hence, the decision of the Taiping to regard men and women as equal was a revolutionary act of unprecedented significance. Women could enter for the state examinations and occupy the same civil or military positions as men. There were women soldiers in special women's contingents in the Taiping army; the binding of women's feet which had been practised in China since the 10th century A.D., especially among the upper classes, was strictly forbidden, and, like prostitution and traffic in girls, was made a capital offence. Monogamy was made obligatory. Women or girls who had no male members of the family to protect them were particularly cared for. Rape was punishable by death. All women were obliged to marry, but betrothal no longer depended on a financial arrangement between families as was usual previously; it rested on the explicit consent of the partners concerned. It should be admitted, however, that couples were sometimes forcibly married against their own wishes by persons in authority. A marriage ceremony, similar to the Western church wedding, was introduced.

4. Temperance: opium, like tobacco and alcohol, was strictly prohibited. According to the reports we have the prohibition was not always observed in the same way, especially later. But in the early years, wherever the Taiping revolution gained control, the opium prohibition, at least, was not simply a matter of theory; it was strictly enforced in practice.

5. Attack on images: in their pseudo–Christian beliefs the Taiping were strictly monotheistic and intolerant of other religions, although they had derived elements from Confucianism, Taoism and Buddhism. The revolutionaries destroyed images, statues and temples of Buddhism and Taoism and did not stop short of the

Confucian ancestor-tablets. By their attack on images the Taiping gave their opponents a powerful weapon to use against them.

6. Treatment of foreigners: as a result of their Christian influence the Taiping regarded all nations as having equal rights and did not regard the Chinese, for instance, as the chosen people. They were hostile to the Catholics, but fairly friendly to the Protestants. Nevertheless, they did not allow even Protestant missionaries from abroad to travel and preach throughout the country, since they believed that they themselves were in possession of the true doctrine and were in the best position to spread this throughout the land in accordance with their own convictions. The Taiping required foreigners in their territory to submit to Chinese jurisdiction, although they had been granted extra-territorial rights by the imperial government. They adopted an emphatically nationalistic attitude and were in favour of equal rights with other nations; they were unwilling to surrender any of the national rights of the Chinese as the imperial government—admittedly under coercion—had done.

7. Calendar reform: the traditional Chinese calendar, which is still widely used and still printed on most calendars alongside the official Western reckoning, was a lunar calendar. The Taiping introduced a completely new calendar, similar to the Julian calendar of a seven-day week (including Sunday) which was officially taken over in the 20th century; it represented a combination of solar and lunar elements.

8. Literary reform: the Taiping relaxed the heavily conventional written style, which was quite different from the spoken language, by approximating it more closely to colloquial speech. Here, too, they were forerunners of the great literary revolution that took place later (see below).

Reasons for the Success and Failure of the Revolution

In order to assess the Taiping better in the context of the Chinese revolution as a whole we shall briefly summarize the reasons for its initial success and its final failure, noting first the most important reasons for its success.

1. The Taiping revolutionaries had, as we saw, a clear, unified religio-political-social ideal, in which they had been trained and for

which they fought. Buddhism, Taoism, Confucianism, opium-smoking, gambling, prostitution, etc., or, on a personal plane, a degenerate dynasty, with corrupt officials and ruthless landlords, were
regarded by the Taiping as representatives of the devil on earth,
and it was their duty to destroy them; they regarded it as their
divine task to create a sort of paradise on earth that would bring
blessing to all. It was this that kept them together and for this
that they risked their lives. In contrast, the government troops
who opposed them in the first years of the revolution were a
motley crew of mercenaries without any common aim.

2. Militarily the insurgents were extremely well organized. Like
the troops, the leaders of the separate contingents felt that they
were servants of the great common endeavour and they co-operated
with each other to the best of their ability. Women and children
did not remain behind at home but followed the army separately;
this, too, guaranteed the loyalty of the soldiers. The government
troops, on the other hand, were badly organized and their leaders
were suspicious of one another and jealous, and made no effort to
co-operate.

3. The revolutionary army had excellent discipline. There was a
list of definite, strictly enforced rules for officers and men, requiring,
for example, participation in religious ceremonies, strict obedience,
co-operation, absolute loyalty—betrayal or desertion were punished
by death—bravery, integrity (i.e. absence of possessions), absti-
nence (from opium, alcohol, tobacco, gambling, etc.). The government troops were undisciplined and depraved; they ravaged,
plundered, raped and murdered without regard for friend or foe.

4. The Taiping leaders were able strategists whose military
technique has been particularly admired and imitated by the
Chinese Communists. Their particular speciality consisted in con-
taining their opponents in weak positions, turning the flank of
strong, well-fortified positions and misleading the enemy as much
as possible. The 'fifth column' also played an important role.

Also in favour of the insurgents was the general situation which
we have already sketched. Thus, the badly armed and poorly
equipped revolutionaries defeated the better armed and better
equipped government troops by reason of superior morale, discipline and organization. The same phenomenon has been prominent

in the initial stages of most Chinese revolutionary movements that have succeeded—for the last time in the conflicts between the Communists and the Nationalists during the 1940s.

All the above traits are particularly characteristic of the first stage of the Taiping movement. Gradually, however, with no abrupt break, changes occurred which led to the eventual failure and defeat of the revolution. The most important reasons for this were as follows:

1. Almost all Chinese dynasties and most partially successful revolutionary movements that have been directed against the existing order have owed their final defeat to the moral failure of their ruling group; so, too, with the Taiping. Soon after the capture of Nanking the 'Heavenly King' and the other rulers, contrary to all the rules of the revolutionary movement, began to preside over a sumptuous court, marked by all manner of luxury, innumerable concubines and a dissolute way of life. This deterioration at the head naturally infected all who stood lower down the chain of command.

2. The Taiping movement had at first a marked revolutionary and anti-traditional character. Gradually, however, this was broken down by many traditional vices. Different, warring factions and cliques were formed based on their different places of origin—a manifestation of traditional Chinese regionalism that does not seem to have been completely overcome even yet. The chief role was played by a Kwangtung and a Kwangsi clique. It was extremely difficult for members of other provinces to obtain higher and more influential positions and nepotism was rife. Later, the close co-operation between the different leaders, that had characterized the Taiping at first, disappeared. The other leaders tried to follow the example of the 'Heavenly King' and live in luxury, and for this they needed large private fortunes. Thus, they violated the rules about common property and adopted the customs of the rich gentry which they had originally fought against.

Whereas the Taiping increasingly lost their revolutionary impetus, important reforms took place on the other side. Reference has already been made to the fact that Tseng Kuo-fan and others had learned how to build a new, well-trained and organized army from the local militia recruited by the gentry for their own protection and that this army gradually gained the upper hand over the rebels, who became more and more demoralized. Previously there had been numerous military commanders under the direct control of the Emperor and they had hardly co-operated with each other at all. Now, Tseng Kuo-fan alone was the leader of a great army. All his subordinate leaders were personally loyal to him and had no direct connection with the government or the court in Peking. This change meant a voluntary renunciation of power by the Manchu dynasty, although this decision was made only reluctantly and under the threat of attack by the Taiping. Tseng Kuo-fan is the ancestor of the later 'war-lords'. After his time the troops were no longer under the direct control of the Emperor and the central government, but of individual leaders, like Tseng Kuo-fan, Li Hung-chang, Tso Tsung-t'ang and later Yüan Shih-k'ai. After the fall of the dynasty political power devolved entirely on the 'war-lords'.

3. Many of the earlier Taiping leaders had fallen in battle or were killed in the great internal struggle of 1856. With the extension of the area affected by the revolution ever greater numbers of able people would have been required for positions of leadership; but such figures were nowhere to be found. In addition, the 'Heavenly King' proved increasingly stubborn and narrow-minded and unwilling to accept advice from anyone. As a result, many able individuals went over to the side of the government. Most of the officers and officials of the Taiping were uneducated. Little was done to instruct and develop genuine talent.

4. Although at first numerous followers of the anti-Manchu revolutionary movements joined the Taiping, the Taiping failed to join with the other revolutionary movements of a similar nature. Neither the revolutionary Triad Society, which had control of Shanghai in 1853–5, nor the peasant revolts known as the 'Nien Rebellion', in the border areas of the provinces of Shantung, Kiangsu, Anhui, Honan and north Hupei, had direct links with the Taiping. Thus, the different revolutionary movements remained independent of each other, and the opposition was thus able to destroy them separately in turn.

5. The final support of the Western powers for the Manchu dynasty, after their initial hesitation at the end of the 1850s,

especially their supply of weapons and support of the voluntary corps, the 'Ever Victorious Army', contributed significantly to the difficulties of the revolutionaries.

6. The educated class in China at that time was still strictly conservative and Confucian and was bitterly opposed to revolutionary ideas. In many respects the ideas of the Taiping were ahead of their time, but incompetent leadership did not help to make them popular among the Chinese people.

The reasons for the rise and fall of the Taiping have been described here in detail, because they may help to explain a great deal in the later Communist movement and help us to see it in true perspective. The Communist leaders made themselves thoroughly acquainted with the Taiping revolution and tried to learn from it. They were concerned to appropriate the good qualities of the Taiping, while avoiding, if possible, their mistakes and weaknesses. But even if the Taiping revolution was in this sense a preliminary stage in the great revolutionary movement of the twentieth century, this does not exhaust its significance for the later period. As a result of the great devastations brought about by the conflicts with the Taiping in the whole of central China and as a result of its surrender of military power to the different generals and its concessions to the threatening Western powers because of internal strain, the Manchu dynasty suffered quite considerable losses of power and prestige, with the consequence that in the new revolutionary movement half a century later it collapsed like a ruined building.

THE REFORM MOVEMENT (1898)

The Situation Abroad at the End of the 19th Century
With the Opium War and its termination by the Treaty of Nanking between England and China in 1842 the West had taken the first strong and decisive measures to extend its imperialistic-colonial aims to China. The Treaty of Nanking, the first of the 'Unequal Treaties', was fundamental and decisive for the development of China's relationship to the West in the following decades.

Brief reference was made at the beginning of the first chapter to the universalistic view of the world and the state among the Chinese. The Middle Kingdom (i.e. China) saw itself as the centre of the world, the central point of all culture and civilization; in fact, it was the world *tout court*. The development of this view, which had arisen out of a naïve view of nature at a very early date, was made easy by China's geo-political position; it was surrounded on all its borders by mountains, steppe or desert, the inhabitants of which were culturally far behind those of the Middle Kingdom. Throughout her entire history these neighbouring peoples have exerted constant pressure on China's borders and China has taken over some of their accomplishments. The lands of the empire were repeatedly overrun by the Mongols and other steppe-people and sometimes even ruled by them, but culturally they were all finally defeated by China and ethnically they were to a great extent absorbed. China's relationships with foreign peoples were fitted into the framework of the tribute system. Foreigners brought natural products of their own country as 'tribute' to the Chinese imperial court, in order to obtain the coveted products of higher Chinese civilization as 'gifts' in return. These 'tributes' and 'gifts' were sometimes of considerable scope, especially if one takes into account the unofficial exchange of goods practised between members of foreign 'tribute-embassies' and Chinese officials and merchants; hence, a certain measure of foreign trade was possible even within the framework of the tribute system. The fact that at many times, because of the military pressure of the steppe-peoples, especially on the northern borders, Chinese 'gifts' were worth much more than the incoming 'tributes' did not lead to the rupture of the system. It took account of the cultural superiority and the corresponding self-respect of the Chinese, without encroaching at all upon the political independence of the neighbouring peoples. This tribute system was for China the only form of international relations. It has been said with some justice that the tribute system played a similar role in Chinese thought to that of nationalism and international law in Western thought of the 19th century.[1]

1. J. K. Fairbank, *Trade and Diplomacy on the China Coast*, Cambridge, Mass., 1953, p. 23.

When China came into increasingly close contact with the states of the West from the 16th century onwards, there was no reason for the Chinese government to see in the peoples of the West anything other than a new species of half-civilized barbarians, possessing primitive natural power, and attracted by the culture, wealth and prosperity of the Chinese Empire. Even when these 'Western barbarians' became more and more aggressive towards the middle of the 19th century this was no reason for China, in dealing with them, to depart from the tribute system which had been used for nearly 2,000 years. China could not know at that time that this system which had been tried and tested in dealings with mountain- and steppe-peoples was completely unsuited for use with the industrialized powers of the West. Yet it was the only method which China had at her disposal at that time for dealing with a foreign people. Hence, the Chinese government accepted the military pressure of the Western powers as something familiar from the past. But it was expected, in view of their previous experiences with other countries, that these barbarians from the West would gradually take note of the cultural superiority of the Chinese and willingly conform to Chinese universalism and the tribute system. According to the Chinese view it was impossible that a foreign state should be on equal terms with China, or a foreign sovereign be on the same level as the Chinese Emperor, the Son of Heaven. The European states, on the other hand, quite apart from their imperialistic activities, regarded the Chinese claim to world dominion, even if it was only theoretical, as intolerable arrogance, a piece of political megalomania, against which the only remedy lay in the use of force. In its collision with the West, China was not only continually powerless against the West's military superiority, but also against its consequent imperialistic penetration and exploitation. China's ruling class met its defeat and humiliation by the Western powers with gnashing of teeth, but still with an initial feeling of spiritual and moral superiority, confidently expecting that one day they would be able to send the foreigners packing.

The essential conditions of the Treaty of Nanking were as follows:

(1) The ceding of Hong Kong to England. (2) The opening of Canton, Amoy, Foochow, Ningpo and Shanghai as 'treaty ports'

for foreign trade, which had previously been limited to Canton, and the appointment of foreign consuls for these places. (3) The payment of a war indemnity. (4) Officials of both countries should correspond with each other on the footing of perfect equality. (5) The release of English prisoners and an amnesty for all Chinese who had worked for the foreigners during the war.

In a supplementary treaty the following year the notorious most-favoured nation clause was added; this was later copied in almost all the treaties made with other nations. It affirmed that all rights which China might at any time grant to other nations would be granted automatically to the treaty-partner in question. The treaty with the English was followed in subsequent years by treaties with the USA, France, Belgium, Sweden, Norway, Portugal, and later with Russia and Prussia also, permitting them trade in the treaty ports.

On the Chinese side there was a great deal of reluctance to implement these concessions, which had been forcibly exacted, and it was hoped, as before, that they would one day be able to get rid of the foreigner. Further encounters were not lacking. England and France made use of—perhaps they deliberately provoked— insignificant incidents for fresh military interventions, in order to obtain further preferences and concessions. In the Treaty of Tientsin in 1858, as a result of a military expedition by England and France, China had to make the following new concessions:

(1) The stationing of foreign legations—at first only an English minister—in Peking. (2) Trading rights for foreigners on the Yangtze and the opening of a number of other places as treaty ports. (3) Freedom for foreigners to travel inland. (4) Regulations concerning customs dues. (5) War indemnity. (6) Freedom to spread Christian teaching.

A later Anglo–French expedition got as far as Peking in 1860. The plundering and total destruction of the great imperial palace outside Peking, Yüan-ming yüan, counts as one of its most particularly notorious deeds. It resulted in the exaction of fresh concessions from China. A clause was slipped into the French treaty after negotiations had been completed, granting French Catholic missionaries the right 'to lease and buy land in all provinces in order to put up buildings there according to their wishes'.[1] This right was then granted to the Catholic missions of other nations on the basis of the most-favoured nation clause. Protestant missions, too, were increasingly able to establish themselves inland, although the formal right to do so was not granted until the American–Chinese treaty of 1903. These events show how closely the Christian mission was connected—greatly to its detriment on a long-term view—with the political and economic invasion of the foreign powers in China. Moreover, the missionaries often gave protection to Chinese converts who had transgressed Chinese laws and enabled them to escape the grasp of the local authority; they often provoked the Chinese, and the incidents caused by such provocation were gladly used by a foreign power as a pretext for attack—as, for instance, later when Germany occupied the Kiao-chow area. Such events brought the missions and Christianity into great odium, which even the sacrificial and exemplary conduct of a great number of missionaries—especially at a later period—could not efface. From the standpoint of the Chinese, therefore, it is not altogether surprising that the revolutionary movement later regarded the Christian mission as a pioneer of imperialism and treated it accordingly (see below pp. 150 ff.).

Until the 1860s the main aim of the foreign powers in China was to extend their trade profitably. But it did not stop there. It was followed by efforts to obtain political strongholds and undeveloped territories for commercial investments. The expansion of their colonial empires became the aim of the great powers, who were also joined by Japan, which had rapidly risen to a position of strength after fundamental political and social reforms. In the 1870s the Russians occupied the Ili area, in 1880 the Japanese took possession of the Liukiu-islands, in 1885 the French exacted Annam (i.e. North Vietnam) and in 1886 the English exacted Burma. But loss of these border areas, which were under Chinese suzerainty although largely independent, was not the end of the matter; in addition to Hong Kong there would soon be other places belonging to China itself under foreign rule. In 1894–5 in the war against Japan China

1. Cf. Wolfgang Franke in *Saeculum V*, 4, 1954, p. 343, and *China and the West*, Oxford, 1967, p. 79.

suffered a serious defeat, which resulted in the surrender of Formosa and the Pescadores islands to Japan and the declaration of independence by Korea. In 1897 on a flimsy pretext Germany occupied Tsingtao and Kiaochow Bay; in the following year Russia took possession of Port Arthur and Dairen, France of Kwangchow and England of Weihaiwei. Extensive concessions for mining, railway-building, etc. in the hinterland had already been granted. In addition some of the powers had been given written promises that certain large areas of China would not be ceded to other powers. In other words, these areas were to remain exclusively within the sphere of influence of the powers concerned and were earmarked by them for later annexation as colonies. Thus, in 1898 China seemed as close to being partitioned by the foreign powers as Africa had been. It was no accident, however, that in this year the Reform Movement reached its climax.

The Ideology and Course of the 'Reform Movement'

The European traders and above all the missionaries brought more and more Western ideas to China. Soon after the Opium War individual scholars and officials had made efforts to obtain better information about the peoples of the West and had indicated that China could learn a great deal from the economic and technical progress of the West. In the 1860s and 1870s there were a number of open-minded officials who could no longer shut their eyes to the view that China must strive to make use of the technical achievments of the West, especially in military matters, and apply them at home, with the aim, of course, of using them in the first instance for defence and liberation from the foreigners. Beyond this, however, they saw nothing worthy of China's emulation in Western culture. 'Chinese learning for the fundamental principles, Western learning for practical application' ran a well-known slogan.[1] Among the younger officials and scholars, however, there were at least a few who realized there must be deeper reasons for China's obvious weaknesses vis-à-vis the foreign powers than simply the lack of cannons and warships. They came to the conclusion that a great number of fundamental changes were required, not only in the technical sphere, but also in the organization of state

1. Chung-hsueh wei t'i, hsi-hsueh wei yung.

and society in China, if the Empire was not soon to disappear completely under the attacks of the foreign powers. The leading figure of this Reform Movement was K'ang Yu-wei from the southern province of Kwangtung, a younger candidate for the upper ranks of the civil service. In 1895 along with a number of like-minded friends in Peking he had founded a 'Society for the study of self-strengthening' (*ch'iang hsueh hui*) to promote the study of Western achievements and possibilities of reform in China; branches of the society or other societies with similar aims as well as newspapers and periodicals, which spread their ideas, quickly sprang into life elsewhere in China. As early as 1888 K'ang Yu-wei had addressed a memorandum on reform to the Emperor; it had been kept back by the authorities, however, because of its contents and had not reached its intended destination. In 1895, after China's defeat by Japan, he composed a second memorandum. It was signed by more than 2,000 scholars from all provinces, who were assembled in Peking as candidates for the metropolitan examination. The memorandum protested against the ratification of the peace treaty and demanded radical reforms in the entire character of the state. But this, too, was kept back and did not reach the Emperor. Only a third memorandum, which K'ang Yu-wei drew up soon afterwards, reached the Emperor through the mediation of the imperial tutor Weng T'ung-ho; it made a strong impression on him. A copy was sent to all governor-generals and governors of provinces, and K'ang Yu-wei himself was appointed secretary in the Ministry for Public Works. In the same year he composed a fourth memorandum, but because of the bitter hostilities of the anti-reform party it seemed inadvisable for K'ang Yu-wei to remain in Peking and he returned to his home-town, where he was successful in developing and spreading his ideas. It was not until the position in foreign affairs became increasingly critical in 1898 that K'ang Yu-wei, in a fifth memorandum, was able to obtain a fresh hearing with the Emperor for his reform plans. Under pressure of events the Reform Movement finally succeeded in winning the Emperor to their ideas. In June 1898 K'ang Yu-wei was commanded to appear before the Emperor and from then on he and others who thought like him were practically the only advisers of the Emperor.

The events of 1898 were decisively influenced by the strong differences between the Emperor and his aunt the Empress Dowager, Tzu-hsi. During the Emperor's years of minority she had conducted the government for him, and even after he came of age (1889) she had retained the reins of government. She was an energetic and capable figure, but also dominating and inconsiderate. A clique that was absolutely devoted to her played the decisive role at court; in addition, among the officials her word counted *de facto* more than that of the somewhat weak and less energetic Emperor. If the men of the reform party found a willing ear in the Emperor and a group of his close friends who were particularly devoted to him, this was not simply the result of concern for the welfare of the state; it was also hoped to strengthen the position of the Emperor and his followers with the help of the Reform Movement and to suppress or possibly eliminate entirely the influence of the Empress Dowager and her clique. In the last analysis it was not so much the opposition between reform and reaction, but the opposition between Emperor and Empress Dowager that mattered. Certain nationalistic, anti-Manchu tendencies also exerted an aggravating influence on the conflict; even if this was not true in the case of K'ang Yu-wei himself, in other publications of the Reform Movement these voices sometimes became dominant.

This false confrontation, the implications of which were not properly appreciated and valued by K'ang Yu-wei and his friends, also affected the fate of the Reform Movement. In a short period of about a hundred days the imperial edicts inspired by the reform party poured forth, having by-passed all other organs of government; their execution would have implied far-reaching changes in the institutions of government. The total exclusion of the Empress Dowager from the government, by force if necessary, was planned. This altogether over-hasty and ill-considered procedure soon brought the opposition under the Empress Dowager into the open. By a sort of armed *coup d'état* the Emperor was taken into custody and interned for the rest of his life on a small island in a lake within the palace grounds. The Empress Dowager took sole charge of the government. The leaders of the reform movement were ordered to be arrested. K'ang Yu-wei, Liang Ch'i-ch'ao, who later became quite prominent, and some others succeeded in escaping to Hong Kong or Japan on foreign ships. Six others were arrested and executed without trial. Among them was the Reform Movement's most brilliant figure, T'an Ssu-t'ung, son of the governor of Hupei. He could have escaped, but in spite of the certain fate that awaited him in Peking he refused to flee and is said to have countered his friends who called on him to flee with the words: 'Political reforms have never taken place in any country without bloodshed; I have not yet heard that blood has been shed in China for the sake of political reform; that is why China has not succeeded.'[1]

K'ang Yu-wei and his circle were the first to be convinced that it was not enough for China to take over the practical and technical achievements of the West, but that a change in the whole political system was absolutely necessary. The leaders of the Reform Movement, however, who belonged to the gentry, the educated upper class, unlike the leaders of the Taiping revolution, were still too bound by the traditional Confucian view of the world and state for them to contemplate a complete break with the Confucian tradition. Hence, in accordance with tradition they turned to the sacred Confucian classics to find a way of deliverance out of the misfortune of the present. The result of this study of the classics was the conclusion that the original tradition had been corrupted and falsified in the course of the history of the last 2,000 years. Everything depended, therefore, on rediscovering the true model of the earliest period. K'ang Yu-wei and his friends discovered completely new truths in the texts of the Confucian classics and their interpretation of Confucius and his teaching was in strong contrast to the orthodox exegesis of the tradition officially accepted for several centuries. Thus, they wished to find references in the Confucian classics to numerous achievements and institutions of the West which they admired and hoped to introduce in China, such as, for example, the participation of the people in the government by means of a parliament, the training and organization of a professional civil service—the Chinese civil service at that time had only a general (though intensive) humanistic and literary education, but no professional training—a school and educational

1. Liang Ch'i-ch'ao : *Wu-hsü chêng-pien chi*, biography of T'an Ssu-t'ung.

system similar to the modern one, etc. The reforms in Russia under Peter the Great and even more frequently the reforms of the Meiji period in Japan since 1868 were popularly cited as foreign parallels and examples. At the time everyone knew from experience how the little island-state of Japan, subjected to the caprice of foreign powers at first, like China, had become a modern, powerful state within a few decades and was already beginning to play a part in international politics. The imperial edicts inspired by the Reform Party during the brief 100-day era of reform dealt with the following topics: the introduction of scientific, especially technical, studies and courses of instruction on the Western model, the improvement of agricultural methods of production, the introduction of military training on the Western pattern, the establishment of a university at Peking, the modernization of the school system, the abolition of the traditional civil service examination system, the drawing up and publication of an annual budget for government expenditure, the abolition of sinecures, the dismissal of officials who opposed reform, etc. After the victory of the reactionary party under the leadership of the Empress Dowager all these decrees were immediately annulled; but the new ideas had been publicized everywhere by the reform edicts as well as the publishing activity of the Reform Movement and had found a considerable response, especially among the younger intelligentsia. Thus, a large number of the reforms announced in the reform edicts and later revoked were rearranged in a more cautious form in the course of the next decade and gradually put into practice. The Reform Movement contributed substantially towards preparing the ground for the coming revolution.

In spite of all their detailed criticism of the Reform Movement, which has been described as 'bourgeois-capitalistic', present-day Chinese historians have continued to regard it as a significant forerunner of the revolution and the six who lost their lives in the reaction, especially T'an Ssu-t'ung, have been commemorated as martyrs. T'an Ssu-t'ung was also by far the most radical in his ideas within the Reform Movement. Among other things he repudiated the traditional strict family hierarchy, advocated the emancipation of women, praised democracy in contrast to autocracy, etc. He believed that all these principles were justified in the light of the teaching of Confucius, if this was restored to its original form. Despite his criticisms T'an remained rooted in tradition; in this he differed fundamentally from the intellectual leaders of the May 4th Movement, which sought to reject the entire Chinese tradition (see below pp. 99 ff.).

According to Chinese Communist historians the Reform Movement was bound to fail, because it was only the concern of a comparatively small group within the gentry and could not rely on a large, powerful popular movement. This criticism is certainly not without justice; but even without great popular support the Reform Movement might have succeeded if its leaders had had more political acumen and foresight and instead of getting involved in a false confrontation with the Empress Dowager had tried to win her over to their ideas. She was not totally opposed to reform in principle, but after the experiences of 1898 she regarded all attempts at reform as an attack on her own position; hence she allied herself in the following period with the most rooted reactionaries of her entourage. This led to the events of 1900, which would have looked very different if the attempts at reform in 1898 had been successful.

It is important in connection with the Reform Movement to notice that here for the first time the influence of Japan begins to make itself felt. In what follows it is inextricably interwoven with the revolutionary movement. It even prepared the way for the Communists in a certain sense, as will be shown later (see below pp. 179 f.). As long ago as 1905 Otto Franke described this, as he did the importance of the Reform Movement as a whole, very accurately and in a way that could hardly be bettered even today:

There are two chief instances, which in an estimate of the reform period stand out sharply and in which we can recognize without difficulty the seeds from which events in the following period developed—in all their formative importance: firstly, the cautious, but cleverly calculated and successful encroachment of Japan on Chinese intellectual life, and secondly the reaction of China against foreign pressures. We know today that the two are psychologically connected. We have had more than one opportunity of seeing how the Reform Movement, which grew at first out of hatred of what was foreign, gradually and perhaps unconsciously at first came under Japanese influence, as it drew a large part of its examples and leading ideas from Japan and as its persecuted representatives also found asylum there. Japanese policy was too clever to become more heavily involved at this stage: its hour had not yet come. It let the storm blow over quietly, for it foresaw that when the passions abated the movement would revive, given more appropriate and more capable leadership. This expectation was not disappointed, even if the frenzy in Peking lasted longer than had been assumed in Japan. But since 1901 a quieter China has returned to the self-same reforming measures which in 1898, more for personal than objective reasons, aroused such rage. . . .[1]

THE BOXER UPRISING (1900)

The critical events of 1900 in Peking and northern China, which are known as the 'Boxer Riots' or 'Boxer Uprising', resulted from the combination of two different movements. One of these stemmed from a secret religious sect, the other from a clique at the palace, which was planning the complete elimination of the Emperor, who had already been excluded from the government in 1898.

Reference has already been made (pp. 14 f. above) to the fact that the great revolution of the 14th century, which led to the expulsion of the Mongols from China and the founding of the native Chinese Ming dynasty, went back to the 'Sect of the White Lotus', a popular Buddhistic–Taoistic–Manichæan cult associated with magic and superstition. After the official founding of the Ming dynasty it was forbidden by the first ruler Chu Yüan-chang, who had himself been a member of the 'Sect of the White Lotus'. It continued to exist in secret, however, and reappeared in the Ch'ing period. In 1796, under the watchword of driving out the Manchus and restoring the Ming dynasty, it unleashed a great revolt, which spread beyond the provinces of Hunan, Hupei, Szechwan, as far as Shensi and Kansu and could only finally be stamped out in 1804. The 'Sect of the White Lotus' was again strictly forbidden and in an imperial edict of 1813 the numerous sects that had branched out from it were also forbidden. This included the I-ho ch'üan, literally 'the Boxers of Honesty and

1. Otto Franke, *Ostasiatische Neubildungen*, p. 91.

Concord'. In spite of all prohibitions most of these sects continued to exist and after the 1890s some of them, especially in Shantung, became increasingly prominent. The reasons were the usual ones: mismanagement by the government, intolerable living conditions among the peasants, aggravated by natural disasters. These secret societies were characterized by a particularly strong element of superstition. For example, they were convinced that their followers could develop supernatural powers by means of certain mystical practices and could be invulnerable to rifle-bullets. The aims of the different revolutionary movements, among which the sect of the Boxers finally proved successful, were, as with all revolts of this sort, of a purely social-revolutionary character at first, directed against the ruling-class of officials, namely, against the gentry. As a religious sect it was hostile to those of different convictions and thus also to Christians. Moreover, many people blamed their misfortune on foreign missionaries, who had established themselves throughout the country and whose behaviour was not always calculated to arouse sympathy for Christianity. Such a view was not entirely unjustified, in so far as apart from the inner collapse of the dynasty the economic consequences of foreign penetration of China were responsible for bringing about a constant deterioration in living conditions. It was believed, moreover, that Christian converts, who were not always recruited from the best elements of the native population, could bewitch non-Christians by means of foreign, mystical influences. Hence, the attacks on churches, foreign missionaries and native Christians by the Boxers. The local authorities tried to suppress the movement by force sometimes; sometimes they tried to reach agreement. The latter choice was made less from convinced sympathy for the Boxers than because they were unable to control the movement. As a result of opportunist leaders and the influence of interested government parties the anti-foreign character of the Boxers became more and more prominent; the social-revolutionary and anti-Manchu elements receded and finally disappeared altogether and their motto became: 'Support the Manchu dynasty and destroy the foreigners.'[1] In the years following 1895, because the authorities in Shantung more or

1. *Fu Ch'ing mie Yang.*

less tolerated the Boxers, there were numerous clashes with foreign missions. The government in Peking was afraid that this would lead to growing complications with the foreign powers and therefore, towards the end of 1899, dispatched a new energetic governor (Yüan Shih-k'ai) to Shantung with orders to suppress the Boxer movement. Consequently the centre of the movement was transferred to the province of Hopei (at that time called Chihli) where it was generally tolerated by the authorities, even if not protected. By 1900 a strong group was firmly established in Tientsin, the most important centre of foreign trade in northern China.

The *coup d'état* of the Empress Dowager in 1898 had practically excluded the Emperor from the government, but as soon as the aged Empress Dowager breathed her last the Emperor would resume control and it was to be expected that he would then bring the members of the reactionary clique in palace and government to justice. It was these people who were personally responsible, along with the Empress Dowager, for the *coup d'état* of 1898. In order to forestall their inevitable punishment the reactionary clique tried—probably with the connivance of the Empress Dowager—to dethrone the Emperor or to kill him and replace him with another prince. In addition there were the customary palace intrigues which were always rife at the imperial court of China and were not fundamentally a matter of reaction or reform. The successor of the Emperor who was to be deposed was to have been a son of Prince Tuan Tsai-i. The planned change of ruler, however, foundered on the opposition of a number of governor-generals in the provinces, who had large armies and consequently no fears for their own security, and on the opposition of the foreign legations in Peking. Prince Tuan had to be satisfied with naming his son as successor to the throne. This failure provoked his anger—he had already shown himself to be a very stubborn, reactionary prince—against the foreign legations and the somewhat more progressive provincial governors and led to his alliance with the Boxers. He thought that with the help of the Boxers and their supernatural capabilities—apparently he believed in these—he would be able to expel the foreigners from China and then use the Boxer movement for his personal ends. Among other things he bears primary responsibility for the consequent alliance of the court under the leadership of

the Empress Dowager with the Boxers and for the entry of the
Boxers into Peking. This resulted in the hostilities against foreigners begun at the command of the Empress Dowager, the blockade
of foreign legations by the Boxers, together with regular troops,
and a reign of terror in the city. Numerous high-ranking officials,
who had shown themselves progressive and disposed to reform or
were in any other way unpopular with Prince Tuan and his clique,
were condemned out of hand as alleged traitors. No one dared
speak out against this, unless he were willing to risk his own life.
Outside the palace the masses raged in a nationalistic and religious
frenzy. Among the foreigners the first victims were a Japanese
legation secretary and the German minister. The Chinese themselves also had felt the terror. Not only were all Christians or
supposed Christians, who could be caught, put to death, but also
all those who had or had had anything to do with foreigners, either
commercially or privately. The nickname given to these Chinese
was the 'The secondary hairy ones' (*êrh-mao tzu*), a reference to
foreigners who were called 'the hairy ones' (*mao-tzu*), since the
hair-growth of Europeans is usually stronger than that of the
Chinese.

The events which followed—the blockade and relief of the
foreign legations in Peking, the arrival of the international
expeditionary corps under the leadership of Count Waldersee, the
flight of the Empress Dowager and the court, the plundering of
Peking by foreign troops, the defeat of the Boxers, the return of
the court to Peking and the international 'Boxer protocol' with
its harsh terms for China—are not of fundamental importance for
the history of the revolution and may therefore be omitted here.
Moreover, there are numerous accounts in Western languages in
which the events are excellently described.[1]

Modern Communist historical writing regards the Boxers as a
spontaneous popular movement, directed against foreign imperialism, but lacking in organization and intelligent leadership, with
the result that the reactionary court-clique were able to exploit
them for their own purposes. The measures of the Boxers against
foreigners and against those Chinese who were connected with them

1. See bibliography, below.

arouse their sympathy. The provincial governors and the other high-ranking officials, who—less from sympathy for the foreigners, in our opinion, than from greater insight into the folly of the undertaking—were against an alliance of court and government with the Boxers, are regarded by the Communists as traitors. The invasion of the foreign powers enabled the outbreak of violent xenophobia, which at that time was limited to northern China, to be put down. But the foreign powers did not gain sympathy or respect by their handling of the affair, and their stock of crimes against China rose even higher as a result. Moreover, the events of 1900 dealt another severe blow to the Manchu dynasty and it was not long before it collapsed completely.

3   The Republican Revolution
of 1911 and its Antecedents

The Taiping revolution as such was suppressed in 1864, by which time most of its leaders had met their deaths. The active supporters had numbered several hundred thousand, however, and neither the survivors nor their ideas could be wiped out so quickly. Even if the Taiping movement as a whole was scattered and its organization dismantled, this did not prevent the survivors taking shelter in various secret societies. It is not known in detail, of course, where the remaining Taiping went, but there is no doubt that many of them joined the Triad Society and the 'Society of the Elders and Brothers' (*Ko-lao-hui*).

The Triad Society had been associated with the beginning of the Taiping revolution (see above pp. 26 and 29). It stemmed from the 'Heaven and Earth Society' (see above pp. 26 f.), which was founded by loyal supporters of the defeated Ming dynasty at the beginning of Manchu rule, viz. about the middle of the 17th century. 'Overthrow the Ch'ing and restore the Ming' was their chief slogan. Their following consisted mainly of the poorest and lowest stratum of the population. The society was particularly widespread in south China and among the overseas Chinese communities in Indo-China, Siam, Malaya, Indonesia, Hawaii, etc., which came from the southern provinces of Kwangtung and Fukien. The Triad Society constantly fomented rebellions, even after the Taiping revolution; it was active in Kwangtung, for instance, in 1886.

The 'Society of the Elders and Brothers' probably had similar origins and a similar character to the Triad Society. It, too, went back to a branch of the 'Heaven and Earth Society', established

5—C.C.R.

at the beginning of Manchu rule by partisans of the Ming in Fukien and Chekiang. It did not take the name 'Society of the Elders and Brothers' until after the Taiping period, when it was joined by survivors of the Taiping and parts of Tseng Kuo-fan's Hunan army, which was largely disbanded after the final defeat of the Taiping revolution. The 'Society of the Elders and Brothers' had also spread in the Yangtze provinces of Hunan and Hupei as far as Szechwan, Yunnan and Kweichow. In fact, the movement had a lot of supporters and occupied a very influential position in southwest China even until quite recently. The Communist government has taken serious measures against them in recent years and their leaders have been imprisoned or put to death, but it is still not known what success has attended the attempts to eliminate once for all the 'Society of the Elders and Brothers' and other related secret societies.

Both societies were involved in numerous revolts in different parts of the Empire and were destined to play a part in the approaching revolution. They were well organized, widespread and ready to initiate rebellions and undertake terrorist action. It is true that apart from the slogan 'overthrow the Ch'ing and restore the Ming' they had no definite plans of a political or even purely social nature. They consisted predominantly of the poorest and most oppressed elements of society, men who were dissatisfied with existing conditions: poor peasants and tenant farmers, transport workers—especially from the ships and harbours of the Yangtze— small tradesmen, artisans, soldiers, bandits and smugglers together with a few from higher social positions. The really revolutionary ideas, however, did not come from these uneducated masses. The advocates of the revolutionary idea were the progressively minded, educated young intellectuals, who came chiefly from respectable gentry-families, or from merchant, artisan or peasant circles, usually in south China. These circles also had their own secret societies to some extent; at first they limited themselves simply to a study and discussion of questions of political and social progress, but later they spent more time in preparing for a revolution.

One—but, seen in retrospect, probably not the most outstanding —of these young revolutionaries was Sun Wen who later became most famous and was even called the 'father of the Chinese

Revolution'. In the West he is better known by his fancy-name
Sun I-hsien (in Cantonese pronounced Sun Yat-sen) and in China
best known as Sun Chung-shan. He was born into a small peasant
family in a village near Canton in 1866. One of his elder brothers
went to Hawaii to trade and Sun Yat-sen, who was twelve years
old at the time, went with him to Honolulu. He went to an Anglican
mission school, where he learnt English; three-and-a-half years
later he returned home but left again soon afterwards (1883) in
order to attend a college in Hong Kong and prepare himself for
university study. His Christian education in Hawaii had made a
strong impression on him and he was baptized as a Christian by
an American missionary in Hong Kong. From 1887 to 1892 he
studied medicine in Hong Kong and subsequently settled down as
a doctor in Macao. He is thought to have had some contacts with
the 'Society of Elders and Brothers' at that time. But apparently
he did not find the desired sounding-board for his ideas; in 1894
he founded the 'Society for the Development of China' (*Hsing
Chung hui*) in secret together with some like-minded, progressive
Cantonese. According to their initial announcements the society
aimed at reform rather than revolution. Their methods, apparently,
were those of the Reform Movement of K'ang Yu-wei and his
friends—memoranda and suggestions to the throne. There was no
talk at first of using force to overthrow the Ch'ing dynasty and
establish a republic. Their first objective was to remove certain
abuses and set up a constitutional monarchy. Yet the Society
found itself in increasing opposition to the Ch'ing dynasty and the
existing régime, which was regarded—not unfairly—as the main
obstacle to any progress. In 1895 Sun Yat-sen moved from Macao
to Canton and in the same year the first attempted putsch of the
'Society for the Development of China' took place—unsuccessfully,
of course. Sun Yat-sen escaped to Hong Kong and from there
overseas. A second attempt at rebellion in 1900 in the province of
Kwangtung, planned on a larger scale and undertaken in conjunc-
tion with the Triad Society, also failed. Superficially the old-style
secret societies seemed more radical, in that they aimed at overthrowing the dynasty; but it was only in order to replace it with
another dynasty. Sun Yat-sen and the 'Society for the Development of China' were not initially committed to abolishing the

dynasty, but their fundamental aims went much further. The change to a constitutional monarchy which they sought was much more radical than the solution envisaged by the followers of K'ang Yu-wei and it would have had much more serious consequences in the total political and social structure than a simple change of dynasty, which would have made little or no difference to the constitution and the structure of society. Sun Yat-sen and his friends were the active intellectual and practical leaders of the 'Society for the Development of China' but they were not in a position to raise the significant amounts of money needed for such a revolutionary movement unaided. Sun Yat-sen describes in his diaries how extraordinarily difficult it was for him in the early years to find sympathy and support for his ideas and plans among his fellow-countrymen—both at home and abroad. At first it was chiefly the workers and small craftsmen in Chinese overseas communities that gave material help to Sun Yat-sen, whereas the more prosperous business people at first inclined more to the party of K'ang Yu-wei and Liang Ch'i-ch'ao. Liang, too, was in exile and was very active in Japan and America. It was some time before Sun Yat-sen and his friends succeeded in winning these circles over.

Chinese business people realized that they were always at a disadvantage in commercial and industrial undertakings compared with foreigners. As a result of the low import controls laid down by the 'unequal treaties' foreign goods could enter the country very cheaply and no real protection could be given to help the development of incipient native industries. The government, under the impact of the traditional Confucian anti-commercial orientation, recognized no distinction between foreign and domestic trade. Thus the government and its officials, who were largely corrupt and greedy, sought to indemnify themselves against losses on foreign imports at the expense of the domestic trade; they raised internal tariffs and other supplementary taxes on a great variety of pretexts, which did not apply to the foreign merchants and their goods because of their privileged position. It was impossible for domestic goods, therefore, even if they could be produced much more cheaply, to compete with foreign goods. The best openings for investments in railway construction and mining, etc., were also held primarily by foreigners. Many Chinese saw that they could often develop their activities abroad better than at home, because (in spite of discrimination) conditions were more lawful and stable there. Hence it is easy to see that Chinese business people at home and abroad had little sympathy for a dynasty that was impotent in the face of foreign powers and for an officialdom that was corrupt; they saw themselves exploited and robbed at their whim. Naturally, therefore, they had a deep interest in changing existing political and economic conditions. In order to develop their business undertakings they needed a stable government which was capable of giving them protection at home and overseas. These are the groups known in Communist parlance as 'national capitalists' (*min-tsu tzu-pen-chia*); theoretically, at least, they are recognized as full members of the new economic order. They lived abroad mostly and have given increasing support to the revolution since the end of the 19th century; without their financial aid, in fact, the revolution would hardly have been possible. Even in recent times the majority of them were not opposed to the rule of Mao Tse-tung. These national capitalists are quite separate from the 'comprador' class (*mai-pan chieh-chi*) which consisted of business-people who worked for foreign firms, or made their living from commercial undertakings abroad and who up the end of the 1930s also lived for the most part in the leased territories or in the foreign concessions of the treaty ports, where they were protected against the intervention, justified or otherwise, of the Chinese authorities. Such circles as these were naturally opposed on the whole to any revolutionary movement; conversely the present Communist régime did not recognize their right to exist. It is true, of course, that these two groups of business-people could not always be sharply distinguished and many individuals would not claim to belong to either group. Nor did they belong strictly to entirely different social groups; it is quite possible, for instance, that one brother would belong to one and another brother to a different group and that they would later change groups because of a change of employment. The two groups, however, did represent fundamentally different interests, and consequently their attitude to the Communist revolution was also basically different. The 'national capitalists' were not exactly the 'guiding lights' of the revolution but they were the most important source of financial support.

About the same time that Sun Yat-sen formed the 'Society for the Development of China' in southern China and abroad, other societies of a similar nature such as the 'China Advancement Society' (*Hua-hsing hui*) and the 'Restoration Society' (*Kung-fu hui*) sprang up independently in other parts of China. The former of these was founded under the leadership of Huang Hsing in the province of Hunan in 1903 by a group of revolutionary intellectuals who had studied in Japan. Huang Hsing came from a well-known gentry family in Hunan, where he had engaged in revolutionary activities at the end of the 1890s in his home province and had taken part in an attempted *coup* in 1899. Consequently he had to flee to Japan temporarily and there he met other Chinese revolutionaries. In south China the 'Society for the Development of China' was closely associated with the Triad Society; similarly in Hunan the 'China Advancement Society' was closely associated with the 'Society of the Elders and Brothers'. In Chekiang about this time the 'Restoration Society' came into being under the leadership of Chang Ping-lin, who is best known as a scholar; he was joined by other important people such as Ts'ai Yüan-p'ei, who was one of the leading personalities in the cultural and academic life of China until his death in 1940. The members of both societies came largely from the young progressive intellectuals of well-to-do gentry families.

All these revolutionary movements increasingly made their headquarters in the Japanese capital, Tokyo, which became the asylum of the various revolutionary leaders, when they had to flee from their native country. They were able to get to know one another in Tokyo and discuss their mutual aims and plans in peace, supported by Japanese friends and under the benevolent protection of the Japanese government. Chinese students of science and technology also began to go to Japan in great numbers; in 1905 there were 8,000, in the following year more than 13,000. Revolutionary ideas found a ready response and a sympathetic hearing among them. Since then Chinese students abroad—not only in Japan but also in Europe and America—have always been an important factor in the Chinese revolutionary movement. In 1905 the three societies we have referred to formed themselves into an alliance in Tokyo—the 'Chinese Revolutionary Alliance' (*Chung-*

kuo ko-ming t'ung-meng-hui) which later grew into the 'National Party' (*Kuo-min tang*). Members representing seventeen provinces, i.e. all except Kansu, were present at its inception. Sun Yat-sen was elected leader. As a sign of their protest against the Manchu dynasty the revolutionaries cut off their pigtails, as the Taiping revolutionaries had done (see above p. 29). Their emphatically anti-Manchu attitude goes back to the tradition of the old secret societies and the scholars who were loyal to the Ming in the early Ch'ing period; but it was strengthened by nationalistic ideas from the West which the revolutionaries had become familiar with— mostly as a result of Japanese mediation.

The Chinese revolutionaries were not just treated with sympathy and tolerance in Japan; they were given substantial support towards realizing their plans. Many Japanese personally took an active part in the Chinese revolution. Important material aid, particularly in the shape of weapons and armaments, came from Japan. Sun Yat-sen's *coup* in 1900 had to be abandoned chiefly because Japan lost interest as a result of internal political developments which meant the active support expected for the Chinese revolution did not materialize. Leaving aside some individual Japanese, who supported the revolutionary cause and Sun Yat-sen out of idealism and sympathy, Japan's policy of supporting the Chinese revolution was already pointing in a definite direction, even though its plans were still fluid. Up to the Second World War Japan welcomed all types of political refugees from China, whether they were revolutionaries who were plotting to overthrow the existing government, or supporters of a government that had just been overthrown. The best way of serving Japanese interests, it was thought, was by helping to power those who were well disposed towards Japan and who needed Japanese support in order to maintain their position (see below p. 87). The first half of the 20th century made it quite clear that the aim of Japanese policy was Japanese predominance in East and South-East Asia and the exclusion of Western influence under the battle-cry of 'Asia for the Asians'. Soon after the end of the Japanese–Chinese war of 1895, the Japanese, by means of clever propaganda emphasizing their common Asian race and culture, had succeeded in diverting the hatred and hostility of China from themselves and directing it against the real common enemy, the West. It was not only the leaders of the Reform Movement and the revolutionary movement who were strongly influenced by Japan; even within China the Japanese developed lively channels of information and propaganda especially as a result of the 'East Asian Cultural Union' which was founded in Tokyo in 1898. In the following year the origin and purpose of this Union were described by a Chinese newspaper appearing in Japan as follows:

The world is divided into four continents—Asia, Europe, Africa and Australia. Recently the Europeans have gradually become stronger, the Asians weaker. In the war of 1894 Chinese and Japanese crossed swords; nations that live together attacked each other and treated each other like scum. Consequently Europe displayed even greater disdain for the people of Asia. China, Japan and Korea are the three neighbouring powers in East Asia; they are related to each other like tooth and jaw and should give each other mutual support. If they do not act together and combine now, they will soon be enslaved by others. In Japan the educated classes are extremely concerned about this prospect, and in their concern they have founded the East Asian Cultural Union. Its aims are as follows:

1. the preservation of the *status quo* in East Asia
2. the raising of popular educational standards and the development of all talents and skills
3. the strengthening of national forces.

The president of the Union is Prince Konoye and the headquarters are in Tokyo. In addition branches will be set up in Hankow, Peking, Shanghai, Foochow, Canton and Korea, each with its own President.[1]

To crown everything Japan's victory over Russia in 1905 added considerably to her authority and esteem in China. People in China saw how a small island, which had previously been despised, had risen to a position of strength in a very short space of time by modernizing military, economic and political conditions, in other words, by modernizing the state, and had been able to defeat one of the dreaded big powers of Europe in a short war without foreign help, and to drive it back from its advanced position in East Asia. It is easy to imagine what effect this Japanese victory must have

1. Quoted from Otto Franke, *Ostasiatische Neubildungen*, pp. 136–7.

had on the Chinese, who were subject to the constantly growing pressure of Western imperialism. What Japan, a small island, could do, China, which was so much bigger, must also be able to do. It was only necessary to create the right conditions, i.e. modernize China like Japan. Japan was regarded as the pioneer of freedom in East Asia; it was time to learn from Japan and imitate her. Thus, Japan's victory not only marked a significant advance in her own Asian programme; it was also grist to the mill of the Chinese revolutionaries.

THE IDEAS OF THE REVOLUTIONARY MOVEMENT

Sun Yat-sen came to occupy an increasingly important role in the revolutionary movement and his ideas had considerable influence on its development. It is true, of course, that his teaching was not given its most characteristic shape until after 1911 and by far the greatest number of his writings came from this later period, but the framework of Sun's basic ideas began to take shape much earlier, soon after the formation of the Revolutionary Alliance. In the 1890s Sun was still greatly influenced by the Reform Movement of K'ang Yu-wei and, as we have already noted, his primary objective was reform of the existing system of government while retaining the ruling dynasty. The programme of the 'Society for the Development of China' from the beginning of the 1890s was drawn up with this in mind and contains no mention of an appeal to overthrow the dynasty. Gradually, however, Sun came to the conclusion that it was impossible to expect any thorough reform of the constitution from the existing Ch'ing dynasty, which was already in serious difficulty both at home and abroad and which was, in fact, itself the real obstacle to any fundamental reform. Only its overthrow could clear the way for a new development. Sun's journeys abroad both before and after 1900, together with the impression made by the republican constitution of the USA, may not have been without influence in altering his outlook. His association with the older secret societies, which sought to overthrow the Ch'ing dynasty and restore the Ming, may have contributed to his anti-dynastic views. The programme of the Revolutionary Alliance of 1905 contains a clear demand for a republic. Thus, Sun Yat-sen and his friends came into sharp conflict soon after 1898 with the group of reformers led by K'ang Yu-wei and Liang Ch'i-ch'ao, who had fled to Japan after the failure of the Reform Movement. They supported the figure of the Emperor (see above p. 46) as before and set up their organization in Japan on the same lines, calling themselves the 'Party Loyal to the Emperor' (*Pao-huang tang*). They emphasized their loyalty to the Ch'ing dynasty by adopting 'constitutional monarchy' as their objective, an aim which Sun Yat-sen had originally campaigned for.

The programme of the Revolutionary Alliance (*T'ung-mêng hui*), which Sun Yat-sen headed, contained the following four basic points:

1. Expulsion of the Manchus. The Manchus are a foreign, barbarian people, who entered China 260 years ago, and have oppressed and enslaved the Chinese. It is time to liberate China from this yoke. Those who surrender, when the revolution takes place, are to be spared; those who resist are to be disposed of without scruple. This applies not only to the Manchus, but also to their Chinese collaborators.

2. Restoration of Chinese rule. After the deposition of the Manchus the Chinese themselves are to rule China once more.

3. Establishment of a republic. All inhabitants of China are to be considered equal and enjoy the same political rights. President and Parliament are to be elected by the whole nation.

4. Equalization of land rights (*Ping-chün ti-ch'üan*). In view of its particular importance this point is reproduced verbatim:

The prosperity resulting from civilization should be equally enjoyed by all people of the nation. We should improve our social and economic organization, and assess the value of all the land in the country. Its present value shall still be considered the property of the owner, but all increases in value resulting from social reform and progress after the revolution shall belong to the state, to be enjoyed by all the people in order to establish a socialist state, where each family within the Empire will be well supported, each person satisfied, and no one fail to secure employment. Those who dare to control the livelihood of the people through monopoly shall be ostracized.[1]

1. *Chung-shan ts'ung-shu*, Vol. 4, *Hsüan-yen*, pp. 2–3. For the English translation cf. Ssu-yü Teng—John K. Fairbank, *China's Response to the West*, Harvard University Press, Cambridge, Mass., 1954, p. 228.

This is the first reference to the problem of land which became so important later in the revolution. Sun had observed how land values in Europe and America had soared as a result of modern industrial development; he had also studied Western theories of land reform. His idea of 'equalization of land rights' goes back chiefly to John Stuart Mill and the English 'Land Tenure Reform Association' which Mill had founded after 1870.[1] Sun thought he could foresee the same development in China as in the West, and planned that the accruing profit should be for the general good. At that time the land problem had no great importance for the revolutionaries and social problems were not yet in the forefront of men's thoughts. In 1907 Sun Yat-sen expressed himself as follows in a speech setting forth the aims of the revolution:

China does not at present suffer from social problems although it will do so later. At the moment the social question is not yet as pressing as the urgency of the first two questions (i.e. the national and the political revolution, entailing the termination of Manchu rule and the formation of a Republic). Few people in China are concerned about the social question; but our view must reach beyond the immediate present: we must work to prevent the problem before it comes upon us and while it is still possible to protect ourselves in advance against it. If we wait until we are overcome by the problem it will be difficult to counteract its influence. The social question in Europe and America is extremely difficult to solve; although this is not true of China yet, it is bound to be important in the future. Then it will be impossible to solve without an economic revolution. But revolutions do not occur until people are driven to do something; alternatively economic revolution following the anti-dynastic revolution, following the change of political system, would be disastrous for the people. Our political revolution must find means of improving the social position sufficiently to prevent the necessity of an economic revolution in the future. . . . Our aim is not simply to establish

1. See Charles Gide and Charles Rist, *A History of Economic Doctrines*, London, 1932, pp. 587 ff. Sun Yat-sen was strongly influenced by Henry George. He draws his idea of the 'equalization of land rights', however, from Mill. Cf. Harold Schiffrin, 'Sun Yat-sen's Early Land Policy. The Origin and Meaning of 'Equalization of Land Rights', *Journal of Asian Studies*, 16:4, 1957, pp. 549–64.

democracy, but to improve social conditions. For Europe and America this is a very difficult problem, but for us it is simpler.[1]

Sun Yat-sen may well have underestimated the difficulties. Further development has shown that the social question in China is different from that in the West, but its solution is no easier. Sun was right, however, in his prediction of the disastrous social revolution that would confront China with particular severity if it were neglected at the time of the political revolution. Even then, however, the social question was so important for Sun Yat-sen that he included it—admittedly, in third place—in his 'Three People's Principles' (*San min chu-i*) as 'the principle of the people's livelihood' (*Min shêng chu-i*) alongside 'the principle of nationalism' (*Min tsu chu-i*) and 'the principle of the people's rights' (*Min ch'üan chu-i*). This theory of 'The Three People's Principles', which later became so important, had already been developed in rudimentary form in *The People* (*Min Pao*), a newspaper published in Tokyo by the Revolutionary Union; it was only fully elaborated, however, in Sun Yat-sen's later writings (see below pp. 120 ff.).

The basic idea of the 'Five Power Constitution' (*Wu ch'üan hsien-fa*) can also be traced to this period. The classical Chinese state knew no sharp distinction of functions within the state, certainly not between executive and judiciary. In many cases both were administered by the same authorities or even the same official. In addition to the legislative, executive and judiciary, however, there were two institutions which played a special role in China and which have not been developed in such a consistent form by any Western state; viz. the examination system for the selection of civil servants and the censorial system. The importance of the first does not need explaining: by means of regular examinations of a uniform nature and open to everyone they had to choose the candidates who would enter the civil service. The Chinese system had a direct as well as an indirect influence on similar institutions in other countries.

1. Quoted from the French in *Bulletin de l'École Française d'Extrême Orient*, 7, Hanoi, 1907, pp. 445–6.

The most important task of the censorial establishment, within its numerous agencies, was to supervise government action and to uncover any violation of the law or failure of duty on the part of officials. This was meant to prevent caprice, inadequacies and corruption in the administration and also to put into practice the prevailing Confucian political doctrine. Thus Sun Yat-sen combined the three powers which developed in the West—legislative, executive and judiciary—with the two traditional Chinese powers of examination and censorship to make the 'Five Power Constitution'.

Three periods were scheduled for carrying through the revolution. The first was the period of military rule lasting until the monarchy or its representatives had been overthrown and the enemies of Revolution destroyed. This period was to last three years. Every district (*hsien*) should constitute a unit in itself. If in any district the necessary preconditions were fulfilled within three years, the second period would begin: 'the rule of the provisional constitution' (*Yüeh-fa chih chih*), during which the elected representatives of the people and elected officials in a particular district were responsible for administering local affairs on the basis of a provisional constitution agreed upon with the military government. The third period (constitutional government) was to begin after six years. At that stage the whole power of government was to be transferred from the military to the hands of the president chosen by the people, and into the hands of Parliament, which was also to be elected by the people, and of the executive bodies appointed by them. The basic ideas of this rather rigid theory were preserved by the Kuomintang in a modified form after Sun's death.

It is important to notice the attitude of the revolutionaries to the big foreign powers, which had political and economic interests in China. The revolutionaries had reached the conclusion that unless they could rely on the foreign powers at least remaining neutral the revolution could hardly hope to succeed. It was of fundamental importance, therefore, not to prejudice the foreign powers against the revolution in advance. The futility of open outbreaks of hatred against foreigners had been demonstrated by the events of 1900. Hence, the call to arms sounded by the revolution was directed exclusively against the Manchus. In fact the national, anti-Manchu aspect of the revolutionary movement may perhaps have been overemphasized in order to divert popular feelings and anger from the real oppressors of China to the foreign, but now fully naturalized, Manchu dynasty. As early as 1907 seven basic points were drawn up for revolutionary policy as it affected foreign powers:

1. Treaties made by China with foreign governments were to remain in force.

2. Indemnities and debts would continue to be recognized and paid from maritime customs duties as previously.

3. Foreign concessions and settlements were to be respected.

4. Foreigners and their property in areas controlled by the revolutionary military régime would be protected.

5. All treaties, concessions, recognition of debts and other agreements, signed by the imperial government after this declaration (1907), would not be recognized by the military government.

6. Foreigners who supported the imperial government against the revolutionary army would be regarded as enemies.

7. Any goods of military significance delivered to the Manchu dynasty by foreigners would be confiscated.

THE OUTBREAK OF THE REVOLUTION

Developments after 1905 favoured the revolutionary movement, and their first objective, the overthrow of the Manchu dynasty, was fulfilled more quickly perhaps than their leaders had expected. In 1908 both the Emperor Kuanghsü and the Empress Dowager Tz'u-hsi died. The new Emperor Hsüan-t'ung, Prince P'u-i, was still a minor and his father, Prince Ch'un Tsai-feng, the brother of the deceased Emperor, became regent. Even during the lifetime of the Empress Dowager far-reaching reforms, many of them similar to those of the Reform Movement of 1898, had been announced and some were already being put into practice: provincial assemblies were set up, and it was promised that a parliament would be convened and the people given a share in the government; a constitution was to be published and the state was to become a constitutional monarchy. One of the most decisive measures was the abolition of the official examination system by an edict of 1905. Consequently, it could no longer be assumed that the gentry and the scholar-officials, who had served as pillars of the Chinese state for one-and-a-half millennia would be uniformly indoctrinated and trained in Confucianism. Further, there was no longer any criterion for distinguishing the privileged ruling gentry-class from the large mass of common people, who were just subjects. Thus, the abolition of the examination system inevitably resulted in the dissolution of the existing political and social order. The importance of this measure for the final collapse of the traditional system which soon followed cannot be overestimated. Other reforms, however, were executed perfunctorily and promises made by the government were constantly postponed. It soon became obvious that the Manchus were not really ready to surrender any of their claims to rule or any of their special privileges in the political and social structure of China. As a result increasing numbers finally withheld their loyalty to the Manchu dynasty and expressed sympathy with the revolution, without committing themselves unreservedly to the programme of the revolutionaries.

The most important element in the revolutionary movement both then and later consisted of young intellectuals and students. A large proportion of them was undoubtedly carried along by idealistic enthusiasm for the high ideals of the revolution and by a commendable desire to save their country. Included in their number were many extremely well-educated people, such as Chang Ping-lin, Ts'ai Yüan-p'ei and others. But among some of the Chinese students in Europe, America and Japan there was also a great deal of snobbish arrogance, immature pretension, poor education and limited understanding of the realities of their own culture and tradition. Moreover, they had a very limited knowledge of Western civilization and education; they had no real ability or skill and their one thought was to find a lucrative official post in the coming new republican government. But even if only a minority of the students who returned from abroad pledged their active support for the revolution, they were on the whole— especially in view of the respect enjoyed by the educated and even half-educated in China, and all the more so if they had studied abroad—a destructive influence on the traditional culture and the existing order. Thus, even if only destructively, students helped to prepare the ground for the revolution.

Further support for the new ideas came from the new army contingents which had been trained on the Western pattern; they were now beginning to surpass the traditional Manchu soldiery in importance. The young officers, particularly, who had been given a modern military training—often abroad—and had consequently received rapid promotion, usually favoured the revolution, whether for idealistic reasons or personal ambition. Ultimately, their participation in the revolution was to prove decisive, and in the years that followed they exercised considerable influence on China's fate. The support for the revolution in large sections of commerce and industry especially among overseas Chinese has already been mentioned (see above p. 59).

Apart from Sun Yat-sen, the revolutionary intellectuals and students largely came from well-to-do families of civil servants or merchants, families which had the means to allow their sons to study at home or even to send them abroad. Even the students who were selected by the authorities to study abroad at the country's expense belonged to the same circles. It was taken for granted until very recently that sons of relatives or friends of the leading officials would receive first consideration for the government scholarships to study abroad, which were usually extremely well endowed. The new ideas picked up by individual members of the family, whether at home or abroad, were often not without influence on the other members of the family. Hence, even in the ruling gentry-class the conviction spread that a fundamental change in the constitution was necessary, even if it entailed a revolution. Other sections of the gentry-class, of course, remained staunchly conservative, and loyal to the ruling dynasty. In fact, the gentry-class as a whole, and sometimes a single gentry family, contained all sorts and shades of opinion—from the ultra-conservative supporters of the traditional system to the most radical republicans. It was a time when the traditional system of family and society began to disintegrate; the strict hierarchy within the individual gentry family was no longer possible. Moreover, whereas possession of an academic degree obtained by the traditional official examinations had been a necessary condition of membership in the gentry-class, the abolition of the examination system meant the disappearance of this criterion, even if the traditional examination was partly replaced in general esteem by a modern academic education. The absence of an absolute criterion, however, inevitably resulted in the gradual collapse of the gentry-class as a clearly defined, unified, ruling class. This process was only slow at first, but since the 1920s and especially since the beginning of the last war in 1937 it has accelerated rapidly. Even in 1911, however, the gentry were no longer a unified group, solidly supporting the ruling dynasty, as they had done during the Taiping revolution. This was another factor that helped considerably towards the success of the revolution.

Between 1905 and 1911 the leaders of the revolutionary movement made frequent journeys, both at home and abroad, in order to establish revolutionary organizations in every province and in every large town; they were active in disseminating propaganda and making all the preparations necessary for the revolution; and, in addition to all this, they began to collect the money required to carry through the revolution, especially for weapons and munitions. The headquarters of the Revolutionary Alliance were initially in Japan. But since the Japanese government wanted to avoid unnecessary complications with the Manchu government Sun Yat-sen and other revolutionary leaders were ultimately banished from Japan. Sun transferred his headquarters to French Indo-China, where he was given a friendly reception by the French authorities. Between 1906 and 1908 an increasing number of places were the scene of attempted rebellions, either organized by the Revolutionary Alliance or at least associated with it, but none was very successful. Sometimes the insurgents proceeded from Vietnamese territory, where they could retire again if necessary under French protection, safe from the intervention of Chinese authority.

The period from the end of 1908 to early 1910 was, on the surface, comparatively peaceful. In secret, however, the revolutionaries were working all the more intensively to build up their organization. When the government discovered a revolutionary secret organization, parallel organizations in the same place or even elsewhere often came to light at the same time; in such cases their members were arrested or put to death and the organization disbanded. The revolutionaries, therefore, changed their practice

6—C.C.R.

and set up separate organizations, which were often working side by side in larger towns or in the same province without any knowledge of the existence or membership of other similar groups. Only in central places were all the threads brought together and then under conditions of the utmost secrecy. The disadvantage of this, of course, was that in the case of attempted insurrections it was sometimes difficult to distinguish between friend and foe.

A new attempt to start an uprising, this time on a larger scale, was made in the spring of 1910 in southern China; the attempt failed and this helped to spark off a difference of opinion among the revolutionaries as to whether the revolutionary emphasis should continue to be placed on the southern provinces of Kwangtung and Kwangsi before advancing into central and northern China after the manner of the Taiping or whether it might be better to transfer the emphasis to central China and the Yangtze valley, since the government was particularly on its guard in the South because of previous attempts at rebellion there. Sun Yat-sen's plan was to start revolutions simultaneously in as many different parts of China as possible.

Before unanimity on this issue could be reached a favourable opportunity to revolt presented itself as a result of the railway loan in Szechwan. This was exploited accordingly by the revolutionaries and it proved the prelude to general revolution. In the spring of 1911 the imperial government had finally decided to nationalize the remainder of the railway system of China, including the part that was still in course of construction, which was in private hands. The money required for this was to be raised by means of a loan from the Big Four powers (England, France, Germany, USA). The announcement of the intended nationalization roused considerable opposition, especially in the provinces that were chiefly concerned, Hunan, Hupei and Szechwan. For the main issue was that the central government was taking charge of the construction of the Hankow–Canton and the Hankow–Chungking–Chengtu lines, which had been started by private companies with loans from the provinces concerned. The opposition to the plans of the government came chiefly from the interested parties in the provinces, which had promised to undertake and finance the project; they were opposed to the centralizing policy of the government. The revolutionaries' propaganda cleverly exploited this dissatisfaction for their own purposes. They reproached the imperial government with wanting to barter away important national interests to the foreign powers by borrowing money simply to strengthen their own position and with suppressing the initiative of their own economy in favour of the foreign powers. In justification of their measure the government pointed out that the railway companies had embezzled some of the money, and far from being in a position to complete the construction of the railways, were not even making progress. In fact, the line from Hankow to Canton was not finally completed until 1936 and the stretch from Chungking to Chengtu not until 1952. The line from Hankow to Chungking is still not built even today. When the government was going to repay the capital to the private companies and their shareholders, it tried to implement a regulation which was objected to by these creditors and open riots broke out in Szechwan, which was particularly involved. Geographical factors have always kept Szechwan politically, economically and intellectually distinct from the rest of the country. Almost as big as Germany in 1937, with a present population of probably more than 70 million,[1] the province has always held itself apart from the central government. Hence, the government's attempt to gain direct control of the projected railway, which would be the most important line of communication into the province as well as within it, met with particularly stiff resistance. The opposition came from the local gentry who saw their provincial interests threatened. To strengthen their position against the government in Peking members of the gentry made use of their influence on the 'Society of the Elders and Brothers', which was particularly strong and powerful in Szechwan, and on other secret societies, to incite a mass movement. Ever since their inception the secret societies had opposed the Manchu rule (see above pp. 26 f., 55 f.) and they were permeated with members of the Revolutionary Alliance, who knew how to guide movements that were originally inspired by purely regional motives on to general national, revolutionary lines. Since there were many supporters of

1. According to the Census of 1953, Szechwan had 62·3 million inhabitants.

the revolutionary movement among the gentry also, whose propaganda worked in the same direction, the 'movement for the
protection of the railways' (*Pao-lu yün-tung*) quickly became an
armed insurrection which gripped the whole province. Even before
the officials and troops dispatched by the imperial government
succeeded in quelling the rebellion in Szechwan, there was an
insurrection in the garrison of Wu-ch'ang on the Yangtze on 10th
October, 1911, by revolutionary soldiers, who soon gained control
of the whole town. The revolt was the signal for revolution;
carefully prepared by the Revolutionary Alliance and the secret
societies, it spread throughout China. Hence, 10th October became
a day of national celebration until eventually the Communists
substituted their own festivals. Although parts of Wu-ch'ang were
reoccupied by Manchu troops at the end of the year, the leading
cities and most important places in the other provinces were
captured by the revolutionaries without any serious bloodshed.
Hupei, Hunan, Kiangsi, Anhui, Chekiang, Fukien, Kiangsu,
Yunnan, Kweichow, Kwangtung, Kwangsi, Shensi, Shansi, Szechwan, Shantung declared their independence from the imperial
government one after the other at the end of October or beginning
of November. In January, 1912, the somewhat remote north-
western province of Kansu followed suit. Even the three north-
eastern provinces of Manchuria slipped out of the central
government's control. Only in Chihli (later Hopei) and Honan were
attempted revolts suppressed by loyal imperial troops and these
two provinces remained firmly in the control of the Manchus for the
time being. A few days after the outbreak of the revolution in
Wu-ch'ang the imperial government recalled Yüan Shih-k'ai, who
lived in retirement in Honan, and entrusted him with the task of
overthrowing the revolution. Yüan Shih-k'ai had been responsible
for deceiving the Reform Party and making possible the arrest
of the Emperor on the orders of the Empress Dowager in the
coup d'état of 1898 (see above p. 46). He was a clever, energetic
figure, one of the few important men in the last two decades of the
dynasty, and gradually through the favour of the Empress Dowager
he became the most important figure in the government. His
opponents exploited the death of the Empress Dowager in 1908
to procure his exile by decree of the regent, who could not forgive

him the wrong done to the Emperor, his brother, in 1898. Now, in October, 1911, the court regarded him as the only one who could save the dynasty. Yüan obeyed the request which was put to him in this way, but he realized that the ruling house, now without head, was beyond rescue. He began to negotiate with the revolutionaries at first in the service of the imperial government but later for his own ends. On 12th February, 1912, the dynasty finally announced in a solemn edict that 'Yüan Shih-k'ai has full power to organize a provisional republican government' and with these words abdicated.[1] Sun Yat-sen was in the United States when the revolution broke out. Immediately after his return to China on 29th December, 1911, he was elected acting President of the Republic in Nanking by delegates from sixteen provinces, all of which belonged to the Revolutionary Alliance or were closely associated with it.

The following year, 1912, counts as the first year of the Republic. A provisional government was set up in Nanking, which was to become the capital once more, and on 5th January the foreign powers were informed that a Republic had been formed. The revolution had succeeded; the dynasty was overthrown; thus, in name at any rate, if not yet in fact, a Republic had been created. The real power, however, lay in the hands of the army, not of Sun Yat-sen or the other revolutionary leaders. The government in Nanking had no troops worth the name at its disposal or under its direct command. Hence, Sun Yat-sen and the provisional government found they were unable to exercise their authority and on 13th February, 1912, they stepped down in favour of Yüan Shih-k'ai, who had been named as its successor by the defeated dynasty. On 10th March Yüan administered the oath to the Republic; Peking remained the capital. Thus, as acting President, Yüan Shih-k'ai became the most powerful man in China.

THE SIGNIFICANCE OF THE REVOLUTION OF 1911

The revolution of 1911 and the consequent establishment of a republic had a quite extraordinary significance, far exceeding that

1. *Hsüan-t'ung chêng-chi*, 70, 13b.

of the abolition of monarchies in European countries such as France in 1870 or Germany in 1918. In China the year 1911 put an end to a development stretching over 2,000 years or even longer without any serious break. The Confucian view of the state (see above p. 1 f.), continuing earlier traditions, had held sway in China without serious opposition since the beginning of the Christian era. In the course of the centuries this universalistic view of the state and the world had been modified and developed in detail, without any of its essential foundations, such as the position and authority of the Emperor as Son of Heaven, being seriously affected. Even the foreign dynasties—Tungus, Mongols and Manchus, etc.—which ruled China temporarily, for the most part adopted the Chinese view of the state. Only in the 19th century, as a result of changed conditions, did it become clear that this traditional view was untenable and that the Confucian idea of the state was simply Utopian. Hence the revolution of 1911 meant the final overthrow of a structure that had been shaken by Western imperialism from without and slowly but surely undermined and ruined from within ever since the Taiping revolution, not least by the abolition of the official examination system (see above pp. 68 f.). It is important to notice that the revolution of 1911 was not just another of the many changes of dynasty which China had often experienced, even though it had many of the characteristic elements of such changes and was soon followed by an attempt to establish a new dynasty. Nor was it, as it may perhaps have seemed at the beginning, the introduction of a new era of division and strife, with each ruler declaring himself the legitimate successor of the Son of Heaven. It was much more the conclusion of an era, an era of more than 2,000 years, the irrevocable end of the Confucian state and indeed of Confucianism. Since the beginning of this century and particularly since 1911 China has found itself in a tremendous crisis, the dimensions and significance of which have rarely been seen in the history of the world; the number of those involved in this crisis is about equal to the entire population of Europe. All traditional political, social, intellectual and moral foundations, which had for centuries been regarded as inviolable dogma, indubitably true and self-evident, were reduced to absolutely nothing, to a mere shadow. China has been compared to an old man, who has spent his whole life in the service of a certain idea, believing in its truth and making important contributions based on this idea, and who has suddenly realized in extreme old age that all his presuppositions and ideas have been false and untenable.

These far-reaching consequences of the revolution may have been clear to only a few—inside and outside China. Sun Yat-sen and his followers were full of idealistic and unselfish aims and they deserve credit for having administered the final blow to the tottering Confucian state. In a sense, therefore, their work was essentially destructive. They were not in a position, however, to do anything conclusive or radically new to replace the old order they had destroyed. Their ideas about building up the republic, such as the Three People's Principles and the Five Power Constitution, were too theoretical and took no account of the existing situation. The theoreticians of the revolution lacked insight into the political possibilities afforded by the historical conditions. They lived in a world of theory rather than reality. It was no new experience in Chinese history to have elaborate theoretical systems drawn up and discussed without reference to their practicability; and it would be unfair to expect the revolutionaries to have erected even the foundations of a new structure, while the old decaying structure was still collapsing. The politically inexperienced, idealistic revolutionary theoreticians were confronted by the politically cunning and unscrupulous 'war-lords' and their followers. By far the most capable among them was Yüan Shih-k'ai. He possessed political experience and subtlety, knew what had happened in the past, and could make an accurate assessment of the present situation while exploiting the personal opportunities open to him. He had at his disposal everything that the revolutionaries needed, but he lacked their idealism and sense of responsibility. His activities served no higher purpose or aim than his own ambition and desire for power.

The collapse of the dynasty and the traditional view of the state meant the end of the only bond that had held China together throughout long centuries of real political division. The centrifugal regional forces in the different parts of the country which had slumbered for several centuries, began to reawaken. New centres of power began to form in the provinces, which were already known to be political units. Szechwan, for instance, which has already been mentioned, was one such unit. There was similar pressure for independence from the central government in other provinces, especially in those lying more on the periphery, such as Kwangtung-Kwangsi, Yunnan, Kansu, Shensi, etc. The dependencies of Tibet, Sinkiang, Mongolia and Manchuria established *de facto* independence soon after 1911. The revolution led to a period of constant internal conflicts, in which regional factors often played at least as important a role as ideological factors, if not more so. This was one of the main reasons why Sun Yat-sen resigned the Presidency; he realized he would not be able to hold the country together. Those who controlled the central and southern provinces would have recognized his Presidency—at least *de jure*—but not the provinces of the North. Yüan Shih-k'ai seemed to be the only one of whom it could be hoped that he would be able to preserve the unity of the Empire. He succeeded only in part; his Presidency was the prelude to the period of the great civil wars. Thus, the overthrow of the monarchy which meant a revolution of the constitution was the prelude to the serious disturbances and consequent suffering which China was to experience in the following decades.

THE BEGINNINGS OF THE REPUBLIC

It was primarily the organization and initiative of the Revolutionary Alliance under the leadership of Sun Yat-sen that led to the formation in 1911 of a broad, united revolutionary front which was successful in getting the Ch'ing dynasty to abdicate and in establishing the Republic. But the united front came to an end with this success, and it soon became clear that the numerous different forces which had been united by the common aim of overthrowing Manchu rule were pulling against one another again once their first aim had been achieved. New fronts which were hostile to one another soon formed. Thus, the overthrow of the ruling dynasty by the revolution of 1911 shows largely the same features as similar events in the past. Even so the characteristics of the peasant revolt (see above pp. 19 ff.) do not stand out: it is much more like the frequent military insurrections against the ruling

dynasty in the past. In 1911, of course—as not infrequently before—both elements are to be found, but the latter was clearly
predominant. These traditional elements in the form of the
revolution do not exclude its deeper significance, which we tried
to characterize in the last section as something completely new,
without parallel in Chinese history.

When Sun Yat-sen resigned his acting presidency in favour of
Yüan Shih-k'ai in February, 1912, he relied on Yüan to make the
cause of the revolution and the republic his own. This trust says
much for Sun's idealism and optimism, but not for his knowledge
of human nature or his judgment of the real situation. His expectations were soon disappointed. Yüan Shih-k'ai enjoyed the trust of
the military as well as the Revolutionary Alliance. He was regarded
as the only person who could possibly control the new and difficult
situation. The provisional government of the revolutionaries had
established itself in Nanking and in deliberate imitation of the
first rulers of the Ming dynasty it had decided to make Nanking
the capital of China once more. It was decided to remove the
republican capital from the atmosphere of Peking at the very
beginning because Peking combined cultural refinement and
traditional modes of life with decadence, intrigue and corruption—
in short, all the good and bad features of the old régime. Yüan
Shih-k'ai, whose military and political power was based on the
North, had his own reasons for not moving the capital to Nanking.
As a result of military revolts, which broke out—possibly at his
own secret instigation—in Peking and other places in northern
China at the very moment when he was due to arrive in Nanking
it was clear that his presence in Peking was absolutely indispensable. Thus despite the annoyance of the more radical revolutionary
elements from southern and central China Peking continued to be
the capital.

Reference has already been made to the weakness of these
radical revolutionaries. They wanted to introduce ideas and
institutions of freedom, constitutional government and democracy
from the West where the ethos and structure of society were quite
different, into a China for which these ideas and institutions were
alien and unsuitable. These ideas and the institutions associated
with them were a historical development from western civilization

and had been able to develop successfully only in the West. The Chinese revolutionaries, who were full of Western ideas, spoke a language that was to a certain extent foreign to their own country-men, and they were not understood. Apart from Sun Yat-sen and a number of other idealists, who were genuinely seeking the best for their country, the revolution had attracted a very mixed group of people, some of whom were only interested in seeking office and in the illegal financial gain which was easily combined with this, or in other personal advantages. Thus, the parliamentary elections, which took place at the beginning of 1913 and which gave the Revolutionary Party—now called the Kuomintang, 'the National Party'—a majority of seats, were a farce. The results were deter-mined almost entirely by bribery and terror. The election issues were not political programmes or convictions but the benefits accruing to individuals and groups, for whom the victory of their party was a vital question financially. By their preparation for the revolution the Kuomintang had built up the most effective and widespread organization. Apart from the centres of the revolution-nary movement abroad, the revolution's headquarters in China itself were in the southern province of Kwangtung, especially in the provincial capital of Canton, where Western influences had first found entrance along with Western trade. The provincial government of Kwangtung, which was largely independent of the central government in Peking, consisted largely of the newcomers from the revolutionary movement. An accurate first-hand descrip-tion of the prevailing spirit in Canton is to be found in a contem-porary French observer, who wrote as follows:

This youthful provincial government was composed of journalists, students from abroad, sons of industrialists, merchants and pre-viously rebellious petty officials. In their eyes the spirit of tradition was the enemy of progress; it was to be attacked in all its forms. They were to teach the opposite of what had been taught in the past and make an absolutely fresh start. The advocates of this theory were not, as one might imagine, ideological philosophers, full of abstractions. At the head of the direction of industry there was to be found an industrialist who had worked for many years in the factories owned by his father-in-law in the South Sea; finance was in the hands of a large merchant from the southern ports. Other branches of the administration were the responsibility of specialists. Frenchmen wrongly think that the Chinese of the new generation are theoreticians and fanatical disciples of Rousseau and our encyclopaedists; in fact very few of them have read them. The young rulers of Canton are practical men with purely mercantile interests, i.e. utilitarians. They condemned the forms of the old civilization because they seemed to be hindering the economic progress of the country. They presented the Republican régime as the most suitable framework for commercial and industrial development, a broad, flexible framework which, they thought, would not hold back either the individual or the group. In their opinion the apparatus of government had to be reduced to its simplest form, because social activity was the chief requisite. . . .

Overseas Chinese were noted for their fairly emphatic disregard of government affairs, and they devoted their energies to the questions of exploiting the sources of wealth. These immigrant Chinese may be regarded as displaced persons, who were maimed or deformed by their contact with different cultures. At the same time it should be recognized that they wanted action; they wanted to do something useful; and they were enterprising in outlook. But precisely because they lived abroad, in a cosmopolitan environment, they were hardly aware of forces which were hostile to the renewal of which they dreamed. . . .

These young reformers, who were not dependent on Chinese education, had been particularly subject to the influence of American protestantism and American education. The American citizen was the model for the Chinese of tomorrow. The American's active life, independent, in a world without restrictions, completely dominated by the profit motive, was a very powerful attraction. China's young people were convinced that such a blossoming of human personality was only possible if differences of social hierarchy disappeared and privileges and prerogatives of class were unknown. The first and most important lesson was that there should be equality of opportunity; prejudices and received opinions, family and other ties must be abolished, in order that the individual might be free to engage in the struggle for wealth.[1]

Because of tendencies such as those described above the revolution of 1911 has been called the 'bourgeois revolution'. These bourgeois elements existed not only in Canton but also in other seaports and they spread considerably in the following period.

1. Translated from Albert Maybon, *La République Chinoise*, Paris, 1914, pp. 171–5.

They also had a certain amount of influence in many local government offices. They were only one element, however, and by no
means the most decisive, in the revolution of 1911, so that it
hardly seems justifiable to refer to it as 'bourgeois'.

Bourgeois elements did not have as great a share in the revolution, especially in the provinces of the West and South, as the
regional forces represented by local gentry or merchants and
artisans, who were chiefly concerned not about the choice between
monarchy or republic, but about being as little dependent as
possible on the central government and paying as little as possible
in taxes to the capital. The dispute over the nationalization of the
railways, for instance, had revealed not only the existence of such
tendencies but also their parallelism with the trends of the revolution. Administration under the Ch'ing dynasty had been strongly
centripetal. By stipulating that no one should hold a leading official
position in the government of his own province or of his own
prefecture or county, regional interests were largely eliminated.
This regulation was immediately abolished by the Provisional
Government, partly perhaps for purely idealistic and theoretical
considerations of local self-administration—which had existed for
many years alongside official government agencies in many
branches of the administration—without regard for the practical
consequences. In addition the regional forces may also have made
their fateful influence felt in order to advance their own interests.
The abolition of this regulation meant that the road was clear for
regional forces, and the break-up of the state's cohesion in the
following decades was the inevitable result. Yüan Shih-k'ai, in
contrast to the revolutionaries, sought to follow the centralizing
tradition of the Manchu government and later reintroduced the
relevant regulation of the Ch'ing period. He was not in a position,
however, to see that it was implemented everywhere, because of
the power which regional forces had already regained.

The revolution and the collapse of the imperial government
rendered the position of the prefects and magistrates largely impossible, in so far as they were not taken over and protected by the
new holders of power. Newly dispatched prefects and magistrates
were usually unqualified and inexperienced and consequently were
not usually in a position to enforce their orders. Not infrequently

they were attacked and driven from their area of office, if they did not have sufficient military protection. This was often the case in the southwestern provinces particularly. The *de facto* government of a prefecture or a district then fell into the hands of the local notables, who generally belonged to the local gentry, and not infrequently of the leaders in the secret societies, especially the Society of the Elders and Brothers. They were aware only of the interests of their own small regions and were often independent, in practice if not in theory, not only of the central government in the capital but also of the provincial government in the provincial capital. This is the reason why in a province like Szechwan, for instance, which at the beginning of the century was one of the best governed and most orderly in the whole country, the mismanagement and caprice of the local holders of power after the revolution assumed increasingly worse forms and the general insecurity constantly increased. These regional forces in the South and West had sided on the whole with the revolutionaries, since they looked to this quarter for protection against the centralizing efforts of Yüan Shih-k'ai and the North.

The new 'republic' was characterized not only by increasing decentralization and the breakaway of provinces from the central government but also by the retreat of the civil power in the face of the military. In the classical Chinese state civil and military power stood side by side. Normally the civil power was predominant, and in theory, at any rate, was always so. The president and the officials of the Ministry of War were always civil officials as well as the provincial governors and governors general who were particularly influential in recent centuries. Civil officials were often entrusted with military tasks. Even in the event of war the executive power remained, theoretically at least, in the hands of the civil authorities. Of course, this did not prevent the government of particular regions or even the whole country being assumed by the army and its leaders in times of unrest. Several of the founders of new dynasties were originally rebel military leaders; however, they always restored the power of the government to the civil authorities as soon as they had assumed control.

What followed the revolution of 1911 was somewhat different. Yüan Shih-k'ai was a general and his power rested chiefly on his military strength; three of his four successors as presidents before 1927 were also war-lords. Military leaders often acted in a civil capacity at the same time; in the provinces the military leaders were often simultaneously provincial governors and their subordinates were not infrequently prefects and magistrates. The civil authorities were usually helpless in the face of the army and could not maintain their position without their protection.

It only remains to mention the role played by the great mass of the people, particularly the peasants, in the revolution and the early years of the republic. Apart from the collaboration of the secret societies in central and southern China in the revolution of 1911, the role of the great mass of the population was purely passive. Politics continued to be the preserve of a very small group, and the great majority of the people was not concerned with the revolution and the republic. For the time being, at any rate, the traditional social structure continued almost unaltered. It was only very slowly that the new ideas and the new patterns of life and economics, which were to destroy the traditional order, began to penetrate the Chinese people; but the effect of these new patterns was all the more continuous and lasting. This process of the disintegration of the traditional order has not yet been concluded. The revolution resulting in the overthrow of the monarchy inaugurated this process and this is the reason for the particular importance ascribed to this event.

The Cultural Revolution:
The May 4th Movement
of 1919

In the capital, Peking, the atmosphere was quite different from that in Canton. Yüan Shih-k'ai, a former leading government official and a conservative Northerner, was fundamentally opposed to a democratic government and had little sympathy for the new ideas of the revolutionaries from central and southern China, most of whom had combined under the able leadership of Sung Chiao-jen in the new National Party, the Kuomintang. Between Yüan Shih-k'ai and his followers—who included the army officers, later known as the Pei-yang group, and also the civil servants taken over from the previous imperial government—and the radical revolutionaries were the moderate conservatives, who were likewise composed of various smaller groups.

After entering on his provisional presidency Yüan Shih-k'ai took further steps to consolidate his power. With the help of foreign loans he was in a position to support a large army and bribe venal elements in the civil and military power structure. Opponents whom he could not win over he sought to render innocuous by cunning and force. Sung Chiao-jen was assassinated in the spring of 1913 on the instigation of Yüan. Thus Sun Yat-sen and the members of the Kuomintang soon realized that their revolutionary cause had been betrayed by Yüan's dictatorial and reactionary methods, and in the summer of 1913 started a violent insurrection, the 'Second Revolution', against Yüan and his clique. Yüan's well-trained and well-equipped troops, however, had no difficulty in gaining the upper hand and swiftly quelling the movement. Popular sympathy at that time was on Yüan's side, with the result that Yüan's power and prestige were considerably enhanced by these events; moreover the South—especially Kwangtung—which had previously been in the hands of the revolutionaries, was now brought firmly under Yüan's centralized control. Sun Yat-sen and the other leaders of the insurrection who managed to escape Yüan's clutches fled to Japan.

After this notable success Yüan Shih-k'ai was no longer satisfied simply to head a provisional government. By subjecting the parliament, which had been elected at the beginning of 1913 and was assembled in Peking, to the increasing pressure of generosity coupled with threats to confine it under military guard he persuaded it to 'elect' him President on 6th October, 1913. Recognition of the new state by foreign governments followed. Soon afterwards Yüan ordered the dissolution of the Kuomintang and the arrest of a large proportion of its membership because of 'connections with the rebels'. Parliament, now reduced to less than half, lost its quorum and was dissolved shortly afterwards. This was followed by the proclamation of a constitution which gave Yüan almost dictatorial powers; it was soon revised to confer the presidency on him for life and even gave him the right to determine his successor. There was no longer any doubt where the path would end, and at the beginning of 1915 preparations were begun to proclaim Yüan Shih-k'ai as Emperor. In the spring, however, these plans had to be broken off for the time being because of Japan's 'Twenty-One Demands'.

Like China, Japan had been forcibly opened to foreign trade in the middle of the 19th century and had been similarly subjected to foreign interference and humiliations. As a result of radical reforms in the constitution, however, Japan quickly learned to adapt herself to the demands of a new situation and, following the example of the Western powers, initiated its own active, imperialistic policy on the mainland opposite by seizing the Liukiu islands, Formosa and the Pescadores (P'eng-hu tao), and severing Korea's tribute relations with China. Japan's attempt to set foot on the mainland was forestalled by the Shimonoseki intervention of Russia, France and Germany in 1895, but her victory in the Russo–Japanese war of 1904–5 allowed her to attain her first objective on the mainland: the occupation of the Russian leased territory of Liao-tung together with Dairen and Port Arthur and the Russian-built South Manchurian railway, and the virtual surrender of Korea. The final annexation which set the seal on the previous development did not occur, however, until 1910, without any opposition by the great powers.

As we have seen, Japan's external expansion was paralleled by its attempt after 1890 to exert influence on internal Chinese politics by providing asylum and help for all sorts of political refugees from China. The chief obstacle to further political and economic expansion by Japan on the mainland was the presence of the Western powers. The outbreak of the First World War in 1914, which concentrated the attention of the Great Powers on Europe, therefore presented Japan with a favourable opportunity to pursue its own aims in the Far East. Japan's entry into the war on the side of the Allies enabled her to attack the German-occupied leased territory of Kiaochow and to occupy the province of Shantung. As a result of Japan's attempt to exploit the situation even further, China was presented with the famous 'Twenty-One Demands' at the beginning of 1915. This action went back in part to the memorandum of a radical nationalistic group, the Black Dragon Society, which demanded that the involvement of the European Great Powers in their own affairs should be fully exploited and that full use should be made of an opportunity which was unlikely to present itself again to establish lasting Japanese predominance in China. The authenticity of this memorandum, which was published against the wishes of the Japanese government, was disputed by the Japanese, but has since been proved; certainly, subsequent Japanese policy widely confirmed its contents. The Japanese demands were transmitted to President Yüan Shih-k'ai by the Japanese ambassador in Peking on January 18th, 1915; they were in five parts and consisted of twenty-one points. The first section concerned the transfer of German rights and interests in Kiaochow and Shantung; the second concerned special Japanese interests in Manchuria and Inner Mongolia; the third concerned Japanese control of the largest Chinese ironworks, the Han-yeh-p'ing works, in which Japanese capital was already involved; the fourth stipulated that places on the coast should not be leased to any third power; and the fifth dealt with the extensive use of Japanese 'advisers' in all political, military, economic and

7—C.C.R.

cultural institutions throughout China, so that Japan would virtually control the entire public life of China. Acceptance of these demands in this form would have made China *de facto* a Japanese protectorate. The Chinese government, therefore, strenuously resisted the Japanese demands, and both England and America intervened when they saw that their own interests were threatened by the Japanese proposals. Discussions followed and the Japanese demands were considerably modified. Only the points of the first section remained unchanged, while those of the second, third and fourth sections were accepted after modification. The fifth group were completely omitted and postponed for later agreement. Japan only succeeded in enforcing the revised demands after an ultimatum on 7th May, 1915, which the Chinese government was forced to accept.

Yüan Shih-k'ai had not endeared himself to the Japanese since his first official contact with them in the Korean capital in the 1880s and 1890s, before the outbreak of the Sino–Japanese War. They had no sympathy for the clever, determined, energetic leader who gave little indication of complying with their wishes. A further strengthening of the Chinese central government under Yüan, which seemed the natural outcome after the success of 1913, was incompatible with Japanese interests. Hence, the Japanese hoped to force Yüan on to a course acceptable to Japan by means of the Twenty-One Demands, and at the same time to strengthen the revolutionary elements as well as certain movements towards independence in Manchuria and Mongolia in opposition to Yüan. In fact, the Japanese had a good case for threatening to give active support to the revolutionaries if their demands were rejected by the Chinese government, for Sun Yat-sen had given the Japanese government written assurances of extensive political and economic concessions in return for their desired help against Yüan Shih-k'ai. Resentment against the Japanese demands was felt strongly by all who were at all interested in politics, and tension was high. Most of the revolutionaries who had taken refuge in Japan availed themselves of Yüan Shih-k'ai's amnesty and returned to China. Only Sun Yat-sen and his closest friends remained in Japan, and their action lost them a great deal of support in China. If Yüan Shih-k'ai had had the resolution to reject the

Japanese ultimatum and to call the people to armed resistance if necessary, he would have won the enthusiastic support of the whole people—including the greater part of the revolutionaries—and he would have been recognized as the leader of the nation. But he was not ready to take this very risky and momentous step. This damaged his prestige in China very considerably. If he continued to seek to become Emperor, he would have to take into account Japanese objections, and further Japanese support for the revolutionaries, for Yüan's policy of centralization offered the Japanese little chance of pursuing their special local interests in Manchuria or southern China with any success. The idea of a divided China ruled by two figures, both of whom were completely dependent on and loyal to Japan, was much canvassed in Japan. The view expressed later by some Chinese historians, that the acceptance of the Japanese ultimatum was the price for Japan's recognition of Yüan as Emperor, hardly corresponds to the facts.

Shortly after the Japanese ultimatum an official central organization, *Ch'ou an hui*, was set up in Peking to see that petitions came in from all the provinces and organizations asking Yüan Shih-k'ai to accept the imperial title. Yüan acceded to this 'unanimous' request of the 'whole' nation and announced his accession to the throne for the following year, 1916. This announcement had the effect of bringing the opposition into the open. Naturally, radical revolutionaries in the South and abroad viewed Yüan's plans for a monarchy with disquiet. A great number of Yüan's former supporters, the moderate conservatives, also openly turned away from him, as far as they dared—among them men such as Liang Ch'i-ch'ao, who had for a time been influential in the Republican government under Yüan and who, as one of the most important and progressive scholars of his day, enjoyed an outstanding reputation among all educated Chinese. When Yüan's intentions became clear, Liang Ch'i-ch'ao gave up his office and left Peking for one of the foreign concessions of Tientsin, and from there he published a long attack on Yüan's monarchical ambitions, an attack which because of the prestige of its author carried a great deal of weight.

The leader of the general revolt against Yüan Shih-k'ai, commonly known as the 'Third Revolution', was Ts'ai O, an ambitious young general and politician who had been educated in Japan. Although he did not belong to the radical revolutionary party, he had taken part in the revolution of 1911 as commander of the troops stationed in Yunnan, a body which, because of the proximity of the border with Indo-China, was large and well trained. Yunnan was one of the first provinces to declare its independence in 1911. After the revolution Ts'ai O remained in Yunnan, at first as military governor, but he was subsequently given a post in Peking by Yüan, who did not trust him and therefore wanted to have him near him. In Peking Ts'ai O was in close contact with Liang Ch'i-ch'ao and other members of the moderate conservative group. In spite of the close watch that was kept on him, he succeeded in leaving Peking secretly in the second half of 1915 and reached Yunnan via Japan, Hong Kong and Indo-China. He had already resumed secret connections with his friends there and by the end of 1915 the resistance movement of the 'National Protection Army' led by Ts'ai O from Yunnan was in operation against Yüan Shih-k'ai. In all probability it was supported by Japan, secretly if not openly. The province of Yunnan declared its independence of the central government; it was followed by Kweichow, Kwangsi, Chekiang and Szechwan. Yüan realized his authority was at an end and in March 1916 he revoked his plans and measures to re-establish the monarchy. But the movement against Yüan, once it had come into the open and achieved success, could not be halted. By revoking his plans for a monarchy Yüan showed that he was no longer possessed of the same prudence and power as in his earlier years and that his authority was finished. Even in northern China the authority of the Peking government began to collapse. The resistance movement compelled Yüan to retire and the Presidency was transferred to the Vice-President, Li Yuan-hung. On 6th June, 1916, Yüan died suddenly and unexpectedly after a short illness, and thus provided a peaceful solution to a number of questions.

Yüan Shih-k'ai's death was the beginning of the so-called war-lord period which lasted for over a decade. The area controlled by Yüan's successors extended no further than the power of their own troops—insofar as they had troops under their command—or of the war-lords who supported them. None approached even remotely the position of strength which Yüan Shih-k'ai had enjoyed. More-over, the Parliament dissolved by Yüan, although temporarily recalled, was unable to exercise any real influence. The real authority was held by the various war-lords, who were fighting to gain control of the capital or were consolidating their control over groups of provinces or even single provinces. Even within a single province there were often several war-lords struggling for power. Various foreign powers contributed to the general state of disorder by assisting sometimes one of them, and sometimes another. The events that followed cannot be discussed here in detail. It is important to notice, however, that before 1927 all the groups and individuals fighting for power in Peking and northern China were very conservative, if not reactionary, and they were hostile to the revolutionaries around Sun Yat-sen. In fact, in 1917 the general Chang Hsün, with the support of his troops, attempted to restore the last Ch'ing Emperor (Hsüan-t'ung), an attempt in which K'ang Yu-wei, who had achieved fame in the Reform Movement of 1898 and who was still loyal to the dynasty, was also involved. The attempt misfired, however; Chang Hsün was unable to maintain his position for more than a few days. The interlude was brought to an end by another general, Tuan Ch'i-jui. Chang Hsün took refuge in the Dutch Legation and thereafter played no significant part in events.

In the same year China entered the war against Germany on the side of the Allies. The official explanation—the German declaration of unlimited U-boat warfare—was only a pretext. The real reason for such a step, which provoked considerable conflict within the government, was largely a matter of internal politics; rival groups were struggling for power and each saw the declaration of war as being to their advantage or disadvantage. No less important, how-ever, were Allied influences, especially American. Among Chinese who were able to look further than the question of their own power and position American pronouncements had raised hopes of their being able to exert in future some influence on the peace treaty. It was hoped to win back the former German rights and deeds of ownership in Shantung, which had been forcibly surrendered to Japan as a result of the Twenty-One Demands. The secret promises regarding German rights in Shantung made to Japan by England

and France before China's entry into the war were unknown to China at this time. China's resentment, therefore, was to be all the more bitter when peace was concluded in 1919.

THE EXTERNAL EVENTS OF
THE MAY 4TH MOVEMENT

As one of the powers involved in the war against Germany, China sent a large delegation with five official delegates to the peace conference at Paris. Great hopes were placed on this conference by the Chinese, particularly because of the fifth point of the declaration of President Wilson before the end of the war, when he predicted a free, impartial and absolutely unprejudiced settlement of all colonial questions. The Chinese delegates in Paris presented a memorandum which would have ensured China a position of equality among the victor nations of the First World War. This memorandum dealt with a general adjustment of the situation in China deriving from the unequal treaties in the following seven points: (1) renunciation of spheres of influence or interest; (2) withdrawal of foreign troops and police; (3) the withdrawal of foreign post offices and telegraphic agencies; (4) abolition of extra-territorial consular jurisdiction; (5) relinquishment of leased territories; (6) restoration to China of foreign concessions and settlements; and (7) tariff autonomy. Further demands included the transfer of German rights in Kiaochow and Shantung and the abrogation of the Twenty-One Demands enforced by the Japanese in 1915. Organizations of Chinese students throughout Europe lent their energetic support to the requests of the official delegation by resolutions and demonstrations. But the Chinese point of view won little support, not only among the Japanese, which was to be expected, but also among the majority of other delegates to the conference. Discussion of the seven points was referred back on the ground that the conference was not competent to deal with them. England, France, and Italy had already made secret commitments to Japan about the transfer of German rights in Shantung and China was unable to advance its claims in the face of these promises. Moreover, Japan threatened to leave the conference if Chinese wishes were made a matter of serious discussion. American support, which China was relying on, did not materialize. Hence, articles 156–8 of the Treaty of Versailles came to read as follows:

Article 156. Germany renounces, in favour of Japan, all her rights, titles and privileges—particularly those concerning the territory of Kiaochow, railways, mines and submarine cables—which she acquired in virtue of the Treaty concluded by her with China on March 6, 1898, and of all other arrangements relative to the Province of Shantung.

All German rights in the Tsingtao–Tsinanfu Railway, including its branch lines, together with its subsidiary property of all kinds, stations, shops, fixed and rolling stock, mines, plant and material for the exploitation of the mines, are and remain acquired by Japan, together with all rights and privileges attaching thereto.

The German State submarine cables from Tsingtao to Shanghai and from Tsingtao to Chefoo, with all the rights, privileges and properties attaching thereto, are similarly acquired by Japan, free and clear of all charges and encumbrances.

Article 157. The movable and immovable property owned by the German State in the territory of Kiaochow, as well as all the rights which Germany might claim in consequence of the works or improvements made or of the expenses incurred by her, directly or indirectly, in connection with this territory, are and remain acquired by Japan, free and clear of all charges and encumbrances.

Article 158. Germany shall hand over to Japan within three months from the coming into force of the present Treaty the archives, registers, plans, title deeds and documents of every kind, wherever they may be, relating to the administration, whether civil, military, financial, judicial or other, of the territory of Kiaochow.

Within the same period Germany shall give particulars to Japan of all treaties, arrangements or agreements, relating to the rights, title or privileges referred to in the two preceding Articles.

When the Chinese public got to know what had been decided in Paris there was a great outcry and agitation, especially in the academic circles of Peking and Shanghai. The fourth anniversary of the delivery of the Japanese ultimatum to China was 7th May, 1919. Three days previously, on 4th May, on the initiative of the University of Peking, several thousand students assembled for a mass demonstration in front of the T'ien-an Men (Gate of Heavenly Peace) in Peking. They carried banners with slogans such as 'China belongs to the Chinese', 'Restore Chinese rights in Shantung', 'Reject the Twenty-One Demands', 'Refuse to sign the

Paris Peace Treaty', 'Punish all traitors'. The last slogan was a reference to the three pro-Japanese politicians who were thought to be responsible for accepting the Twenty-One Demands. The government, led at that time by Tuan Ch'i-jui, refused to enter into discussions with the students. Excitedly they marched to the house of the Minister of Communications, Ts'ao Ju-lin, whom they regarded as one of the traitors. As it happened, the other two politicians who had been branded as traitors were also there. The students forced their way into the house; in the mêlée that followed, the police, who had been quickly alerted, intervened, some shots were fired and part of the house was set on fire. The three politicians escaped with slight injuries and a number of students were arrested. There were no further incidents that day. With the exception of what happened at the house of the Minister of Communications the action of the students had been peaceful, orderly and without bloodshed.

The arrest of a number of students, however, provided grounds for further action. The students of the Peking colleges and universities who were subsequently joined by students from colleges and universities throughout China, formed a National Students' Union in Shanghai (*Ch'üan-kuo hsüeh-sheng lien-ho-hui*). A large number of professors and lecturers declared their sympathy with the students—including the President of the University of Peking, Ts'ai Yüan-p'ei—although they did not actually take part in the student demonstrations. Further demonstrations and strikes followed throughout China and there was an appeal to boycott Japanese goods. The boycott spread quickly and while it lasted— for about a year—affected Japan's trade to China very considerably. The movement which had begun with the students soon affected other groups. Large sections of the trading population went on strike for a time in support of the boycott on Japanese goods. For the first time Chinese workers held public demonstrations on a large scale in Peking, Tientsin, Shanghai, Hankow and other cities, thus uniting themselves with the general national movement inspired by the students.

Confronted by such a national movement, which continued to expand, the Peking government was finally compelled to give way, in spite of being friendly to Japan and quite averse to any active anti-Japanese policy. The three politicians who were regarded as being responsible for accepting the Twenty-One Demands resigned, and the Chinese delegation in Paris was instructed not to sign the treaty. The aims of the student movement were thus substantially achieved.

THE POLITICAL AND ECONOMIC BACKGROUND

The events just mentioned may not seem very important, when compared with the events of 1898, 1900 or 1911. Prior to the last decade Western commentators have paid little attention to the May 4th Movement. It has usually been briefly mentioned in passing or even ignored altogether. In China, however, the May 4th Movement has been regarded as an event of extraordinary significance, if not the most important event in the Chinese revolution. Most modern Chinese historians make the period of 'modern history' that begins with 1840 end in 1919 with the May 4th Movement; 'contemporary history' begins in 1919. Mao Tse-tung expressed himself as follows in 1940:

The May 4th Movement was an anti-imperialist as well as an antifeudal movement. Its outstanding historical significance is to be seen in a feature which was absent from the Revolution of 1911, namely, its thorough and uncompromising opposition to imperialism as well as to feudalism. The May 4th Movement possessed this quality because capitalism had developed a step further in China and because new hopes had arisen for the liberation of the Chinese nation as China's revolutionary intellectuals saw the collapse of three great imperialist powers, Russia, Germany and Austria-Hungary, and the weakening of two others, Britain and France, while the Russian proletariat had established a socialist state and the German, Hungarian and Italian proletariat had risen in revolution. The May 4th Movement came into being at the call of the world revolution, of the Russian Revolution and of Lenin. It was part of the world proletarian revolution of the time. Although the Communist Party had not yet come into existence, there were already large numbers of intellectuals who approved of the Russian Revolution and had the rudiments of Communist ideology. In the beginning the May 4th Movement was the revolutionary movement of a united front of three sections of people—Communist intellectuals, revolutionary petty-bourgeois intellectuals and bourgeois intellectuals (the last forming the right wing of the movement). Its shortcoming was that it was confined to the intellectuals and that the workers and peasants did not join in. But as soon as it developed into the June 3rd Movement, not only the intellectuals but the mass of the proletariat, the petty bourgeoisie and the bourgeoisie joined in, and it became a nation-wide revolutionary movement. The cultural revolution ushered in by the May 4th Movement was uncompromising in its opposition to feudal culture; there had never been such a great and thoroughgoing cultural revolution since the dawn of Chinese history. Raising aloft the two great banners of the day, 'Down with the old ethics and up with the new!' and 'Down with the old literature and up with the new!', the cultural revolution had great achievements to its credit.[1]

It is not necessary to accept all Mao Tse-tung's views in detail. The May 4th Movement was primarily a national movement and it can hardly be regarded as part of the proletarian world revolution. Nevertheless, Mao's statements may help us to see the significance of the movement in a wider context. It was not the events of May 4th or June 3rd as such—the beginning of the strike in Shanghai—that gave these dates importance, but the whole movement of this period which was associated with these dates and which found concrete expression in the events of the May 4th and the following weeks.

As already mentioned the decade following the death of Yüan Shih-k'ai was marked by conflicts between individual war-lords and their supporters struggling to gain control either of the central government or a part of the Empire or a single province. These clashes were very similar in character to those of the past when a failing dynasty was about to give way to a new one; even the centres of power, which were determined by natural, geographical factors, were usually the same as centuries, or even millennia, before, e.g. Shansi, Szechwan, the Yangtze delta, etc. The only difference from the past was the absence of the Confucian idea of a united state with a central ruler. Many of the successful military leaders of the past—perhaps even the majority—had regarded themselves implicitly or explicitly as the future central ruler, whose task was to unify the state, and hence they had been able to

1. 'On New Democracy' from *Selected Works of Mao Tse-tung*, Vol. II, Peking, 1965, pp. 373–4.

inspire their troops with the same idea. Even if traces of the traditional Confucian view of the state could still be found, they had lost all power to exercise any fundamental influence since the failure of Yüan Shih-k'ai and Chang Hsün. The purely personal interests of the various war-lords and their concern with power politics became all the more open and prominent. Every war-lord was more or less absolute dictator in the region he controlled. On the whole, of course, they limited themselves to raising money to support their troops—at the cost of the people, especially the peasants. Some of them also sought new sources of help in industrial and mining works. But there was no thought given to fundamental political and social reforms. It was not unnatural, therefore, that a large proportion of young intellectuals should devote serious thought to the question of how to escape from the maladministration which was ruining the whole of China or that they should seek new ideas and ways of doing this. Whereas the imperial dynasty before its 'overthrow and also to a certain extent Yüan Shih-k'ai had, so far as possible, suppressed the publication and spread of revolutionary or other undesirable new ideas, the war-lords at first showed little concern about such matters. Hence, the new ideas which led to the May 4th Movement circulated freely among young intellectuals throughout China, so long as they did not directly prejudice the interests of particular war-lords.

The situation was different from that in 1911, not only politically but also economically. As a result of the war the economic activity of the European powers in China had been substantially curtailed. European industry was devoted primarily to the war effort, and European goods gradually disappeared from the Chinese market. To a certain extent the decline in European imports was offset by an increase in Japanese and American imports. But, this apart, China now had an opportunity to extend its own industry, which had been very limited until then. During the war years the textile industry and corn milling as well as the production of matches, cigarettes, cement, tinned foods, etc., had increased considerably. Chinese banking had also expanded. Cities like Shanghai, Hankow and Tientsin were extensively industrialized during this period. Important railway junctions, such as Tsinan, Hsüchow, Shihkiachwang, etc., became new economic centres. All these industrial cities attracted large numbers of peasants, and a new class of industrial workers began to develop on a scale not known in China before. This working-class population was ready to accept new views and ideas, especially since they had become increasingly independent of the ties of the traditional family structure which was essentially economically based. For the traditional Chinese family was, apart from its other functions, an economic unit, and the absolute authority possessed by the head of the family depended largely on this. The peasant family whether viewed as a consumer or a producer, was very much a self-contained unit. For the most part it produced its own food and clothing and had few links with the outside world other than with a narrow circle of neighbours. All the economic enterprises of the past had been managed on a particularist basis, apart perhaps from the large building projects, for which large numbers of unskilled workers were recruited on a temporary basis; such workers returned to their families when the work was finished. Modern economic enterprises, however, especially in industry, cannot select their labour force according to consideration of family or clan relations; they have to pay attention primarily to the individual's qualifications and capacity for work. This does not mean, of course, that the individual qualification and ability was insignificant in traditional China; one need think only of the craftsman, for instance. If an apprentice, who had been chosen because he belonged to a certain family or clan, proved incompetent, another apprentice was sought—but again on the basis of family or clan relations. Such a procedure would be impossible in modern industry with its constant need of skilled or semi-skilled labour, for not every worker is equally adept at adjusting himself to the technical skills required. Industrialization offered the peasant family in particular not only the opportunity of additional income through the employment of individual members of the family but also, for the individual or married couple, the possibility of an independent existence outside the larger family unit. This gave the individual the chance to escape from the authority of the head of the family, if he wished, or alternatively to use this possibility of withdrawal as a means of getting his own way in spite of pressure from the family. This undermined what had been the almost absolute authority of the head of the family and the structure of the family lost its stability. It is easy to see, therefore, that industrial workers who had experienced such emancipation formed the basis of a new proletarian class, who were fairly ready to join mass movements either of a nationalistic or communistic nature, in contrast to the peasants who were mostly conservative and held fast to the old norms and ties.

Economic development during the First World War contributed not only to a significant increase in the working class but also to a considerable increase in the numbers of entrepreneurs and merchants. With the decline of foreign commercial activity the number of Chinese businessmen who were not dependent on foreign trade, the 'national capitalists' (cf. above p. 59), increased, and in the port cities the business class gained an importance it had not previously possessed. They were interested in a strong national government which would give them internal security from the caprice and greed of the war-lords and their corrupt officials and which would be able to represent the interests of Chinese commerce abroad. Such considerations had prompted a large proportion of the business community to give their support to the revolution of 1911, although their hope of a strong national government had not been realized. But, as before, the entrepreneurs and business-people, whose numbers had increased, continued to be sympathetic to all nationalistic ideas of revolution. Even before 1919 a boycott of certain foreign goods was practised in some places, and the appeal by the intelligentsia to boycott Japanese goods found strong support in these circles. The boycott of 1919, therefore, which spread throughout China surpassed all previous actions of this sort in scope and effectiveness.

INTELLECTUAL BACKGROUND AND SIGNIFICANCE

General

Reference has already been made to the fact that intellectuals were the starting-point and driving force of the May 4th Movement. The ideas they stood for were given expression by the 'New Culture Movement' (*Hsin wen-hua yün-tung*). The Reform Movement of 1898 also began among intellectuals, but it was directed towards reform rather than revolution and in spite of many new ideas its basic presuppositions followed traditional norms. The main aim of the revolution of 1911 was the overthrow of the Manchu dynasty and except among a very narrow circle close to Sun Yat-sen there was no intention of a complete break with the past. Even Sun Yat-sen and his followers did not reveal the features which characterized the later revolution, viz., externally the struggle for complete national sovereignty against the privileges and claims of foreigners and internally the fight against traditional norms and practices and against the traditional social structure—in Communist terminology, the fight against imperialism and the fight against feudalism. In the May 4th Movement these elements came sharply to the fore for the first time. Old and new were clearly opposed to each other in a way that had not been true of 1911. Representative of the new ideas were the students and the progressive-minded lecturers of the colleges and universities which were established throughout China after the overthrow of the dynasty. 'They wanted to overthrow the ancient intellectual tradition of China and advocated learning from the advanced foreign civilization in order to create a new independent national Chinese culture'—writes a modern Chinese historian.[1] The followers of the new ideas, therefore, stood in sharp opposition to the teaching of the past, especially Confucianism, which they regarded as the main representative of traditional order and thought and therefore as an obstacle to all progress. In opposition to this New Culture Movement, the conservative reactionary groups of the war-lords and their followers—officials, politicians and scholars of the old style—supported Confucianism and the traditional ways of life and thought.

As a result of the developments set in motion by the Opium War the political universalism on which Confucianism rested was increasingly shaken and finally disproved: similarly its ethical-

1. Hua Kang, *Chung-kuo min-tsu chieh-fang yün-tung shih*, Shanghai, 1951, p. 577.

political doctrine also collapsed as a result of the Reform Movement, the abolition of the traditional examination system and the establishment of the Republic. Many of the leading supporters of Confucianism may have felt this instinctively, even though they were not clear about the ultimate consequences of what was happening. Metaphorically speaking, they wanted to decorate the superstructure of a building whose foundations had already been destroyed. Confucius should be worshipped as God and Confucianism in China should play the role played by Christianity in the West. The followers of these ideas dated the years from the birth of Confucius, just as the Christian calendar numbered the years from the birth of Christ. Conservative circles in Shanghai in 1912 had established the 'Confucian Society' (*K'ung-chiao hui*). Its aim was to secure the maintenance of Confucian tradition by proclaiming Confucianism the state religion. Two of the leading figures behind this move were K'ang Yu-wei, formerly leader of the radical Reform Movement, and now a zealous guardian of Confucian tradition, together with his pupil, Ch'en Huan-chang, known for his work (written in English) *The Economic Principles of Confucius and his School*. A series of widely circulating magazines publicly canvassed the idea of Confucianism as the state religion, especially through contributions by K'ang Yu-wei. This propaganda fell on fertile soil in the case of the conservative Peking government. In 1914 Yüan Shih-k'ai reintroduced the cult of Confucius, which he regarded as useful for his monarchical ambitions. Succeeding presidents and war-lords showed they were no less disposed to Confucianism since they regarded it as a protection of their own power against revolutionary forces.

To counteract this reactionary trend the magazine *New Youth* (*Hsin Ch'ing-nien*) was founded in 1915, first published in Shanghai; it soon became a rallying point for leaders in the struggle for progress. Its contents consisted of criticism of Chinese tradition together with a discussion of Western civilization and its representatives. Ch'en Tu-hsiu, the founder and editor of *New Youth*, had studied in Japan at the beginning of the century but had at that time not joined the revolutionary movement there. During and immediately after the revolution of 1911 he played an active part in his home province of Anhui, but after the failure of the 'Second

Revolution' he had taken refuge in the foreign concession of Shanghai, where he had set up his magazine. In 1917 the open-minded President of Peking University, Ts'ai Yüan-p'ie, invited him to join the staff of the Faculty of Literature there. Gradually many others who belonged to the *New Youth* circle followed him to Peking, among them Hu Shih, Wu Yü, Lu Hsün, etc. Thus, the University of Peking became the intellectual and organizing centre of the May 4th Movement.

The Struggle against Confucianism

Two of the most zealous and eloquent antagonists of traditional Confucian teaching and its moral and ethical standards were Ch'en Tu-hsiu and Wu Yü. Ch'en Tu-hsiu started from foreign Western ideas and wanted to replace the traditional teaching by these new Western ideas, whereas Wu Yü based himself predominantly on purely Chinese presuppositions and marshalled his opposition to Confucius from China's own history.

During the lifetime of Confucius and in the centuries immediately following Confucian teaching did not occupy a position of exclusive importance. It was not until it was made the official doctrine of the state in the Han period that it was able to prevail over numerous other doctrinal systems. Opponents of Confucianism were not lacking even then, but eventually orthodoxy, represented by the power of the state, began to strangle all opposition at birth. Under the last dynasty anything that was contrary to orthodox teaching was no longer even permitted to be published, and the great literary inquisition of the 18th century was not limited to the suppression of contemporary heretical writings, but also made a wide-ranging attempt to ban heretical publications from previous centuries. Thus, the works of the last most outstanding opponent of Confucianism, a man who was extremely famous in his day, Li Chih, better known as Li Cho-wu (1527–1602), fell into obscurity during the last two centuries and his name was almost forgotten. Wu Yü brought him to life again by publishing a biographical study of him: his grave near Peking was restored, some of his works were republished and he became the subject of a number of scholarly essays in China, Japan and the West.

Wu Yü had studied law in Japan and had come into contact

there with the Chinese revolutionaries and with Western ideas. Both may have influenced him. Even before the overthrow of the Manchu dynasty he began to publish his views discriminating against Confucianism. His writings were consequently banned and he himself was to have been arrested, but he was able to hide in the country until the revolution in 1911 saved him from the threat of arrest by the imperial authorities. Even after the Republic was established, however, the power of past tradition was so strong that in Chengtu, the capital of Wu Yü's home province of Szechwan, a magazine was banned because it had published articles of an anti-Confucian nature by Wu Yü. After that no newspaper or magazine in Szechwan was willing to publish any contribution which attacked Confucian teaching. *New Youth*, edited by Ch'en Tu-hsiu in Shanghai, reached Wu Yü in Chengtu: he made contact with Ch'en and quickly became an active contributor to the magazine. A number of earlier, as well as more recent, essays by him were subsequently published in *New Youth*. The titles of Wu Yü's articles are sufficient indications in themselves of the nature of his attack on traditional Confucianism: 'The family system as a source of despotism', 'Cannibalism and the Doctrine of Etiquette', 'The harmful effects of the class system propagated by Confucianism', 'Taoism and Legalism in opposition to traditional morality', 'The passive revolution of Lao-Tzu and Chuang-tzu', 'Refutation of K'ang Yu-wei's thesis that the traditional relationship between prince and subject cannot be altered'. Wu Yü saw the contemporary hollowness of a great deal of Confucian moral teaching. He saw that the lofty concepts of Confucian ethics were often only a cloak for the lowest sort of self-seeking: the traditional patriarchal organization of the family, based on reverence for elders, often led to the head of the family oppressing and exploiting the other members of the family in the most brutal and selfish manner, in the same way that the authority and dignity of the Emperor and the officials gave them an excellent opportunity to extend their own power and wealth at the expense of others. Encouraged by the example of Lu Hsün (cf. below p. 111), whose story *The Diary of a Madman* lampooned the hollowness and falseness of traditional society and morality, Wu Yü in his article, 'Cannibalism and the Doctrine of Etiquette', sought to examine the historical development of this incongruity between theory and practice in Confucian morality. He wrote:

When I read Lu Hsün's *The Diary of a Madman* in *New Youth*, it unexpectedly evoked a variety of responses in me. The most curious fact about us Chinese is that we are cannibals and yet are able to speak of the Doctrine of Etiquette. Cannibalism and the Doctrine of Etiquette are extreme opposites in origin, but in the history of the last five hundred years of the pre-Christian era they have come together in harmony. This is quite unique!

In *The Diary of a Madman* it says, When I open a page of history and begin to read it, the words 'humanity, righteousness, morality and virtue' are to be found everywhere. I read it attentively half the night and realized then, reading between the lines, that the whole book consisted of nothing more than two words—'eating, men' (*ch'ih jen*).

I think one perceives quite clearly from this diary that the real content of history is cannibalism, while humanity, righteousness, morality and virtue is only a façade. All those man-eaters, slippery, cunning people, hiding under a cloak of the Doctrine of Etiquette have had the cloak removed by him [i.e. Lu Hsün].[1]

Wu Yü then adduces a number of examples of actual cannibalism by followers of Confucianism in the late Chou and Han period. He concludes with the following words:

If one preaches the Doctrine of Etiquette of Master Confucius and takes it to its ultimate, to kill and eat men is inevitable. What an extremely grim thought! In one period of history people may talk about morality and virtue or humanity and righteousness, whilst on a similar occasion, directly or indirectly they eat human flesh. Even if people alive today have not, in fact, eaten men, their intention to eat men and devour a few morsels, in order to give vent to their anger, is not yet purged.

It is time we realize that we do not live for the princes! Nor for the sages and the wise men! Nor do we live for the principles of the Doctrine of Etiquette. What does 'distinguished sir' mean? What does 'devoted sir' mean?[2] Such words are only the snares which those cannibals have laid to fool us. It is time we realize that 'to

1. *Ch'ih jen yü li-chiao*, 1a-b, collected prose, *Wu Yü wen lu*, Chengtu, 1936, Vol. I.
2. Posthumous Confucian honorary titles.

eat men' is the same as 'to preach the Doctrine of Etiquette'. To preach the Doctrine of Etiquette is cannibalism.[1]

It is not necessary to agree with all Wu Yü's rather one-sided statements; but they do contain a great deal of truth. Confucianism has often served to disguise the most extreme cruelties. And Confucian narrow-mindedness, arrogance and orthodoxy have in the name of morality and virtue, humanity and righteousness, the Confucian cardinal virtues, been responsible for innumerable crimes. A glance at Chinese history is sufficient to confirm this. On the other hand Confucianism has produced not a few outstanding figures and broad-minded characters, and its politico-ethical doctrine of the state held China together for almost 2,000 years. But since the Sung period and especially under the last dynasty Confucianism was increasingly confined by a narrow-minded orthodoxy within a hollow system of forms and rules, from which almost all life had disappeared. All too often in the 20th century Confucianism was used by reactionary holders of power in family or state merely as a cheap means of suppressing all opposition to their own mismanagement and corruption. Yüan Shih-k'ai and those who succeeded him as President together with the local warlords held Confucianism in high regard in this sense. In the 1920s and even at the beginning of the thirties the Kuomintang was still predominantly anti-Confucian; simultaneously with its increasing inward decay, it began more and more to stress the traditional virtues. Finally, the most striking example was the reintroduction of the sacrificial cult of Confucius and the propagation of Confucian ideas by the Japanese during their occupation of northern China in the years 1937 to 1945. From the third decade of our century Confucianism has represented the traditional social and economic order, an order full of cracks and holes in domestic affairs and impossible to maintain in China's international relations in view of the revolutionary global changes of the 20th century. This was clearly realized and expressed as early as 1927 by O. Franke in a lecture:

We can now give the answer to the question of the role played by Confucianism in the present crisis. The answer is 'none'. Or, at

1. *Ch'ih jen yü li-chiao*, 6a–b.

least, no more than that of a dead man in a ruined house. Anyone who thinks he can or ought to rescue Confucianism from the ruins of the old China, should realize that he is carrying a corpse.

The worship of Confucius and Confucianism, which has become fashionable in quarters under the influence of unhistorical ideas in the West, is observed with surprise or with a smile in China.[1]

Of course, from a purely aesthetic point of view, the Chinese scholar official of the old style, whose composed personality had a dignity which represented the unique traditional Chinese civilization, was a much more pleasant figure than the modern revolutionary intellectual. It is understandable that many a Western observer of Chinese conditions, who has some experience of traditional China, has been influenced by this and still sees the ideals of Chinese tradition in what remains. No amount of respect for these ideals of the past, however, should blind one to the fact that this appealing tradition concealed a great deal of sham and hypocrisy, as was clearly recognized and stated for the first time in China by those who participated in the May 4th Movement.

Democracy and Science

Among the revolutionary opponents of Confucianism Wu Yü represented only one particular trend in arguing primarily in forms of traditional Chinese concepts and in following closely those who had opposed Confucianism earlier in Chinese history. There were also others, such as Hu Shih, who pointed to the possibility of picking up the threads of earlier trends of Chinese thought, which had been cut off in the course of the centuries under the pressure of Confucian orthodoxy. The overwhelming majority of those actively contributing to *New Youth*, however, were very much influenced by Western thinking, not least Ch'en Tu-hsiu, the editor of the magazine and the guiding spirit of the Peking students in the May 4th Movement. For him and his followers 'Democracy' and 'Science' were the two leading concepts, which initially were transcribed quite phonetically into Chinese as *te-mo-k'o-la-hsi* and *sai-yin-szu*. It was not until later that a translation based on the content of the words was arrived at. Ch'en Tu-hsiu rejected

---

1. 'Das Konfuzianische System and sein Ende', *Zeitschrift für Missionskunde und Religionswissenschaft*, Vol. 44, No. 3, 1929, p. 83.

traditional Chinese culture altogether, not only Confucianism but also Taoism and Buddhism, on the ground that Chinese culture had made people inactive and incapable of a positive response to the challenge of the West. The reason for the activity and vitality of the West and its superiority over China was quite simply democracy and science. Ch'en Tu-hsiu's and his followers' knowledge of the West was very superficial. Everything before the 18th century was ignored. They did not take the trouble to go to the roots of Western civilization and its thought; their concept of democracy was that of the Manchester school of liberalism. Its aim was the liberation of the individual from all restraint by the ties of tradition, especially Confucianism, in the belief that the individual who was thus freed from all ties would then be able to achieve successes similar to those in the West. Similar ideas, even if less well reasoned and systematic, had been popular immediately after the revolution of 1911 within the revolutionary provincial government of Canton, which consisted largely of overseas Chinese. Ch'en Tu-hsiu and the people close to him regarded 'science' primarily as a weapon against superstition, meaning by 'superstition' all religious beliefs without exception. Science would serve to break down the traditional social order, which rested on certain basic religious conceptions, not only in the fight against Confucianism but also in the fight against all other religious teaching and traditions which had a religious sanction. This anti-traditionalism, combined with an uncritical superficial admiration of Western political and social patterns and of Western thought, was characteristic of most progressive Chinese intellectuals at that time, and, so far from having withered, this attitude could be observed quite often in more recent times too. As a result of American cultural propaganda, which increased considerably after 1911, America and the American way of life became more and more the ideal pattern. In 1919–20 the American philosopher John Dewey gave a series of lectures at the University of Peking; these had a quite extraordinary influence, which lasted into the thirties and even later. Dewey's positivistic thought, directed to the practical life, commended itself particularly to Chinese academic teachers and students. His stimulus contributed to a certain degree to the deepening of the concept of democracy in China.

An article in *New Youth* referring to Dewey, entitled 'The basis for the realization of democracy', by Ch'en Tu-hsiu, is evidence of this.[1] For the first time Ch'en Tu-hsiu spoke of grass-roots democratic organization in the smallest units of geographical neighbourhood and daily work, and in doing so he referred to certain institutions of local self-administration and professional or other associations that had existed in China for a long time. There were wide areas of life not touched by the official administration of government in traditional China; these were left to the initiative of the people. This reference made by Ch'en Tu-hsiu could perhaps have proved fruitful for the advancement of really democratic methods in China, but unfortunately he did not follow it up. Soon afterwards Ch'en Tu-hsiu subscribed exclusively to the ideas of Marx and Lenin. Some of those who were associated with the May 4th Movement followed him sooner or later, although others retained their liberal ideas of these early days or even, like, for example, Hu Shih, gradually adopted a more conservative position.

Irrespective of their position, however, they all helped to prepare the intellectual ground for the later stages of the revolution, especially for the victory of Communism. That the Communists in 1954–5 launched an attacking campaign against Hu Shih, who at that time lived in retirement in the USA, was probably the result of the great debt the Communists owe him. Even to this day he may have quite a few secret friends and followers among Chinese intellectuals. His main service was in connection with the 'literary revolution'.

The Literary Revolution

The fight of young Chinese intellectuals against tradition was not limited to the political and social order. The picture of the May 4th Movement would be incomplete without reference to the momentous 'literary revolution' (*wen-hsüeh ko-ming*). For a true appreciation of the significance of this change it must be realized that the Chinese script is not phonetic like most other scripts but consists of ideographs, developed from an ancient picture form of writing. Every character—and Chinese literature since the 5th

1. *Shih-hsing min-chih ti chi-ch'u,* collected prose writings, *Tu-hsiu wen-ts'un,* Vol. I, pp. 373–89.

century b.c. has used about forty or fifty thousand—represents a certain concept. Five to ten thousand of these are used regularly. But for the pronunciation of this great number of characters, each with very fine shades of meaning, the vernacular of northern China today has little more than 400 different monosyllables, which when given four different tones results in a total of 1,600 sound combinations. The spoken language to a large extent combines different monosyllables which have the same or basically similar meaning to form a compound word. Thus, Chinese conversation is as intelligible as any other language and the possibilities for misunderstanding are limited to a few exceptional cases. One result of this incongruity of written Chinese and the vernacular is that the two diverge and go different ways. Knowledge of Chinese writing, which is much more difficult to learn than a phonetic script, has since ancient times been the privilege of a very small élite that has controlled political and social power, and this has remained true into the 20th century. Mastery of the characters as such is only the first of the difficulties to be overcome. In the course of time literary Chinese developed an extraordinarily refined and complex style, which could only be fully mastered after long study and intensive practice. Any text written in the literary style and read aloud was unintelligible without seeing the characters with the eye. The sacred books of Confucianism, which in their present form come from the beginning of the Christian era and constitute China's 'classics', were the foundation of all literary education and the sole content of official state examinations for many centuries. Knowledge of the classical literature and literary language was the criterion for membership of the ruling élite. Poetry, too, was written in this literary language, but after it had reached its peak in the T'ang and Sung period it gradually became more and more of a learned game of words and literary allusions—often without real content. There were, of course, songs, plays and novels in the vernacular apart from these purely literary products, and some of these had great poetic value. In literary circles, however, they were officially regarded as common and coarse, and were not counted as literature. That they were actually widely read and known was not acknowledged publicly. Consequently the authors of many novels and plays were reluctant to link their names with their work.

In practice, therefore, literary education was the privilege of the ruling gentry-class. Who else had time and means for undisturbed extended study? The gentry, however, formed only a small percentage of the total population. There were other social groups, especially in the larger cities, who had received a certain elementary education and possessed a limited knowledge of the written language; but the majority of the population could neither read nor write. Thus, before there could be any revolution in the political and social structure of the country, it was necessary to break through the barrier of literary education with which the gentry had surrounded themselves, and to make education universal. The leaders of the Reform Movement of 1898 (and some people even earlier) had demanded the abolition for examination purposes of the purely formal 'eight-legged' essay, which depended on a more or less formal sequence of literary quotations and phrases. With the abolition of the examination system this demand was practically fulfilled. The introduction of new, Western expressions and ideas together with the numerous translations from Western languages resulted in considerable changes of literary style. In this connection Liang Ch'i-ch'ao is particularly significant for his creative work. But the traditional written style was not displaced. The real literary revolution did not occur until the May 4th Movement. The first open thrust in this direction was an article in *New Youth* on January 1st, 1917, written by Hu Shih, who was at that time a student in the USA. In this article, called 'Suggestions for a literary reform', he put forward a programme of eight points:

1. What you write should have meaning or real substance.
2. Do not imitate the writings of the ancients.
3. Pay attention to clear, grammatical construction.
4. Do not write that you are sick or sad when you do not feel sick or sad.
5. Discard stale, time-worn literary phrases.
6. Avoid the use of classical allusions.
7. Discard the parallel construction of sentences.
8. Do not avoid using vernacular words and speech.[1]

1. *Wen-hsüeh kai-liang ch'u-i*, Collected Prose Writings, *Hu Shih wen-ts'un*, 1st series, Vol. I, pp. 7–8. Cf. Chow Tse-tsung, *The May Fourth Movement*, Cambridge, Mass., 1960, p. 274.

Hu Shih's theses found a considerable response. Ch'en Tu-hsiu, in an article, 'On the literary revolution', also published in *New Youth* shortly after Hu Shih's article, brought together Hu Shih's purely literary viewpoint and the general revolutionary trend and put forward the following three fundamentals for the literary revolution:

1. Down with artificial, untrue, aristocratic literature! Create a natural, simple, lyrical people's literature!
2. Down with rotten, unrealistic literature based on quotations! Create a new, true, realistic literature!
3. Down with the obscure, unclear, difficult literature of woods and hills which is remote from life! Create a clear social literature which is popularly understood![1]

It is remarkable that both articles are still written in a somewhat modified literary style. Not until his article 'On a constructive literary revolution' in April, 1918, did Hu Shih write in the vernacular (*pai hua*). The long novels of the 17th, 18th and 19th centuries, which were written in the vernacular (some of which have become known in the West through translations) served as stylistic models. Most of those associated with *New Youth*, among them Ch'en Tu-hsiu, Wu Yü and many others, followed the example of Hu Shih and chose to write in the vernacular. This was the beginning of the triumph of the vernacular, which also soon established itself as a medium of fiction and poetry, finding its most outstanding representative in the famous writer Lu Hsün, who has already been referred to as the author of *The Diary of a Madman*. Lu Hsün was one of those who had studied in Japan at the beginning of the century and had joined the revolutionary movement. His novels and essays, most of which have been translated into English, pilloried the abuses of traditional Chinese society and its hypocritical morality very vividly in poetic form. Young people of the 1920s, 1930s and 1940s, whose aim was to create a new social and moral life in China, were influenced by his writings more than by those of any other author; his name stands high on the list, therefore, of the influential writers of the May 4th Movement. Sometimes he is referred to as the Chinese Gorky. He

1. *Wen-hsüeh ko-ming lun*, Collected Prose Writings, Vol. I, p. 136, also in Hu Shih, Collected Prose Writings, 1st series, Vol. I, p. 25.

certainly counts as the most significant 20th-century writer produced so far by China. He reflects, of course, the same naïve anti-religious optimism of faith in science and technology which characterized the intellectual leaders of the May 4th Movement and which is still strong in China to the present day.

Hu Shih based his fight for the literary revolution mainly on a purely literary standpoint. The quite unique significance of the literary revolution in relation to the social and political revolution, however, has been indicated already by the three theses of Ch'en Tu-hsiu. As the vernacular gradually became the standard written language, the way was opened for the universalization of education. Knowledge of written Chinese ceased to be limited to, by and large, one privileged stratum of society and became a common right. The monopoly of the gentry over the contents of literature had to cease also, and the way was open for a popular literature. The literary revolution was understood in this general revolutionary context by the overwhelming majority of its protagonists. Lu Hsün's writings abound in reflections such as the following, which he made in 1935, a year before his death, in a statement to a journalist:

Unless the old literature is abolished, China must fail in the competitive struggle with other countries; its complexity will never allow our culture to progress. The people have no share in the nation's culture and do not even understand their own misery. I have struggled hard with the old Chinese literature and know it fairly well. I am quite sure that a new language will be able to conquer the mass of the people who have been so impeded so far. Even now, as soon as the new language established itself, it had a fruitful influence on literature. Unfortunately it was impeded by political measures. Perhaps these politicians were afraid that the people would become clever as a result and the insights gained from literature could be used as political weapons. They may well be right; but it is senseless to seek to impede this development which has already been initiated. I represent the view that the literary revolution must be linked with the people's revolution and advance hand in hand with it. . . .[1]

1. Quoted from the German translation by Wang Chêng-ju, 'Lu Hsün. Sein Leben und Werk', *Mitteilungen der Ausland-Hochschule an der Universität Berlin*, 42, 1939, p. 75.

The conservative opposition also regarded the literary revolution in the context of the political-social revolution. There were, in fact, attempts to persuade the government to use force to suppress all publications in the vernacular, since it was being used to disseminate radical ideas that were harmful to the people. But the rapid success of the literary revolution could not be halted. In the official textbooks of the lower and middle schools the classical written language increasingly gave way to the written vernacular. Newspapers and magazines appeared in a mixed style, but the vernacular element constantly increased. Only the style used for official writing and for correspondence remained largely unaltered. The Communists were the first to be able to effect a change here, although remnants of the traditional official style are still to be found in documents of the People's Republic.

MARXISM AND LENINISM

The Beginning of Marxism in China

The first issues of the most progressive and most radical Chinese magazine, *New Youth*, discussed a great variety of Western thinkers and intellectual movements, without referring to Marx or Marxism in any detail. In less radical magazines Marx was not even mentioned. It should not be assumed that no one among the authors in *New Youth* had access to Marx's teaching or that it appeared too extreme. Open-minded Chinese intellectuals of that period accepted the most up-to-date and most radical Western ideas quite readily, so there must have been a different reason for the failure to pay attention to Marx. Marxism in its original form, prior to Lenin, referred to a highly industrialized society and according to Marx the revolution of the proletariat and the creation of a new order of society would begin where capitalism and industrialization were most advanced. Countries such as China, which were backward in these respects, would not play a significant role in the coming world-revolution. Hence, Marxism had nothing to say to Chinese intellectuals at first; it seemed irrelevant to China.

It was not until the October Revolution in Russia that Marxism, in the interpretation and dogmatic form given to it by Lenin, suddenly began to attract attention in China, too. It was realized that in a country scarcely less backward in Marx's sense than China a numerically small proletariat could, if it were strictly organized under the leadership of intellectuals, depose a monarchical government and a privileged ruling élite. The revolutionary wave spread also to other countries such as Germany, Austria and Hungary and it seemed as if it would spark off the world-revolution predicted by Marx of proletariat against capitalist, exploited against exploiter. Lenin proclaimed as the messianic message of the revolution not just the liberation of the working class from exploitation by capitalists, but the liberation of colonial and semi-colonial peoples from the yoke of Western imperialism. The united front of the Western powers against these people was thereby broken; in addition, the Soviet Russian government announced soon after the revolution that they would renounce all concessions and rights, including the right of extra-territorial jurisdiction, which the Czarist government had had. This news was communicated officially a few days after the May 4th Movement. Soviet Russia was one of the first Western powers to extend equal rights to China. The next country to renounce its treaty rights was Germany in 1921—not voluntarily, however, but only because it was compelled to do so by the Allies under articles 128–134 of the Treaty of Versailles after the First World War. The advantages that this reluctant German renunciation brought to future German–Chinese relations may give some idea of the even greater sympathy which Russia's voluntary act evoked in China.

One of the first visible effects of Marxism was the 'Society for the Study of Marxism' set up by Li Ta-chao in the spring of 1918 at the University of Peking, the centre of the May 4th Movement. Li Ta-chao had also belonged to the Revolutionary Alliance during his time as a student in Japan, like the majority of those associated with *New Youth*; he was now a professor at Peking University and director of the University Library. As such he was the immediate superior of Mao Tse-tung, who in the winter of 1918–19 worked in a subordinate position at the library and was a member of the Society. Most of the Society's members were university students, many of whom, such as Chang Kuo-t'ao, in addition to Mao

Tse-tung, were later to play an important role in the Communist movement. At first, as its name suggests, the Society's aim was limited to a study of Marxism. Gradually, however, individual members, especially Li Ta-chao, came to the conclusion that the messianic message of the Russian Revolution could not be separated from the theory on which it was based. Thus, the Society for the Study of Marxism gradually became the precursor of the Chinese Communist Party. In 1920 or even earlier Ch'en Tu-hsiu, the editor of *New Youth*, embraced Marxist–Leninism; from that point Communist tendencies became more and more pronounced in the magazine.

A direct result of these new Marxist–Leninist ideas was the first attempt of the students to organize and mobilize industrial workers after the May 4th Movement. Their efforts led to the strike of workers in the new industrial centres in the June 3rd Movement, which was really a continuation of the May 4th Movement, and contributed considerably to its success, however limited.

The Russian Revolution, therefore, and the new form of Marxism propounded by Lenin were not entirely without influence on the May 4th Movement in China. On the other hand the view of Mao Tse-tung (quoted above), also followed by other Communist writers, that the May 4th Movement was part of the world proletarian revolution of that time—a Communist action, so to speak, without any Communists—may be exaggerated and one-sided. The May 4th Movement was primarily a nationalistic movement; socialistic ideas played only a subordinate part.

The Establishment of the Chinese Communist Party

Reference has already been made to the fact that one of the most outstanding intellectual leaders of the May 4th Movement, Ch'en Tu-hsiu, had become a convinced follower of Marxist–Leninism by 1919 or 1920 at the latest. It was particularly the messianic expectation of a world-revolution, the freeing of the exploited classes from their masters, that filled him with enthusiasm. He saw everything in terms of black and white; the whole world was involved in a struggle between workers and capitalists irrespective of national differences. At first he paid little attention to the numerous problems connected with the realization of the aims of the revolution, especially the political organization of a communist party in China. He has been called a 'Proto–Trotskyist',[1] a precursor of Trotsky, because of his ideas of universal world-revolution, which had no place for nationalism.

Later in the year of the May 4th Movement, Ch'en Tu-hsiu left conservative Peking for the freer, more progressive atmosphere of Shanghai, where he quickly became the centre of a very varied group of revolutionary intellectuals. There were anarchists, Marxists, various shades of Socialists, as well as followers of Sun Yat-sen and anti-Confucianists. With their help he organized a Socialist Youth Corps in 1920 with the aim of organizing the workers and filling them with revolutionary zeal. Li Ta-chao organized a similar group in Peking.

In the same year the Comintern sent their first agent, Gregor Voitinsky, to China. He opened an office in Shanghai and regarded it as his first duty to weld together the heterogeneous elements round Ch'en Tu-hsiu and to place them organizationally under the Comintern in the hope of gradually making useful communists (in the Comintern's sense of the word) out of these young intellectuals, who were so different in their ideas and often rather confused. It is interesting that some of Sun Yat-sen's close associates, such as Hu Han-min and Tai Chi-t'ao, both of whom later joined the extreme right wing of the Kuomintang, were to be found in this group. For them the idea of the class struggle in Marxism was unimportant; they were attracted, however, by Lenin's theory of imperialism and of the struggle of oppressed colonial and semi-colonial peoples against imperialist powers, and they thought they could make use of these ideas for their aim of national liberation from foreign encroachment. The intervention of a foreign power in the form of the Comintern in internal Chinese party politics, however, soon made Tai Chi-t'ao and Hu Han-min determined and bitter opponents of the Communists. For the time being, however, this conflict was not as sharp as that between Ch'en Tu-hsiu and the anarchists. Meanwhile, Ch'en Tu-hsiu was becoming more and

1. Benjamin Schwartz, *Chinese Communism and the Rise of Mao*, p. 29.

more convinced by Voitinsky that, in order to implement the new order of society proclaimed by Marx and Lenin, it was necessary to have a tightly organized group of leaders, who could exercise authority; there could be no revolution simply by theorizing and without a practical point of view. Ch'en regarded the anarchists as nothing but a continuation of passive, Chinese Taoism, which he condemned in the sharpest possible terms. It may be that anarchism fell on less fertile soil in China because of its complete denial of the state, whereas Marxist–Leninism with its strong emphasis on a state led by an élite was successful because it linked up unconsciously with Confucian influences in Chinese thought. Perhaps, too, the 'Trotskyist' ideas of Ch'en Tu-hsiu, that we have referred to, may unconsciously reflect traditional, universalistic Chinese thought-forms.

During this same period Mao Tse-tung tried to organize a revolutionary movement on Marxist lines in his home province of Hunan. After a stay of six months Mao had left Peking, where he had first become acquainted with Marxism–Leninism, shortly before the May 4th Movement. In the summer of 1921 there were Communist groups apparently in existence in Peking, Canton, Shanghai and in the province of Hunan. It is remarkable that the revolutionary groups that came together in the Revolutionary Alliance under Sun Yat-sen in Tokyo in 1905 had emerged in the same places, with the exception of Peking, at the turn of the century. Communists from different parts of China met in Shanghai and their delegates founded the Chinese Communist Party. No record of the proceedings has been preserved; hence, neither the exact date nor the names of all the participants are known. Later, however, 1st July, 1921, was fixed as the foundation date and duly celebrated. References to those taking part are conflicting; there were approximately twelve and Mao Tse-tung was certainly one of them. Several of them later joined the anti-Communist camp, such as Chang Kuo-t'ao, for example; he was Mao Tse-tung's rival for a long time but left the Communist movement in 1938. The leading role in the organization was played by Ch'en Tu-hsiu and Li Ta-chao. A Communist Youth Corps had been formed by Chinese students in France in the previous year; it included Chou En-lai, Li Li-san and many others, who later played and still do play a leading role in the Chinese Communist Party. A similar group is thought to have existed in Germany also; later members included Chu Te, who studied in Germany at the beginning of the 1920s.

5 The Political Revolution: The Victory of the Kuomintang

The External Development up to 1924

It had become evident that Sun Yat-sen's revolutionary party, which in the course of the revolution of 1911 had unnaturally increased in size, lacked the inner cohesion and the power necessary to establish itself politically. The disintegration of the party was hastened by the Second Revolution, when one section of the party led by Sun Yat-sen clashed with Yüan Shih-k'ai's troops and was defeated, while the other section remained loyal to the government in Peking and continued to sit in the Parliament. The disintegration was complete when the party was banned in the autumn of 1913 and parliament was dissolved the following year. Sun Yat-sen, who had fled to Japan, consolidated his closest followers in Tokyo in 1914 to form a group openly calling itself the Chinese Revolutionary Party, *Chung-kuo ko-ming tang*. The movement, which was directed against Yüan Shih-k'ai's imperial plans, brought together in Canton towards the end of 1916 numerous politicians who had fled from Peking because of their opposition to Yüan. When the attempt to restore the Manchu monarchy in Peking in the following year failed and the extremely reactionary Northern Party under Tuan Ch'i-jui gained power again, Canton became the centre of an extraordinary national assembly of former members of parliament who had fled from Peking. In 1918 they set up a counter-government in Canton, styling themselves 'the military government for the protection of the law'. In the same year Sun Yat-sen became the leader of this military government in Canton. But, as in 1912, this government and the forces that comprised it consisted of very heterogeneous elements; Sun Yat-sen and his supporters formed only a small group. Military leaders from the southern provinces and Cantonese businessmen wielded the strongest influence. The troops who served Sun Yat-sen and his close supporters were no different from other mercenaries: they sold themselves to the highest bidder, not to the highest ideal. Towards the end of 1919 or the beginning of 1920 the name of the party was altered again— this time to Chinese National People's Party, *Chung-kuo kuo-min tang* (abbreviated to KMT), the name still in current use. There was at that time a constant struggle for power between different individuals and the groups whose interests they represented; their only agreement lay in their common opposition to the Peking central government and the war-lords of the North. This did not prevent occasional agreements for tactical purposes between one or another of the southern military leaders and one of the northern war-lords. The centre of government was in the provinces of Kwangtung and Kwangsi; the remaining southern provinces—Yunnan, Kweichow, Kiangsi, Fukien—sympathized with Canton in varying degrees. Sun Yat-sen himself had to flee from Canton several times and on one occasion escaped only by the skin of his teeth. A doctrinaire revolutionary, convinced of the rightness of his own ideal, he was too autocratic and not enough of a politician to be able to work in harmony for any length of time with those who were not absolutely committed to his ideas. Consequently, the revolutionary cause was impeded by this struggle for power and conflict of interests, and although Sun Yat-sen and his closest followers always remained true to their basic principles, the leading role in the revolutionary struggle seemed to have passed in part to the protagonists of the May 4th Movement. At the beginning of the 1920s, however, there was a decisive change in the ideas of Sun Yat-sen and his associates, which resulted in a complete reorganization and reorientation of the party. This was to lead eventually to victory over the numerous war-lords in both South and North.

Sun Yat-sen's Principle of Nationalism

Sun Yat-sen did not alter his basic ideas about 'The Three Peoples' Principles' and 'The Five-Power Constitution', but in many respects he considerably modified his views, and in some respects revised them completely. This was particularly true of his attitude to foreign powers and the social question. In their declaration of 1907 relating to foreign powers it was expressly stated that all agreements which the imperial government had made with foreign powers would be honoured. This meant that leased territories, settlements and concessions, extra-territorial rights, the right to station troops in the legation quarter of Peking and in the foreign concessions, control of the maritime customs and salt tax, together with all other economic and political rights and privileges were specifically guaranteed. Sun Yat-sen expressed himself in a similar vein when he took over as temporary President at the beginning of 1912. Many of Sun's statements—especially to his Japanese friends—did reveal strong anti-Western, pan-Asian tendencies, and both he and his followers were deeply conscious of the injustice of foreign privileges in China. In the last analysis, however, they regarded them as the result of China's weakness and political backwardness, particularly its imperial government and traditional system, rather than as a result of the imperialist character of the Great Powers. The Principle of Nationalism in the Three People's Principles was initially directed exclusively against the foreign rule of the Manchus, not the imperialist Western powers. Sun Yat-sen and his followers were full of admiration for the democracies of the West and their system of government. Sun thought that a democratic system on the Western pattern was necessary in China also, if she was to obtain full equality with other powers. He deluded himself that the foreign powers would give generous help towards the political and economic reconstruction of China and, when this was sufficiently advanced, voluntarily surrender their privileges. The foreign powers, apart from Japan, were kept busy in Europe during the First World War and were prevented from pursuing an active policy in the Far East. There was no reason, therefore, for Sun to change his views. Even his *Plan for the Reconstruction of China*, a comprehensive but unfinished work the last part of which was written in 1919, is based on the assumption of extensive assistance from the Western powers and harmonious co-operation with them. It was with this in mind that he published an English edition called *The International Development of China*, based on the central sections of the Chinese edition, dealing with material reconstruction. Sun hoped that energies released by the end of the war in Europe could be used to build up China. His writings often make reference to the traditional Chinese idea of the 'One World' (ta t'ung), in which all men live in peace and harmony, an ideal that K'ang Yu-wei nursed throughout his life and made the theme of a massive book (Ta t'ung shu).

But Sun Yat-sen was soon to be disappointed. The events of 1919 in Paris were the first indication that the Great Powers—including America—in spite of the apparent promises of President Wilson about national self-determination and a readjustment of colonial relationships, were not willing to surrender any privileges in China and not even ready to help China in the struggle for her rights against Japan. Fresh hopes were raised by the Washington Conference of 1921–2. China demanded the abolition of spheres of influence, the abrogation of consular jurisdiction, full customs autonomy, the termination of foreign postal services, remission of the Boxer indemnity, withdrawal of foreign troops of occupation, return of concessions and of the German rights in Shantung which had been taken over by the Japanese. The results, however, were no more in China's favour than at Versailles. It is true that there were some concessions on unimportant points and a limit was placed on further Japanese advance on the mainland, but the union of the USA, England, France and Japan in the so-called Four-Power Agreement marking off their own interests in the exploitation of China against one another was at the expense of China. China was merely the object, but not a partner of the agreement. The fact that Japan had to yield to American and English pressure and promise to restore Tsingtao and other German rights in Shantung as soon as possible by a special agreement with China does not alter the situation. In fact, Tsingtao was restored to China in the same year, but Japanese troops remained in Shantung to protect special Japanese interests there until 1929. The excuse put forward by the Great Powers for rejecting numerous Chinese requests was the fact that China was not a unified, ordered state. In fact representatives of two Chinese governments appeared in Washington, but only the representatives of the powerless Peking government were officially recognized, not those of the Cantonese government which had been reorganized

under the leadership of Sun Yat-sen in 1921-2. Although some
foreigners were concerned in their personal capacity to help
Chinese unification and reconstruction in order to create a basis for
the restoration of full Chinese sovereignty, the Great Powers'
official policy worked in the opposite direction, in that it supported
one or other of the war-lords in turn and played them off
against one another. Customs dues and salt tax income, which were
administered by representatives of the foreign powers, went to the
Peking government, which was so helpless that it lived almost
entirely on this income and was unable to claim even that it
represented the greater part of China. The Canton government, on
the other hand, received almost no foreign support because of its
revolutionary character.

The Four Powers represented by the Washington Conference did
not include Russia and Germany. The new Russian government
had already informed China in 1919 that they would surrender all
the rights and concessions of the Czarist régime. Soviet Russia,
therefore, was no longer associated with the imperialist powers:
she was on the side of the colonial and semi-colonial peoples.
Similarly, even if less voluntarily, Germany had surrendered all
its privileges in China and in 1921, three years before the Russian
treaty of 1924 with China, was the first nation to sign a treaty with
China on a basis of equality.

These events and the subsequent alliance with the Soviet Union
and the Chinese Communists had a considerable impact on Sun
Yat-sen and were responsible for modifying some of his ideas.
In his lectures on 'The Three People's Principles' in 1924, which go
back to an older version—since destroyed—that was prepared
between 1918 and 1922, the Principle of Nationalism has undergone
revision on important points. Sun Yat-sen divides the world into
two groups: in the one group are oppressed nations, including
Soviet Russia, Germany and all Asian peoples apart from Japan,
and in the other group, the imperialist powers, primarily England,
France, America and Japan. Future wars would take place only
between these two groups, representing the conflict of right and
might. Even if they are expressed rather differently, these ideas
are not very different in substance from those of Marx and Lenin.
Sun Yat-sen went on to speak at length about the political and

economic oppression of China by the imperialist powers and described China as a sort of 'hypo-colony' (*Tz'u chih-min-ti*),[1] which did not have just one colonial overlord, like Korea or Annam (Vietnam) but was the colony of all the foreign powers that had treaty rights in China. Sun also mentions the Wilson declaration about national self-determination, which the Great Powers had used to deceive the oppressed nations. The Paris Conference had shown that the imperialist powers were not willing to give the peoples of Asia the right of self-determination. Sun calls upon the Chinese to rally to the national cause in order to be able to resist the foreign powers. He challenges them to resist passively like India, to refuse to co-operate with the representatives of the imperialist powers and to boycott their goods. These ideas later provide a direct introduction to the 'Fight against Imperialism', one of the chief points in the Communist programme. Sun, however, regarded imperialism simply as a political tool in the service of economic expansion, not as the final stage of capitalism, as it is in Communist teaching. Sun Yat-sen wanted co-operation with Germany and Russia and even had the idea of a close alliance of these three countries. He found little sympathy for his idea in Germany, which was too occupied with its own problems after the defeat in 1918 to be able to give its attention to what appeared such distant matters. He did, however, find sympathy for China's position and a readiness for closer co-operation in Soviet Russia.

Principle of the People's Rights

In the 'Principle of the People's Rights' Sun warns against overemphasis on the demand for freedom. The aim of the revolution was not the freedom of the individual—of which there was clearly too much in China—but the freedom of the nation. He said:

Western revolutions began with the struggle for liberty; only after war and agitation of two or three centuries was the liberty realized from which democracy sprang. The watchword of the French Revolution was 'Liberty, Equality, Fraternity'. Our watchword is

---

1. *Chung-shan ts'ung-shu*, 1, p. 20; Pascal M. D. 'Elia, *Le Triple Démisme de Suen Wen*, pp. 42–3.

'People's Nationalism, People's Sovereignty, People's Livelihood'. What relation do the two watchwords have to each other? According to my interpretation, our Nationalism may be said to correspond to their Liberty, because putting the People's Nationalism into effect means a struggle for the liberty of our nation. The Europeans fought for individual liberty, but today we have a different use for liberty. Now how shall the term 'liberty' be applied? If we apply it to a person, we shall become a sheet of loose sand; on no account must we give more liberty to the individual; let us secure liberty instead for the nation. The individual should not have too much liberty, but the nation should have complete liberty. When the nation can act freely, then China may be called strong. To make the nation free, we must each sacrifice his personal freedom. Students who sacrifice their personal liberty will be able to work diligently day after day and spend time and effort upon learning; when their studies are completed, their knowledge is enlarged and their powers have multiplied, then they can do things for the nation. Soldiers who sacrifice their personal liberty will be able to obey orders, repay their country with loyalty and help the nation to attain liberty. . . .

Why do we want the nation to be free?—Because China under the domination of the Powers has lost her national standing. She is not merely a semi-colony; she has indeed become a hypo-colony. . . .[1]

Here and throughout the 'Three People's Principles' Sun Yat-sen equates freedom with absence of restriction or arbitrariness and in doing so bases himself on Chinese tradition. Traditional China was not acquainted with the idea of individual freedom in the sense that has been characteristic of the West since the French Revolution; nor did the idea occupy any place in Sun Yat-sen's teaching—in spite of numerous references to it. The 'Three People's Principles' already revealed both here and elsewhere tendencies towards a totalitarian state, which the KMT later exerted itself to translate into practice. Sun Yat-sen regarded the Five-Power Constitution, referred to above, as the ideal solution to the form of the state.

---

1. *Kuo-fu ch'üan-shu*, Taipei, 1960, p. 226; *The Three Principles of the People, San Min Chu I*, Taipei (no date), pp. 75–6. The last phrases, printed in italics, are omitted in the English version.

Principle of the People's Livelihood

The 'Principle of the People's Livelihood' occupies third place, after the Principle of Nationalism and the Principle of the People's Rights in the 'Lectures on the Three People's Principles'; but in the *Outlines of the Reconstruction of China (Chien Kuo ta-kang)* which was published in April, 1924, it occupies first place. The much-discussed observation of Sun, which occurs in the famous version of the 'Three Principles', to the effect that his Principle of the People's Livelihood was in general nothing other than socialism and Communism, does not preclude that he considered his Principle of the People's Livelihood as different from and distinctly superior to socialism and Communism. Moreover, Sun expressly disclaims all connection with Western socialism and Marxism on more than one occasion. Although he had a genuine admiration for Marx, he rejects in detail a number of important Marxist principles such as historical materialism, class struggle, and surplus value. He also adduces a number of examples to show that the course of development has been very different from that predicted by Marx. Even if these examples are not always very convincing, they illustrate Sun's decidedly critical attitude towards Marx's teaching. Sun also approaches the social question from a very different starting-point. For Marx production and the means of production provide the starting-point, whereas for Sun it is human needs, a man's livelihood. What Sun understands by this is set out briefly in section two of *Outlines of the Reconstruction of China*.

The most important point of this reconstruction is the people's livelihood. In the four areas of the people's most important needs, therefore—food, clothing, shelter, and transport—the government must work hand in hand with the people. Together they must plan for the development of agriculture in order to satisfy the people's nourishment, for the development of silk production in order to supply sufficient clothes for the people; they must build houses of different types according to a large-scale plan, in order to improve the people's housing conditions; they must construct and maintain roads and canals, in order to promote the people's transport.[1]

1. *Kuo-fu ch'üan-shu*, Taipei, 1960, p. 156 (0).

Sun Yat-sen lays most weight on agriculture which had had an esteemed place in Chinese tradition from time immemorial, but the agrarian problem, the most important factor in the social order, is certainly not given first place in the 'Three People's Principles'. In fact, Sun Yat-sen shows a striking underestimate of the problem when he says:

There are no large landlords in China today, but there are still many small landlords. In this age of the small landlord there is peace and quiet in most areas and there are no serious difficulties between the people and the landlords. It is only recently with the daily increasing influx of European and American economic trends that the various (traditional) systems find themselves in process of change; and thereby the agrarian question is most strongly influenced.[1]

The demand that 'landowning rights should be equalized' had already been sketched in outline in the programme of the Revolutionary Alliance (see above p. 64) and was dealt with more fully in the 'Three People's Principles'. Today Sun Yat-sen's theory seems very academic, especially after the agrarian revolution of the 1940s and 1950s. In spite of many good ideas Sun does not display any deep understanding of the historical development or the actual situation on the land. His view of the historical development manifests all the traits of the traditional Chinese scholar, in whose eyes social contrasts and conflicts do not exist. Nevertheless, in view of the enormous significance of the agrarian question later Sun's views need to be outlined more fully. He writes:

The aim of the KMT's Principle of the People's Livelihood is to equalize the resources of wealth. Thus the Principle of the People's Livelihood is socialism, is Communism. Only the methods are different. Our first method is to be the solution of the land problem. The methods for the solution of the land problem are different in various countries, and each country has its own peculiar difficulties. The plan which we are following is simple and easy—the equalization of landownership. Naturally, as soon as we talk of the solution of the land problem and of the equalization of landownership the landowners are afraid, just as the capitalists are afraid when socialism is mentioned and seek to resist it. If our landowners were

1. Op. cit., p. 266 (9).

like the great landowners of Europe and had developed tremendous power, it would be exceedingly difficult for us to solve the land question. But China does not have such big landowners, and the power of the small landowners is still rather weak. If we attack the problem now, we can solve it; but if we lose the present opportunity, we can never find a way out. The discussion of the land problem naturally causes a feeling of fear among the landowners, but if the KMT policy is followed, present landowners can set their hearts at rest. What is our policy? We propose that the government shall buy back the land, if necessary, according to the amount of land tax and the price of the land. How, indeed, can the price of land be determined? I would advocate that the landowner himself should fix the price.[1]

Sun Yat-sen then explains that if the owner assessed the value at too low a figure he would save in tax but would make a heavy loss, if the government were to make use of its power to buy the land at this price. On the other hand, if the owner assessed the value at too high a figure, he might make a profit when he sold the land, but he would be paying too much in tax. In order to run no risks—thought Sun—the landowner would declare the true value of the land.

After the land values have been fixed, we should have a regulation by law that from that year on, all increase in land values, which in other countries means heavier taxation, shall revert to the community. This is because the increase in land values is due to improvement made by society and to the progress of industry and commerce. . . . The credit for the improvement and progress belongs to the energy and business activity of all the people; therefore the increase in land values after such improvement and progress shall belong to the whole people and not merely to a few private individuals.[2]

This means, for example, that if a piece of land originally valued at 1,000 yuan is worth 10,000 after some decades, 9,000 belong to the general public, i.e. the state, and only the original value of 1,000

1. *Kuo-fu ch'üan-shu*, p. 269 (2–4); the English version, *The Three Principles of the People, San Min Chu I*, p. 177, is incomplete.
2. *Kuo-fu ch'üan-shu*, p. 269 (7–9); the English version, loc. cit., pp. 178–9, is incomplete.

yuan belongs to the owner. This refers only to the ground, of course, and not to any buildings erected on it.

Sun Yat-sen lays special emphasis on agricultural production. He mentions the injustice of large numbers of farmers, who rent their land, receiving on average less than half of what they produce and having to hand over the rest to the landlord.

> When the Principle of the People's Livelihood is fully realized and the problems of the farmer are all solved, each tiller of the soil will possess his own farm (*Kêng-chê yao yu ch'i t'ien*)—that is to be the final fruit of our efforts.[1]

In addition, Sun points to the urgency of finding a solution to this problem in a political and constitutional manner, without, however, giving any hint at a way to implement his policy. There is no discussion of compulsory expropriation and redistribution of agrarian property, apart from the right of the government, in another context, to buy land at the determined price. The statement that the cultivator of the land should own it became very important later, when it was taken up by the Communists and became part of the 'General Directions', a kind of a provisional constitution of 1949 (article 27) when they came to power. In the constitution of 1954, however, it was not retained.

The Periods of the Revolution

The three periods for implementing the revolution were also revised. Originally it was envisaged there could be a period of military rule, a period of rule under a provisional constitution and a period of full constitutional rule. In the *Outlines of the Reconstruction of China*, it now reads:

§5. The course of reconstruction is divided into three periods: (1) The period of military rule; (2) the period of political tutelage; and (3) the period of full constitutional rule.

§6. During the period of military rule the entire administration is in the hands of the military government, which has two tasks—to solve internal problems, by force if necessary, and to propagate the principles of the state, in order to develop

---

1. *Kuo-fu ch'üan-shu*, p. 273 (a); English version, loc. cit., p. 188.

public opinion throughout the country and to strengthen the unity of the nation.

§7. On the day when a whole province is fully under control, military rule is to be succeeded by political tutelage.

§8. During the period of political tutelage the government must send trained officers who have passed their examinations into every county to assist the people to set up their own administration. Counties which are so far advanced that a clear census of all the inhabitants has been taken and that the land of the whole county has been measured, the police reliably installed and all linking roads finished and the inhabitants trained to use their four rights and to fulfil their duties as citizens and to swear on oath that they are willing to put into practice the revolutionary ideas, may elect the county magistrate, who is to direct the administration of the county together with representatives who have to advise on and establish the laws for the county; only then is a county's own independent administration ready to take over.

§9. In a county with its own independent administration the citizens have the right to elect or dismiss their county officials directly, to propose laws or make fresh decisions about the laws directly.

§16. When all counties of a province have reached this stage then it is time to introduce constitutional rule there. . . .[1]

In other words the period of political tutelage is a period of indoctrination in the fundamental ideas of the KMT, which holds itself responsible for the reconstruction of China. As in the Principle of the People's Rights which includes a warning against over-emphasis on personal freedom, the path envisaged here means the surrender of any idea of parliamentary democracy and leads inevitably to dictatorship. The failure of parliamentary democracy to advance revolution or national reconstruction, and the complete chaos produced by parliamentary democracy, had been demonstrated all too clearly by what had happened since 1911. For this reason Sun Yat-sen now thought it necessary that one party, the KMT, should assume control, in order to create the right conditions for developing the revolution and for rebuilding a new state. The KMT as formerly constituted, however, was not fitted for such an important task and a complete reorganization was inevitable.

1. *Kuo-fu ch'üan-shu,* p. 156.

THE REORGANIZATION OF THE KMT
AND THE BEGINNING OF CO-OPERATION
WITH THE COMMUNISTS

In many respects Sun Yat-sen's ideas in the 'Three People's
Principles' had been given a new direction by the altered international situation after the First World War, and directly or indirectly his perception of Russia's new role after the revolution
played an important part in this. It is not surprising, therefore,
that Russian help should assume critical importance in the reorganization of the party and in preparations and plans to implement
the revolution. This initial co-operation with Soviet Russia was
accompanied logically by co-operation with the Chinese Communist
Party (CCP).

The CCP, which had been founded in 1921 (see above), consisted
at first of a comparatively narrow circle of intellectuals, most of
whom had made intensive study of the writings of Marx and his
followers and wished to pursue their aims on strictly dogmatic
Marxist lines. They sought an alliance with the KMT, which they
were well disposed towards although they criticized it, and with
other revolutionary elements, but in accordance with Marx, they
specifically wanted to retain their independence and their character
as the party of the working class, the proletariat. They worked for
a united front of workers, farmers and petty bourgeoisie, who were
to engage in a common struggle against foreign imperialism abroad
and against reactionary war-lordism at home and to implement a
democratic revolution. The Communists were primarily concerned
about the organization of the workers in the cities; they regarded
the farmers at first as less important. In August, 1922, the Comintern representative Maring (his real name was Sneevliet) made the
suggestion that the Chinese Communists, instead of entering an
alliance with the KMT, should join the KMT. Instead of forming
an independent group alongside the KMT they should form a
group within it. In reply to the objections of Ch'en Tu-hsiu and
other Communist leaders, Maring explained that in contrast to
the original theory of Marx, which stated that the parties should
always be instruments of one single class, the KMT was to be
valued as a party of several classes, namely of bourgeoisie, petty

bourgeoisie, workers and peasants. It was only by invoking the discipline of the Comintern, however, that Maring succeeded in carrying his view against the resistance of the Chinese party leaders. Even in July, 1922, the manifesto of the second Congress of the CCP emphasized that in spite of its alliance with the KMT and with petty bourgeois elements—the bourgeois elements in the alliance are not yet mentioned—the CCP must always pursue its own class interests and the workers belonging to its organization were committed to the establishment of soviets.

Apart from Soviet sympathy for the revolution in China the Foreign Office in Moscow at that time was interested in China's recognition of certain rights in Outer Mongolia, in the Chinese Eastern Railway (in Northern Manchuria) and in the creation of a counterweight to Japan on the mainland; for this purpose the Russians set their sights on Sun Yat-sen and his party, after attempts to come to terms with the government in Peking and with Wu P'ei-fu, who was regarded as the 'Best of the war-lords', produced no satisfactory results. The formation of a link with south Chinese revolutionaries, however, did not prevent the Russians from continuing negotiations with Peking. At the beginning of 1923 Sun Yat-sen and the Russian delegate Joffe drew up a joint statement, which presented a further contrast to the manifesto of the Second Congress of the CCP. Its first paragraph read:

Dr Sun is of the opinion that, because of the non-existence of conditions favourable to their successful application in China, it is not possible to carry out either Communism or even the Soviet system in China. M. Joffe agrees entirely with this view; he is further of the opinion that China's most important and most pressing problems are the completion of national unification and the attainment of full national independence. With regard to these great tasks, M. Joffe has assured Dr Sun of the Russian people's warmest sympathy for China, and of (their) willingness to lend support.[1]

This joint statement by Joffe and Sun Yat-sen was the beginning of the discussions which led to the close association of the KMT

1. From Brandt, Schwartz and Fairbank, *A Documentary History of Chinese Communism*, p. 70.

and Russia and the CCP at the First Party Congress of the KMT
at the beginning of 1924. The party political and military organization of the KMT was reorganized on the Soviet pattern. In the
autumn of 1923 a group of Russian advisers led by Michael
Borodin (his real name was Grusenberg) came to Canton as
representatives of the Russian government to assist Sun Yat-sen
in this reorganization. Borodin was an old Russian revolutionary.
Sun Yat-sen had met him while he was in America, where he was
living in exile before the Russian Revolution. Prior to coming to
China, Borodin had spent several months in Turkey as adviser to
Kemal Pasha. At the same time Sun Yat-sen sent Chiang Kai-shek
as his representative to Moscow to study the structure of the party
and the army there; he was there for about three months. Chiang
Kai-shek (Chiang Chieh-shih) had been an officer at the military
Academy in Japan in 1907 and while there had entered the
Revolutionary Alliance; he had gradually become one of the
closest and most trusted collaborators of Sun Yat-sen. At the
Third Congress of the CCP in June 1923 official sanction was given
to the decision made previously at the request of Maring that the
KMT should be regarded as the centre of all revolutionary forces
and that the Communists should as individuals become members
of the KMT, without prejudice, of course, to their membership of
the CCP. The entry of a Communist as an 'individual' member of
another political organization plainly seems a contradiction in
itself and in spite of all assurances to the contrary the Communists
did not act as individual members but formed a tight, closed group
within the KMT. Here, then, from the very beginning was a source
of conflict in this unusual union, even if the leadership of the
revolution was given to the KMT under Sun Yat-sen.

This co-operation was announced by the KMT at its first big
party congress in January 1924—at the same time as the reorganization of the party and its policy was made public. In the highest
permanent organ of the party, the Central Executive Committee
(*Chung-yang chih-hsing wei-yüan-hui*), the Communists were
allowed one-sixth of the seats. The KMT adopted a new statute by
which members were concentrated under a unified leadership in
strict organization on the model of the Communist Party. Chief
party leader was Sun Yat-sen, who had full authority in the last

resort—even over Communist members, who, theoretically at least, had to accept the party discipline of the KMT in everything.

In the same year military reorganization was advanced by the establishment of the Whampoa Military Academy (*Huang-p'u lu-chün chün-hsiao*) on an island in the Pearl River, about twenty miles below Canton. The aim of this new foundation was the creation of a reliable officer corps, committed to the aims of the revolution. Training, therefore, was not limited to purely military matters; party, political, revolutionary training in the Three People's Principles, the ideology of the KMT, in revolutionary propaganda, and in the tactics of revolutionary warfare also played an important part. The military commandant of the Academy was Chiang Kai-shek; equal with him was Liao Chung-k'ai as the representative of the KMT, and after his assassination in 1925 Wang Ching-wei. The organization of the academy was on Soviet lines through the help of a group of Russian military advisers led by General Bluecher (alias Galen). The authoritative deputy leader of the political department was Chou En-lai, who occupied an important position even then in the CCP. The members of the Academy developed a strong *esprit de corps* and later as leaders formed the backbone of the military and political career of their chief, Chiang Kai-shek. They exercised a fateful influence on the destiny of China and the KMT in other ways besides (see below pp. 165, 185 f.). Only a few—most of whom had belonged to the CCP before they entered the Academy—achieved importance as leaders of the Communist forces, such as Lin Piao.

It was clear from the very beginning that this close alliance between the KMT and the Communist Party could only be a temporary affair. Each of the two partners was concerned with the advantages that co-operation could bring their own ends. A temporary alliance of Communists and the working class, which is represented by the party according to Communist interpretation, with other classes and groups is quite in line with Marxist–Leninist thought. The Chinese Communists at that time were only a small group, consisting predominantly of intellectuals. The organization and mobilization of industrial workers to strike and engage in other revolutionary activities experienced a strong set-back in 1923 after some initial successes. Hence, after initial reluctance to join the

KMT, the Chinese Communists hoped, by uniting with the more numerous and widely spread KMT, to extend their own influence, especially among the peasants, and ultimately to choke the KMT. On the other hand, the KMT lacked a firm organization, a convincing technique of political propaganda and a powerful ally to support them in the struggle against imperialism. The KMT found help on all these scores in Russia, among the Communists. The decisive factor was the desire for Russian help; the reception of Chinese Communists into the party was of minor importance. Although after 1924 a number of Chinese Communists occupied important posts in the KMT and in the Whampoa Military Academy, the decisive influence was exercised by the numerous Russian advisers and agents. The Chinese Communists could gradually be absorbed, it was thought. All important questions were discussed and decided between Sun Yat-sen or his delegates and the Russian advisers or the Central Committee in Moscow, often without consulting the Chinese Communists, who had to fit in with Russian arrangements. The CCP at that time was much more directly controlled by the Comintern than was later the case. Borodin, Bluecher, Roy and others had far more say at that time than Ch'en Tu-hsiu and the other Chinese Communist leaders.

Thus, both partners to the KMT–CCP alliance thought that in time one of the two would be swallowed up by the other and each was convinced that they could absorb the other.

THE BEGINNINGS OF THE PEASANT MOVEMENT

Peasant Distress and Organization of the Peasants by the KMT

One of the most important consequences of the new policy laid down at the KMT's party congress in 1924 and of the alliance with the CCP was rural propaganda, aimed at winning the peasant for the revolutionary cause. Special courses were held from 1924 onwards and young people, especially students, were trained for the work of propaganda and organization in the country and then sent out. It was not surprising that the Communists, who now belonged to the KMT, proved to be the most energetic in revolutionary activity among workers and peasants; they were particularly successful in Kwangtung and Hunan. For the time being the

10—C.C.R.

leadership of the KMT did not interfere, for it needed the support of the great mass of peasants to carry out the revolution, especially for the planned Expedition of the revolutionary army from Canton against the North on the pattern of the Taiping.

Social conditions in the country were mentioned briefly in Chapter I above. The particular economic and political conditions which paved the way for the Taiping revolution in the middle of the 19th century (see above pp. 20 ff.) had improved in some respects under the T'ung-chih restoration which followed the overthrow of the Taiping, but could not have changed drastically. Moreover, after the dynasty finally collapsed, the economic situation in the country deteriorated with increasing rapidity. Whereas in northern China more than 70 per cent of the peasants cultivated their own land, and landowners who let their land for rent possessed only a comparatively small proportion of the total land, in central and southern China most of the peasants were tenants on small farmers' holdings; in Chinese terminology they were 'poor peasants', who on average farmed less than an acre. South of the Yangtze about two-thirds of the peasants were tenants, cultivating land that was partly or entirely rented; there were, of course, some better situated farmers or even large farmers ('middle peasants' and 'rich peasants'). These latter, however, were a small, exceptional group and the great majority belonged to the category of the 'poor peasants', who gained only a scanty livelihood, were in debt and constantly oppressed by landlords and creditors. Also in this category were the agricultural labourers, who hired their services to the middle and large farmers. Thus, the peasantry of the South was considerably more open to revolutionary slogans about lowering the rent or even redistributing the land than the more conservative peasants of the North. Western observers have often noted with surprise how the Chinese peasant in both North and South, in spite of his frequently wretched position, was generally frugal and easily satisfied, possessing both external decency and inner dignity. There is a limit, however, to his frugality, if he is given no opportunity of making even a scanty living. Then he can suddenly become a fanatical rebel. Such a critical point had already been reached in many areas in the 1920s.

Both in North and South the constant fighting of the war-lords had brought the peasants, who, because of the general economic situation, had a difficult struggle to keep alive anyway, into even more serious difficulties. Armies had to be paid, the wars financed and opponents bribed. Moreover, every war-lord, great or small, —including his dependants and adherents—wanted to make a profit; and most of them did. Once they had left the political and military stage, they wanted to live a settled life under the protection of a foreign concession, living on the money they had deposited in good time with foreign bankers in foreign currency for safety. According to a report of April, 1928, there were thirty-six former generals in the foreign concessions of Tientsin consuming their spoils. In addition, there were four former presidents, ninety ministers and forty-one provincial governors, living on the same income, namely taxes and duties they had squeezed out of the peasants. Even if the numbers are not exact, they do give a fair picture of the situation. The taxes which had been exacted from the peasants for a variety of purposes and on various pretexts often many years before and sometimes by force were only one drain on the nation's resources. In the areas through which troops passed they took whatever they needed, corn, cattle, tools, etc., from the peasants, without paying or returning anything. Soldiers were often no different from brigands. Often they compelled healthy peasants to work for them. In one contemporary account we read:

Almost daily one can see soldiers leading off men chained together. There isn't a soldier who carries his own pack; and sometimes not even his own rifle. The coolies receive no payment. Often they are compelled to follow the troops great distances. They return weeks later, if they return at all.[1]

No less devastating than wars and soldiers was the disorder created by bandits. Defeated or unpaid soldiers soon became bandits, reverting to soldiers again, if a war-lord needed them and could pay them. They lived on robbery, plunder and extortion. In fact, the young Chinese peasant, like Simplizius in the Thirty Years War, could easily have dreamed of the war-god, Mars, sitting on top of a tree.

Peasant associations had sprung up in northern China and in the northern parts of central China independently of the KMT or the

1. From Mänchen-Helfen, *Die Bauernbewegung in China*, p. 318.

CCP during the 1920s in the manner of the traditional secret societies, sometimes, in fact, as offshoots of them. The Communists tried to encourage such associations for a time. The best-known were the 'Association of the Red Spears' (*Hung ch'iang hui*) and the 'Association of the Long Knives' (*Ta tao hui*), both of which stemmed from the Sect of the White Lotus (see above pp. 14 f.). Occasionally they succeeded in gaining control of large areas and their supporters numbered millions. Their aims were chiefly the extermination of the bandits, expulsion of the soldiers, refusal of exorbitant taxes asked for in advance and of supplementary duties, removal of the war-lords and their greedy, corrupt officials and other camp-followers. These were very moderate, conservative demands; they did not seek to alter the system of land ownership or to overthrow the existing social and political set-up. Only the worst abuses were to be removed.

Conditions were rather different in central and southern China where the KMT and CCP organized the peasant associations. It is natural to assume in the situation described that the poor peasants and tenants were most likely to follow those who promised to improve their position and who pointed the way, even if their methods were fairly moderate. The most important demand called for the overall reduction of rent from 50 per cent of the harvest or more in most cases to 25 per cent (*Erh-wu chien tsu*) in accordance with the decision of the KMT. Among their other objectives were the continuation of the fight against the war-lords, mutual protection against bandits and soldiers, and resistance to extortionate taxes and rents exacted by officials and landowning gentry, including resistance to their hired armed protectors, the so-called 'militia corps' (*min t'uan*). Lastly, but not least, they wanted public works undertaken for irrigation, public roads, co-operative societies of various sorts, education and places of entertainment. There was no mention of expropriation or redistribution of the land; a definitive settlement of the agrarian question in the KMT's programme was postponed to the far distant future. How this was to be managed in detail, apart from the reduction of rents to 25 per cent, was not stated. Too far-reaching demands by the peasant associations were not in the mind of the KMT; they would have alienated the merchants, artisans and petty bourgeoisie of all types whose co-operation was necessary for the revolution. Such people often owned land—even if only on a small scale—which they let for rent, and they were interested in maintaining the existing ownership of landed property.

But even these moderate demands brought the peasants—the poor as well as the middle and the rich—on to the side of the revolution. Only peasants with less than a hundred mou^1 of land were accepted in the peasant associations, however, and landlords who rented out their land and did not farm it themselves were excluded. Since ownership of land and the renting of land had considerable significance for the social status of a family irrespective of any financial gain, by excluding all such groups from membership the peasant associations assumed a very revolutionary appearance in spite of their moderate demands. There were repeated clashes between peasant associations and the militia corps in which the Canton government supported the peasants to the best of its ability. The peasant associations were at first most widely spread near the centre of the KMT government in the province of Kwangtung, but they were not limited to this area.

The Beginning of the Communist Peasant Movement

A special importance attaches to the peasant movement in the province of Hunan. It introduces the last important stage of the revolution, which in 1949 led to victory, and it is the beginning of Mao Tse-tung's rise to power. After staying in Peking during the winter of 1918–19 Mao returned to his home province of Hunan. There he started a Communist organization and tried at first to organize the urban proletariat along orthodox Marxist lines and to incite the workers to revolutionary activity. In 1921 he was involved in the founding the CCP in Shanghai. But Mao made no progress in Hunan by means of orthodox Marxist dogma, which placed exclusive value on the urban proletariat as the most active and leading class of the revolution. Possibly it was his rural origin that persuaded him to concern himself also with rural social questions. And therefore during the years 1925 to 1927 he devoted himself to the task of organizing the peasant associations for the

1. 1 *mou* = approx. 650 sq. metres = 760 sq. yds.

KMT and the Communists in his own province. He travelled throughout the province and gained first-hand knowledge of the position of the peasants and of the possibility of winning them for the revolution. In 1926 he succeeded in organizing 300–400,000 peasants in peasant associations; in the following year the number of members rose to two million, about ten million including families. In March, 1927, Mao Tse-tung described these experiences and the results of his activity in the famous 'Report on an investigation of the peasant movement in Hunan'. Although Mao Tse-tung regarded himself as a convinced follower of Marxism–Leninism, this report reveals a considerable divergence from the orthodox line. Mao's views were not understood by his fellow party members—including the Russian advisers—and were largely rejected. The report indicates the main direction of the revolutionary movement which Mao finally led to victory; it shows that the most important factor in the Chinese revolution is the poor peasants, because without their support the revolution could never succeed. Even as a literary product the account is one of the most brilliant and impressive of Mao's writings. The following extracts are literal translations from the first part:[1]

In a very short time, in China's central, southern and northern provinces, several hundred million peasants will rise like a mighty storm, like a hurricane, a force so swift and violent that no power, however great, will be able to hold it back. They will smash all the trammels that bind them and rush forward along the road to liberation. They will sweep all the imperialists, war-lords, corrupt officials, local tyrants and evil gentry into their graves. Every revolutionary party and every revolutionary comrade will be put to the test, to be accepted or rejected as they decide. There are three alternatives. To march at their head and lead them? To trail behind them, gesticulating and criticizing? Or to stand in their way and oppose them? Every Chinese is free to choose, but events will force you to make the choice quickly.

After these preliminary statements about the impending rising of the peasants throughout China, Mao describes the experiences in

1. From the English version in *Selected Works of Mao Tse-tung*, Vol. 1, Peking, 1965, pp. 23–33.

Hunan, which caused him to make such a forecast:

The main targets of attack by the peasants are the local tyrants, the evil gentry and the lawless landlords, but in passing they also hit out against patriarchal ideas and institutions, against the corrupt officials in the cities and against bad practices and customs in the rural areas. In force and momentum the attack is tempestuous; those who bow before it survive and those who resist perish. As a result, the privileges which the feudal landlords enjoyed for thousands of years are being shattered to pieces. Every bit of the dignity and prestige built up by the landlords is being swept into the dust. With the collapse of the power of the landlords, the peasant associations have now become the sole organs of authority and the popular slogan 'All power to the peasant associations' has become a reality. . . .

The fact is that the great peasant masses have risen to fulfil their historic mission and that the forces of rural democracy have risen to overthrow the forces of rural feudalism. The patriarchal-feudal class of local tyrants, evil gentry and lawless landlords has formed the basis of autocratic government for thousands of years and is the cornerstone of imperialism, warlordism and corrupt officialdom. To overthrow these feudal forces is the real objective of the national revolution. In a few months the peasants have accomplished what Dr Sun Yat-sen wanted, but failed, to accomplish in the forty years he devoted to the national revolution. This is a marvellous feat never before achieved, not just in forty, but in thousands of years.
   To give credits where they are due, if we allot ten points to the accomplishments of the democratic revolution, then the achievements of the urban dwellers and the military units rate only three points, while the remaining seven points should go to the peasants in their rural revolution.[1]

Every revolutionary comrade should know that the national revolution requires a great change in the countryside. The Revolution of 1911 did not bring about this change, hence its failure. This change is now taking place, and it is an important factor for the

1. The sentence in italics is very important; it was not present in the Chinese text of 1951, on which the English version is based. It was obviously felt to be too strong an affront to orthodox Communist doctrine and, therefore, better omitted. The translation is quoted from Brandt, Schwartz and Fairbank, *A Documentary History of Chinese Communism*, p. 85, based on an earlier Chinese text.

completion of the revolution. Every revolutionary comrade must support it, or he will be taking the stand of counter-revolution.

A revolution is not a dinner party, or writing an essay, or painting a picture, or doing embroidery; it cannot be so refined, so leisurely and gentle, so temperate, kind, courteous, restrained and magnanimous.[1] A revolution is an insurrection, an act of violence by which one class overthrows another. A rural revolution is a revolution by which the peasantry overthrows the power of the feudal landlord class. Without using the greatest force, the peasants cannot possibly overthrow the deep-rooted authority of the landlords which has lasted for thousands of years. The rural areas need a mighty revolutionary upsurge, for it alone can rouse the people in their millions to become a powerful force.

It was necessary to overthrow the whole authority of the gentry, to strike them to the ground and keep them there. . . . it is necessary to create terror for a while in every rural area, or otherwise it would be impossible to suppress the activities of the counter-revolutionaries in the countryside or overthrow the authority of the gentry. Proper limits have to be exceeded in order to right a wrong, or else the wrong cannot be righted. . . . There are three kinds of peasants, the rich, the middle and the poor peasants. The three live in different circumstances and so have different views about the revolution.

Mao then describes how the rich peasants were sceptical at first and sometimes positively antagonistic towards the peasant associations, but later after the initial revolutionary successes hesitantly began to join the unions. He continues:

After joining, the rich peasants are not keen on doing any work for the associations. They remain inactive throughout.

How about the middle peasants? Theirs is a vacillating attitude. They think that the revolution will not bring them much good. They have rice cooking in their pots and no creditors knocking on their doors at midnight.

They, too, were reluctant to join the peasant associations.

It was not until the second period, when the peasant associations were already exercising great power, that the middle peasants came

---

1. A quotation from the Confucian Analects. See Legge, *The Chinese Classics*, Vol. 1, p. 6.

in. They show up better in the associations than the rich peasants but are not as yet very enthusiastic; they still want to wait and see. It is essential for the peasant associations to get the middle peasants to join and to do a good deal more explanatory work among them.

The poor peasants have always been the main force in the bitter fight in the countryside. They have fought militantly through the two periods of underground work and of open activity. They are the most responsive to Communist Party leadership. They are deadly enemies of the camp of the local tyrants and evil gentry and attack it without the slightest hesitation.

This great mass of poor peasants, or altogether 70 per cent of the rural population,[1] are the backbone of the peasant associations, the vanguard in the overthrow of the feudal forces and the heroes who have performed the great revolutionary task which for long years was left undone. Leadership by the poor peasants is absolutely necessary. Without the poor peasants there would be no revolution. To deny their role is to deny the revolution. To attack them is to attack the revolution.

This essential first part of Mao's report, which describes and assesses the situation as a whole, is followed by a fourteen-point survey of the activity of the peasant associations, summarized as follows:

After the peasants had been organized into associations, they began their political and economic attack on the landlords, especially on the evil gentry who tyrannize the villages. Politically they were held responsible for illegal financial gains at the expense of the peasants and for any other infringements against them, and according to the severity of the crime, received punishments ranging from a small fine to execution. The economic attack consisted in the banning of grain speculation, prohibiting increases in rents and interest rates and the cancellation of tenancies, and in reducing or abolishing interest on debts. Moreover, the local administration which was dependent on the gentry and its main source of strength, the militia corps (*min t'uan*), were dissolved with the aim of removing the armed power of the landlords and establishing that of the peasants. In this way the county magistracy with its corrupt officials and its police, clerks and runners

1. This refers only to the province of Hunan.

could no longer be carried on without the approval of the peasant associations in the country. The almost absolute authority of heads of families and clans was also to be set aside. Women were to receive equality with men; and war was proclaimed on superstitious belief in gods and spirits. Mao tried to impress upon the peasants that it was only their own strength, organized in the associations, that had altered their position and could alter it further. Gods and spirits could not help. These questions, however, were temporarily unimportant in comparison with the political and economic aims and the propaganda for these aims. Traditional vices, such as gaming, gambling, and opium-smoking, together with numerous other luxuries were strictly forbidden by the peasant associations. When the peasant associations gained power, the bandits usually disappeared of their own accord; otherwise they were liquidated. The improvement and reorganization of primary schooling, the establishment of co-operative societies for buying and selling and for credit facilities, and the repair of roads and dikes were also undertaken by the peasant associations.

THE VICTORY OF THE REVOLUTIONARY ARMY AND THE SEPARATION OF THE KMT AND THE COMMUNISTS

Sun Yat-sen's Death and the Conquest of Central China

At the end of 1924 Sun Yat-sen travelled from Canton via Shanghai to Peking, to take part in a conference with the various war-lords about a peaceful unification of China. The Communists and the Russian advisers disapproved, but Sun felt that all peaceful methods of improving China's position were justified; he was not committed unconditionally to a violent revolution. It is true that at this juncture such a conference promised little hope of success. Sun Yat-sen was already a dangerously sick man. He was unable to take any part in official discussions in Peking and died there of cancer on 12th March, 1925. Some days before his death he composed his final will and testimony in the following words:

For forty years I have devoted my energies to the national revolution. Its aim is freedom and equality for China. From my experience of forty years I know only too well that in order to achieve this aim the mass of the people must be awakened to join with those peoples of the world who treat us as equals in order to wage a common struggle.

The revolution is not yet complete. All my comrades must continue their efforts to achieve this by means of the books I have written, *Plan for the Reconstruction of China, Outlines of the Reconstruction, The Three Principles of the People*, and *Manifesto of the First National Congress of the KMT*.

I hope that there will be a national assembly very soon and that the unequal treaties will be annulled. This ought to happen very soon. I lay this trust on you.

In the areas dominated by the KMT and later throughout China Sun Yat-sen's will and portrait became symbols. In all official ceremonies of party, government, or school his will was solemnly read and all school-children had to learn it by heart. Sun Yat-sen's portrait was given a place of honour in all public buildings, schools and shops and in many homes. He became the object of a regular cult. On ceremonial occasions all those present bowed three times before the specially decorated portrait of the revolutionary hero; this was followed by a reading of his will and a three-minute silence. Three successive bows are an expression of special reverence; they replaced the *K'ou-t'ou*, which was usual on similar occasions previously. Thus, to a certain extent the public homage to Sun Yat-sen took the place of the earlier Confucius cult. Later, of course, under Communist rule Sun Yat-sen's name has become rather less prominent. But even though he is no longer thought of as the semi-divine hero of the Chinese revolution, above criticism, his memory was still honoured—at least before the Cultural Revolution. On the occasion of the ninetieth anniversary of his birth on 11th November, 1956, there were large-scale official celebrations in Peking and elsewhere. Mao Tse-tung and other leading personalities attested their respect and recognition for their revolutionary predecessor. The Communists regarded Sun Yat-sen as their forerunner whose incomplete revolution they inherited and completed.

Sun Yat-sen did not live to see the victory of the movement he created. The victory of the KMT, however, was not in every respect identical with the success of the revolution, and this—as will be shown later—contained the seeds of the later decline of the

KMT's authority. Soon after Sun Yat-sen's death the Canton military government was dissolved and its place was taken by the Chinese National Government, organized on Sun Yat-sen's principles with the help of Soviet advisers. Both the party and the government were headed by a central executive committee (*Chungyang chih-hsing wei-yüan-hui*), consisting of thirty-six members, including a number of Communists. The first president of this central executive committee was Wang Ching-wei, trusted friend and collaborator of Sun Yat-sen since the formation of the Revolutionary Alliance in Japan and soon to be the strongest rival of Chiang Kai-shek within the KMT. The new government was given financial strength by the skill and dexterity of the Minister of Finance, T. V. Sung (Sung Tzu-wen), the brother-in-law of Sun Yat-sen, and later of Chiang Kai-shek; this was particularly important for the Northern Expedition that was planned. Meanwhile in the Whampoa Military Academy increasing numbers of able officers were given a good military training and equivalent political education, ready for service. The work of propaganda and organization among the workers and peasants, which was undertaken by the Communists in the first instance, had prepared the way for the advance of the revolutionary army. The revolutionary troops were proclaimed as the liberators of the oppressed classes of the nation; in fact, political education proved its effects in the different treatment received by the population from the revolutionary troops and from the armies of the war-lords. Thus, in the summer of 1926 the expedition of the revolutionary army under Chiang Kai-shek against the war-lords of central and northern China began. The central areas south of the Yangtze, Hunan and Kiangsi, quickly fell into the hands of the revolutionary army. In August the Yangtze-metropolis of Wuhan was captured. By the end of the year part of the political leadership of the united KMT/CCP transferred from Canton to Wuhan. In addition, Chiang Kai-shek was pressing eastwards, and in the spring of 1927 he succeeded in bringing Chekiang and south Kiangsu under his control. About the same time, T'ang Sheng-chih, one of the war-lords who had joined the revolution, left Hupei for the north and joined up in Honan with Feng Yü-hsiang, one of the northern war-lords—often known abroad as the Christian General. Feng had travelled to Moscow in

1926, where he had joined the KMT, and on his return to China he tried to establish links with the revolutionary South from his base in the Northwest. Thus, about the middle of 1927, directly or indirectly, a considerable proportion of the whole country was under the sway of the KMT.

The Anti-Imperialist Movement

The advance of the revolutionary armies was part of the fight against imperialism and against the war-lords, usually referred to by the Communists as the fight against imperialism and feudalism. The term 'feudalism' here has nothing to do with what is usually understood by feudalism in the West; it refers to the traditional, social and political order in China, especially in rural areas. The military actions of the revolutionary armies were preceded by propaganda, which in most cases was undertaken by specially trained students. The propaganda was directed primarily at the urban workers, but also at artisans, merchants and peasants. Mention has already been made of the peasant movement. In Communist terminology the KMT at the beginning of the Northern Expedition was already a 'united front', consisting of four classes— workers, peasants, petty bourgeoisie and the national bourgeoisie. The same four classes were again recognized as the four pillars of Chinese society after 1949. All these groups of the population were interested in the fight against foreign imperialism and the native war-lords for their own interests, or they could be made interested by appropriate explanation and propaganda. Reference was frequently made to the imperialist pressure of foreign powers burdening China. Foreign concessions, extra-territoriality, and the lack of full customs authority were regarded as the worst infringe- ments of Chinese sovereignty by foreign privileges, and the fight was directed chiefly against the 'unequal treaties', which forced China to recognize these privileges. It was not just these formal foreign privileges proceeding from the treaties, however, that pro- voked Chinese ill-feeling against the foreigners. With a few excep- tions foreigners regarded the Chinese as colonial natives who stood a great way below themselves and they behaved like colonial lords. A Chinese person, for example, who worked for a foreign establishment, whether it was a commercial or cultural undertaking especially the Christian missions and their institutions—on principle received a much smaller wage than a European, irrespective of his qualifications. In certain parks and restaurants or on public transport in the foreign concessions no Chinese were allowed; in short, the native Chinese were often treated like second-class citizens by foreigners. Of course much of this had changed since the 1920s, but even after the Second World War the tendency had not been entirely eradicated. It is easy to see that this sort of treatment must have been particularly offensive in the case of educated Chinese, who were proud of China's culture; and who in spite of poverty and frugality were frequently superior to most of the foreigners resident in China, for these were usually the less well educated.

The growth of the revolutionary movement was accompanied by a greater number of anti-foreign demonstrations, sometimes with serious casualties. They began with the 'Movement of May 30th (1925)' (*Wu san-shih yün-tung*). There was a demonstration in Shanghai by students and workers, and the police of the International Settlement opened fire on the demonstrators at the command of an English sergeant. As a result thirteen demonstrators were killed and a considerable number wounded. The Shanghai incident sparked off big demonstrations against the foreign settlement in Canton on the island of Shameen (Sha-mien). The foreigners lost their nerve apparently and English soldiers began to shoot at the crowd. The result was a large number of dead and wounded. In return the Chinese used the weapon with which they had assailed the Japanese very effectively six years earlier— namely a boycott (see above p. 94). This time it was directed against England, which at that time still occupied the leading position among the great imperialist powers in the Far East. Not only English goods and ships were affected by the boycott, but a substantial number of Chinese workers and employees in English businesses in Canton and especially in neighbouring Hong Kong, and even those who had domestic duties in English families quit their jobs. Those who were working in Hong Kong left the colony and went to Canton. The island of Shameen, the site of the foreign settlements in Canton, was blockaded. The boycott continued for more than a year with undiminished severity—until October 1926.

There was a further Anglo-Chinese incident later known as 'the incident of Wan-hsien' (*Wan-hsien ts'an-an*) in Szechwan in the late summer of 1926. A Chinese war-lord from Szechwan, Yang Sen, tried to seize two English ships at Wan-hsien on the Yangtze for use as troop-ships. In the 'unequal treaties', however, China had had to surrender its sovereignty over inland waterways. Fighting broke out between the Chinese war-lords and the English, and English gun-boats shelled the city. The innocent victims were several hundred citizens of Wan-hsien, who were killed or wounded as a result.

Soon after the National Government was transferred to Wuhan a Chinese crowd forced its way into the British concession there and demanded its return to China. Thanks to the understanding attitude taken by the government in London—which did not always see eye to eye with the English who lived in China—the incident did not develop into anything serious. Soon afterwards the British concession in Kiukiang on the Yangtze, lower down than Wuhan, was also recovered by the Chinese in a similar manner.

Anglo–Chinese relationships, it can be seen, were extremely tense in 1926-7. As a precaution all English, mostly missionaries and business-people, were evacuated from the inland areas of China, and English women and children were evacuated from the British concessions and from the other treaty ports. One of the reasons why Chinese bitterness at this time was directed primarily against England is to be found in the fact that England was the leading foreign power and had the greatest economic and political interests in China. In addition, the Soviet Russian advisers probably exercised a discreet influence. Russian politics at this time were directed chiefly against England and sought to isolate England from other powers; in contrast, Russia was concerned to be on good terms with France and Japan. The USA at that time did not play a very important role in China.

In view of the increasingly critical situation the English and the other nations involved had assembled a considerable number of warships and troops in Shanghai, in order to protect the international settlement against the revolutionary army. Privately it was hoped that the northern war-lords, who were fairly accommodating to the foreigners and who constituted no real danger to their privileged position, would gain the upper hand against the dreaded national troops, who aimed to keep foreigners in their place and assert China's sovereignty everywhere. However, preparations were made to cover every contingency and precautions were taken. In the eyes of the foreigners at Shanghai the revolutionary army was a crew of rebellious Bolsheviks and they were painted in the worst possible colours by the foreign press, particularly the English press, which resorted to every conceivable propaganda. The Shanghai foreigners were in favour of armed intervention even before the occupation of the parts of Shanghai which were under Chinese administration, in order to prevent the success of the revolutionary army. It was only due to the discretion of the governments in London, Paris, Tokyo and Washington that nothing of the sort took place. The hopes pinned by the Shanghai foreigners on the power of the northern war-lords were not to be realized. There was no need even of the national army. Even while the latter was approaching, there was an organized armed rebellion in the Chinese quarters of the city by the workers against the remnants of the retreating northern troops whom they quickly overpowered. The revolutionary army needed only to receive the city formally from the workers. A few days after the fall of Shanghai the national troops occupied Nanking also. In the disturbances between the departure of the last of the northern troops and the arrival of the revolutionary army a few foreigners lost their lives. One or two foreigners had also been killed or wounded in the other incidents. Altogether the small number of foreign losses at this period bears no comparison with the numbers of Chinese who were killed or wounded as a result of foreign encroachment. But in foreign eyes a hundred Chinese did not count as much as one foreigner, even if he was an undesirable vagrant!

The Anti-Christian Movement

Closely connected with anti-imperialism was the anti-Christian movement, which began about 1922 and reached its peak in 1925-7. Although largely identical with the anti-imperialist movement there were also other elements at work in this case; consequently a separate discussion seems justified.

Reference has already been made in connection with the Reform Movement of 1898 to the fact that not only were Christian missions very closely associated with the political and economic invasion of China by the foreign powers but also, over and above this, power to acquire land throughout China and to settle was secretly written into the Chinese text of the Sino–French Treaty of 1860. Hence, for the Chinese, the expansion of Christianity in China was blemished not only by its connection with the political, colonial power of the western nations, but also by its deceit. The Boxer Risings were the first large-scale, violent expression of the agitation against the Christian missions and against the foreign missionaries. Then, as later and until the beginning of the 1920s, resistance to Christianity was compounded largely of traditional elements—Confucianism, Taoism and Buddhism. In the 1920s, however, a change took place. In the first two decades of the 20th century the Christian missions in China, especially the Protestant, had expanded significantly and had developed a considerable interest in the field of education. The mission schools played an important role in Chinese education. In 1922 a conference of the World Student Christian Federation was held in China for the first time. In opposition to this there arose in Shanghai in the same year an 'Anti-Christian Student Union' (*Fei chi-tu-chiao hsüeh-sheng t'ung-meng*), which quickly spread throughout China. Members of other social groups attached themselves and this resulted in the formation of a very comprehensive organization called the Anti-Religious Union (*Fei tsung-chiao ta t'ung-meng*). The driving force behind the union was always students and teachers. In publications, meetings and demonstrations they attacked the Christian missions and the Christian religion with great vehemence. The movement in Shanghai was given new impetus in 1924 by the reorganization of these currents in the 'Anti-Christian Union' (*Fei chi-tu-chiao t'ung-meng*) and especially after the events in Shanghai on 30th May, 1925 (see above p. 148). During the advance of the revolutionary armies in 1926–7 there were repeated attacks on mission property and excesses against foreign missionaries. In isolated cases missionaries were even killed. At this point the anti-Christian movement becomes indistinguishable from anti-imperialism; in both cases the attacks were directed against the Anglo–American representatives; the

Protestant missions were, in fact, chiefly Anglo–American. The Anglo–Americans, too, had been particularly prominent in the field of education. In the course of the evacuation of central and southern China by the English in 1927 more than 3,000 missionaries, mostly English, Canadian and American, left China. The Catholic missionaries, being less prominent, were not affected by the movement to the same extent.

What were the motives behind this movement? In the first place reference must be made to the new ideas of the May 4th Movement, ('democracy and science'—see above pp. 106 ff.), representatives of which wanted to do away for the most part with every religion, including Christianity, as old-fashioned superstition, hostile to progress and science. Religion was totally incompatible with the naïve belief in progress held by most representatives of the May 4th Movement. The anti-Christian movement originated in 1922 from ideas such as these and was given support by figures like Ts'ai Yüan-p'ei, Ch'en Tu-hsiu, Li Ta-chao and Wang Ching-wei. The basically agnostic, purely this-worldly attitude of the educated scholar, which stemmed from Confucian tradition, also exercised an unconscious influence, in that such scholars looked down from their superior position on the religious customs of the people. Others took exception to the activity of the movement, which they criticized as 'a religious anti-religious movement'. It should be left to the individual, they argued, whether he adhered to any religious belief or not; this was the only attitude in keeping with the claims of democracy and science. In the following years the movement coalesced more and more with the nationalist anti-imperialist movement and finally became a part of it. It was joined then not only by pupils and students from Christian schools who had at first stood aloof but also by Christian students. One of its most important demands was the educational sovereignty of the Chinese government. Christian schools were required to accept the authority of the Chinese administration in education, to teach according to the Chinese curriculum, to refrain from the compulsory religious instruction of all pupils, and to make a Chinese person, not a foreigner, responsible for running the school. Previously in mission schools instruction had usually been given in accordance with the system of the missionaries' own country. Specifically

Chinese disciplines, such as the Chinese language, literature, history and geography, etc., were often given little emphasis. It is natural that the Chinese found this situation intolerable, all the more so since it was in the foreign schools that they learned about the principles of national sovereignty and of democracy. The KMT government also insisted vigorously on implementing the demand for educational sovereignty and in most cases was successful, despite the resistance of the foreign missionaries and the protests of foreign governments. Of course, foreign influence in Chinese education remained widespread. The Chinese headmaster was often only a figurehead; for the foreigners had control of the purse. But the mission schools had to adapt themselves to the Chinese system of education; and, in fact, in the 1930s many mission-universities won for themselves a leading position in specifically Chinese studies.

Apart from the two elements referred to—a naïve belief in progress and nationalism—Communism also played a role that should not be underestimated. It is no accident that the Communist leaders Ch'en Tu-hsiu and Li Ta-chao also played an active part in the anti-Christian movement. A great deal of Communist ideology was taken over in the proclamations of the anti-Christian Student Union and other anti-Christian organizations. The period of co-operation between the KMT and the Communists was also the heyday of the anti-Christian movement. The break between the KMT and the Communists in 1927 also brought the anti-Christian movement to an end for the time being.

The Break between the KMT and the Communists

Co-operation between the KMT and the Communists was seriously hindered from the very beginning by fundamental differences of opinion on many points as well as by the conflicting aims and interests of the two partners. In addition, there was a wide division of opinion within the KMT. This was true to a large degree even during Sun Yat-sen's lifetime, but the authority of his personality in leading the party was mostly able to bridge and smooth over these conflicts. As soon as Sun died, however, the differences within the KMT began to be more noticeable. Opinion was most sharply divided on the question of co-operation with the Communists; accordingly, there was talk of a left and right wing without any suggestion that this was an exhaustive description of all the various shades of opinion. In 1925 the left wing, led by men like Liao Chung-k'ai and Wang Ching-wei, proved stronger than the right wing which rejected co-operation with the Soviet advisers and the CCP with the result that many of the leading members of the right wing left the KMT. Even Chiang Kai-shek spoke decisively in favour of close co-operation with the Chinese as well as the Soviet Communists, although some of his statements indicate that he was suspicious of them. And at that time even the Communists thought of him as tending towards the left wing of the KMT. Gradually a new right, anti-Communist wing began to take shape on lines laid down by Tai Chi-t'ao, an old revolutionary and one of the original founder members of the CCP. Chiang Kai-shek, however, soon became the political exponent of this wing. The first difference of opinion between Chiang Kai-shek and leading Communists took place in March, 1926, at Whampoa, an event later known as 'the incident of the gun-boat Chung-shan' (*Chung-shan chien shih-chien*). It ended with Chiang arresting a number of leading Chinese Communists and having them removed from leading positions in the troops directly under his command and in the military academy. The Soviet advisers were also placed under temporary house arrest. Despite this first serious open difference the subsequent expedition to the North was launched with the help of the Russian advisers. The provinces of Hunan and Kiangsi soon fell into the hands of the revolutionary troops, and part of the government moved to Wuhan at the end of 1926. The military headquarters were in Nanchang, the capital of Kiangsi. Military success, however, as so often, led to conflict between the military leaders and the civil organs of the party and government. In this case, ultimately, this was the same as conflict between the new right and left wing of the KMT. It was the intention of the political leaders, after their entry into Wuhan, to refrain from further military undertakings for the present and to give priority to consolidating the authority of the KMT in the newly won areas. Chiang Kai-shek however, the chief military commander, supported by a clique of close associates who had been officers at

Whampoa, wanted to continue the campaign eastwards. He wished
to bring the rich areas of south Kiangsu and his home province of
Chekiang under his control. Personal differences broke out between
Chiang and various members of the government including Wang
Ching-wei, T'ang Sheng-chih and Borodin. As a result Chiang
ordered the advance to Chekiang on his own authority. The conflict with Wuhan went further; the result was a complete rupture.
In March, 1927, Chiang demonstrated his independence by staying
away from the meeting of the Central Executive Committee at
Wuhan. As a result he and his followers lost the leading political
positions they had occupied till then. Their names did not reappear
in the newly constituted, leading political bodies. Chiang decided,
therefore, to pursue his own plans independently of Wuhan. In
Shanghai, where the Communist-led revolutionary workers' organizations had prepared the way for the national army, he suddenly
suppressed the unions and all Communist or leftist KMT elements
in a bloody act of violence. Thousands of Communists, workers'
leaders and others were arrested by Chiang's troops in Nanking,
Shanghai and other places, and a large number of them were
executed. The CCP and the workers' and peasants' organizations,
which were quite unprepared for such a sudden turn of events,
were proscribed and subjected to violent persecution. In Nanking
Chiang established his own government in opposition to Wuhan.

In Wuhan the co-operation between the KMT and the CCP
continued for the time being. The exit of the right wing of the
KMT considerably strengthened the position of the Communists.
Moreover, Moscow issued explicit instructions to the Russian
advisers and the Chinese Communists that, despite the experience
with Chiang Kai-shek, co-operation with the KMT in Wuhan
should continue. But this, too, lasted only a few months. Further
conflicts followed, the details of which can be omitted here. Wuhan
and Nanking reached an agreement, which was apparently a
compromise, but in fact represented a victory for the right wing.
There was a complete rupture, however, between the KMT and
the Communists. Disappointed and defeated, Borodin and the
other Russian advisers left China, a country they had never
understood properly and which was so obviously ungrateful
to them. They had helped the KMT to victory and now their

services were no longer required. The CCP and the peasant and workers' movement were violently suppressed even in areas ruled by the Wuhan government. The CCP was banned and had to go underground. This, then, was the result of the co-operation between the KMT and the CCP—an overwhelming blow for the Communists.

Responsibility for this belonged to the Moscow leaders, who had a totally false idea of the situation in China. In spite of all the warnings that came from China Stalin persisted in continuing the co-operation of the Communists with the KMT. Just before the final break he stated in a letter that the Communists would sooner or later squeeze the KMT like a lemon. Reports of anti-Communist and anti-revolutionary acts by the right wing of the KMT were deliberately suppressed and the CCP was instructed to maintain its present course; as a result the workers' and peasants' organizations, which had been mobilized with great effect, were misled by this attitude and continued to regard the KMT generals as their friends until the very last moment, by which time the generals had already attacked the mass movements. Several contemporary reports indicate that Moscow would have been willing to forgive Chiang Kai-shek even the bloody suppression of the workers' movement in Shanghai, if he had not set up the anti-Communist government in Nanking.

The background to Moscow's attitude to the Chinese revolution was formed by Stalin's struggle for power against the opposition within the Communist Party, especially against Trotsky. Stalin and his associates were more concerned with immediate Russian interests than with the social revolution in China. Their main aim was to gain an ally against England and for this they obviously had more hopes of Chiang Kai-shek and the other KMT generals than of the Communist-led, radical workers' and peasants' organizations. In contrast, Trotsky placed the world-revolution before purely Russian interests. He had rightly recognized that the interests of the predominant groups in the KMT were quite incompatible with those of the Communist-orientated mass movement made up of revolutionary workers and peasants. Trotsky also foresaw the catastrophic result which must follow the subjection of the CCP to the KMT as instructed by Moscow. The very fact, however, that this more accurate view of the situation in China was advanced by the opposition, made Stalin adhere even more firmly to the course he had chosen. And when the final open break between the KMT and the CCP came, he observed that this was the inevitable course of the development, that it was in no way surprising, and that it had been accurately foreseen. Admission of mistaken policy in China would have meant the justification of Trotsky and his group. In accordance with Stalin's methods the man who had carried out Stalin's unsuccessful policy was made the scapegoat. Ch'en Tu-hsiu and his closest associates, who had grave misgivings about the subordination of the CCP to the KMT from the very beginning and accepted it against their better judgment only because of the authority of the Comintern (see above pp. 131f.), were now blamed for the disaster on the grounds that they were 'opportunists who were deviating to the right'. They were relieved of all their offices in the Party and shortly afterwards expelled from the Party. Personal opponents of Ch'en Tu-hsiu within the Party seized the opportunity by the grace of Stalin to assume the leadership. Ch'en Tu-hsiu was succeeded by Ch'ü Ch'iu-pai, a native of Kiangsu and former student of Peking University, who had spent several years in Moscow, which he had left only in 1924.

Some commentators have sought to regard the break between the KMT and the CCP and the resulting interruption of the Chinese revolution as a decisive event in the subsequent development of international politics. According to them the events in China contributed to the final victory of Stalin over the opposition led by Trotsky, as a result of which the international idea of a worldwide revolution was subordinated to the national power politics of Russia. But the consequences which a different outcome to the power struggle in Russia, together with a successful socialist revolution in China, might have had on future international development cannot be measured in full. Such an interpretation probably overestimates the significance of mass movements in China during the 1920s, and it seems very doubtful whether any different outcome could have been expected even if there had been an earlier separation of the CCP—and the mass movement of revolutionary workers and peasants which it organized—from the KMT. Certainly a well-timed, clear delimitation of fronts would have enabled the workers' unions and peasants' associations to know where they stood and many unnecessary sacrifices on their part could have been avoided. It is highly questionable, however, whether a socialist revolution supported only by the peasants and workers—especially in view of the very small number belonging to the latter class—could have succeeded throughout the whole of China or even in the major part of the country. Even if they had had the complete material and ideological support of the Comintern the time was not yet ripe for a thorough-going, large-scale social revolution. The power of tradition and the customary social structure were still too strong; further events were necessary before a social revolution could be carried through successfully. Hence, the outstanding feature of the revolution in 1925–7 is its national and political character.

6 The Social Revolution: The Collapse of the K M T and the Victory of the Communists

THE UNFINISHED REVOLUTION

The Consolidation of the Nanking Government

After the collapse of the government in Wuhan the new National government in Nanking at first made rapid, visible progress towards consolidating its power. Of the war-lords who continued to resist some were overcome by force, others were induced by peaceful means to submit to Chiang Kai-shek and the National government, although they retained their very considerable and real freedom of action. In 1928 Chiang made his entry into Peking, after the government there had been dissolved and Nanking had been declared the official capital of China. In the following year also Manchuria recognized the authority of the National government, until it was violently cut off from China in 1931 by the Japanese. The other dependencies remained more or less independent of Nanking. Sinkiang and Outer Mongolia were under Soviet influence, Tibet largely under English influence. Nevertheless the whole of China, outwardly at any rate, was united under the Nanking government, and the red flag with a white sun on a blue background in the top-corner flew as the symbol of the new government throughout China.

The break with the Communists and with the left wing of the KMT, accompanied by a more moderate approach in the fight against imperialism, soon persuaded most of the foreign powers, in view of Chiang's overwhelming successes, to recognize the new government and to conclude treaties with it on a basis of equality, at least in principle. America, England and France recognized China's customs autonomy in principle; its infringement had always been regarded in China as a particularly discriminatory regulation of the unequal treaties and prejudicial to the economic development of China. Several countries, like Belgium, Italy, Denmark and Spain, declared their readiness from 1st January, 1930, to renounce the extra-territorial rights of their nationals in China, if the majority of the other powers would follow suit. Germany had already been compelled to forgo its rights (see above pp. 114, 123) and had not fared badly as a result. Nevertheless, the Great Powers still retained a number of fundamental privileges. But the National government, in addition to the recovery of the English concessions in Wuhan and Kiukiang in 1926, succeeded in winning back foreign concessions in a number of ports as well as the British leased territory of Weihaiwei; moreover not only was the principle of customs tariff autonomy recognized, but they also obtained practical concessions relating to the customs tariff and the surrender of other privileges, implementation of which was planned for the foreseeable future. The Nanking government never concealed its nationalist character and it prosecuted the fight to abolish the rights granted to the Western Powers under duress in the 'unequal treaties' with constancy and determination, even if in its outward approach, less radically than in previous years. This fundamental attitude finds expression in numerous statements by leading figures of the KMT, not least Chiang Kai-shek.[1] The Communists' reproach that the government of the KMT became a tool of Western imperialism has not been substantiated by convincing proof so far. In fact, the Nanking government obtained as much as could be obtained. It had no power to achieve more. Only the decisive weakening of England and France in the Second World War finally made it possible to abolish the 'unequal treaties' once and for all.

There was also significant progress in domestic affairs and numerous hopeful preliminaries were made towards the rebuilding of China. China's government from 1927 to 1937 was more stable than at any time since 1911. It is true that during this period there were military conflicts with the powerful war-lords, some of whom were still very powerful (others even belonged to the KMT). But Chiang Kai-shek knew how to restore unity, whether it was by

1. For example, in his book *China's Destiny*, where he sets out his aims. See the English trans. by Philip Jaffe, New York 1947, pp. 76–107.

diplomacy, bribery, trickery or force. The only groups that defied any agreement were the Communists, who had organized themselves militarily into individual soviets, and the Japanese, who forced their way into northern China from Manchuria. Nanking, which had been the residence of the Chinese Emperor at the end of the 14th and beginning of the 15th centuries and later became the seat of the Taiping government and the seat of the provisional republican government in 1911 (see above pp. 30, 75), became the new capital. Chiang and his followers wanted to be free from the decadent political atmosphere of Peking and from the control exercised by foreign troops stationed in the legation quarter of Peking; they sought, therefore, to build up an efficient government and administration in accordance with Sun Yat-sen's principles, working in an orderly, honest manner. Their full authority extended only to the coastal provinces of Kiangsu and Chekiang, however; in the rest of China they exercised only partial, varying control. The open break with the Communists and revolutionary mass movements, along with the appointment of T. V. Sung (Sung Tzu-wen), the brother-in-law of Sun Yat-sen and Chiang Kai-shek, and other men of ability to leading positions in the financial and economic administration gave the wealthy Chinese and foreign business community of Shanghai confidence in the new government and made them willing to co-operate with it. Foreign markets also began to show more interest in investing money in China. In accepting foreign aid, however, the Chinese government rejected any political 'strings' and refused to pledge important government revenues as had often been done before. There was close economic co-operation between China and Germany which profited from the fact that Germany no longer possessed any sort of privileges or political interests in China. A very significant victory for the government was the abolition in 1931 of the domestic tariff widely known as *Likin*, which had been raised by various local authorities since the end of the Ch'ing period; this was closely connected with the granting of customs autonomy by the foreign powers. Other measures aimed at centralizing financial, economic, transport, cultural and educational policy followed. The government also made strenuous efforts to reform the system of justice. The political patterns of traditional China no longer corresponded to the changed

situation; similarly, traditional patterns of justice were for the
most part no longer applicable, and the foreign powers wanted to
make their surrender of extra-territorial rights dependent on a
fundamental reorganization of the Chinese judicial system. Before
1927 little had been done in this field. Hence, the KMT government
devoted great energy and thoroughness to preparing a comprehensive legal code. A book of civil law and numerous other laws were
promulgated. This involved the large-scale adoption of continental
European law; both the content and the spirit of traditional Chinese
patterns of justice were ignored. The new law, therefore, was only
intelligible to a small upper class that had a Western education and
it took no account of the needs of the great majority of the people.
Its usefulness was thus very limited. It made the dissolution of
traditional morality and the traditional social order easier, but
was unable to establish new foundations in place of the old. The
old system of justice was no longer valid, but the new was not a
natural growth. It was widely regarded as foreign and not binding.

From Revolution to Restoration

Reference has already been made to the agrarian problem as one
of the most important problems if not the most crucial problem
of China. The KMT government could not at first refuse to recognize its importance. After the peasant associations of 1925–7 had
been dissolved and forbidden, there was a series of attempts with
official or semi-official support to improve living conditions in rural
areas; they were known as 'rural reconstruction'. Foreign missionaries and other foreign institutions joined in to some extent. But
it soon became clear that the question of raising the standard of
living in rural areas was inseparable from the general social and
political situation, especially questions of land ownership and
tenancy. The increasing education of the peasants in connection
with the programme of rural reconstruction contributed to their
growing awareness of their exploitation by landlords and officials
and to their increasing determination to stand up for their own
interests. Fundamental reforms, however, would have entailed
unforeseeable changes in the whole social structure. The government shrank from this, for it was widely influenced by conservative
circles which vigorously rejected not only any alteration in

conditions of land ownership but also even any decrease in the income from the land they owned. Regard for the still powerful local war-lords and their followers, who came largely from the landowning, land-leasing class, made the government cautious lest it run the risk of fresh conflicts with the provincial war-lords. Consequently the attempts at 'rural reconstruction' gradually came to a halt again, and on the whole everything remained as before. The leading circles of the KMT did not see that they were condoning conditions which could not last and which, when exploited by the Communist leaders, would give them the chance of gaining power—conditions in short, which presaged the end of KMT rule.

The failure to deal with the agrarian question was not the only mistake of the KMT régime; it was merely one symptom of its inner weakness. Since 1927 the main aim of Chiang Kai-shek and his supporters in the KMT was no longer revolution, but the creation of peace and order in the country, in other words restoration. Nothing seemed so well suited for this purpose as the traditional Confucian ideology, which had proved an ideal means for securing the rule of a small élite over the large mass of the people for more than 2,000 years. Hence, references to the traditional virtues and traditional morality became more frequent, often with the nationalistic undertone that these were specific values with which China could oppose the West. In the 'New Life Movement', which was launched officially in 1934, these tendencies were given general visible expression. As shown above, Confucianism and the Confucian ethic, its principles shaken, had long since lost its vitality, and the traditional virtues (not very satisfactorily translated by such phrases as 'principles of social conduct', 'righteousness', 'conscientiousness', 'self-respect', li, i, lien and chih, which the New Life Movement sought to revive) had been practically emptied of all meaning. They were repeatedly emphasized—but without any closer definition of content. They were really a means of defending the existing social order and of disciplining the people. It was precisely for this that the May 4th Movement had most sharply attacked Confucian teaching.

Whereas Sun Yat-sen and other revolutionaries had taken the Taiping and similar revolutionary movements of the past as their example and pattern, Chiang Kai-shek did quite the reverse and modelled himself on Tseng Kuo-fan and others (see above p. 31) who had had the Taiping suppressed. The T'ung-chih restoration, which restored peace and order to the country in a conservative spirit after the collapse of the Taiping revolution, became Chiang's guide. He had eyes only for its initial success; he did not see that ultimately it had failed and had been unable to save the traditional order from destruction. Chiang Kai-shek failed to realize that in the seventy years since Tseng Kuo-fan's first successes, Western influence and Western ideas had led to the dissolution of the traditional political, intellectual and social structure of China with increasing rapidity and to call a halt was impossible. Moreover, Chiang Kai-shek differed from Tseng Kuo-fan in one further very important point. Tseng Kuo-fan had been concerned not simply to restore peace and order in the areas devastated by the wars with the Taiping but to reintroduce an honest civil administration and to take comprehensive measures for economic reconstruction in order to lift the peasants' living standards as far as possible above what they enjoyed under the Taiping. But Chiang's restoration in the areas recovered from the Communists consisted primarily in enforcing strict control so that he could cut off any revolutionary activity.[1] Moreover the 1930s saw once again the spread of corruption and nepotism. Sometimes proceedings were taken against comparatively small offences with great severity, but among those close to Chiang Kai-shek no one was charged with such offences. In the capital Nanking there was a frugal, almost puritanical atmosphere. But Shanghai, which was only a few hours distance away by rail, enabled a small group of leading government and party officials who had private means or lucrative appointments to enjoy in the International Settlement or the French concession there all the pleasures and luxuries that were strictly forbidden in Nanking. Even if this charge could probably not be levelled at Chiang Kai-shek himself, he nevertheless did condone such behaviour in people close to him, as long as their loyalty to him was not in question.

1. See, for example, his speech in Chengtu on 14th June, 1935. See *Ausgewählte Reden des Marschalls Chiang Kaishek*, Heidelberg–Berlin, 1936, pp. 60–2.

Although leading civilians in the KMT exercised a certain amount of influence immediately after the establishment of the one party government in Nanking, the ascendancy of the military leaders became more pronounced with Chiang's continuing military successes, with the result that it became more accurate to speak of a military dictatorship than a party dictatorship. Even if the external structure of the party and government corresponded to the system drawn up by Sun Yat-sen, its actual practice had little else in common with Sun's ideas. Chiang Kai-shek was surrounded by a group of officers from Whampoa, who possessed his unconditional and exclusive trust. Chiang appointed members of this clique to almost all important military posts under his immediate command. For them unconditional loyalty to Chiang was the supreme commandment and there was no pardon for those who disobeyed it, whereas all other transgressions were normally treated very indulgently. When he met anyone who did not belong to this group, Chiang was always suspicious. If for political reasons he had to concede such a person a leading position, he usually tried to render him innocuous by constantly by-passing him.

This was not the only abuse that began to sap the inner strength of the KMT in the 1930s. When the government took over a number of formerly private enterprises, several outstanding businessmen, industrialists and bankers were appointed to important official positions. At the same time they and other members of the government continued their activities in private business, industry and banking. The positive side of this was the gain by the government of men of proven ability in financial and economic questions. The increasingly negative side of the picture, however, was that national and private enterprises were not kept strictly separate and government money was used to finance private enterprise, and income that should have come to the government went into private pockets. This mixing of public and private interests was condoned by Chiang Kai-shek and it was started in the circle closest to him, namely by his brother-in-law, T. V. Sung, and the husband of Chiang Kai-shek's wife's sister, H. H. Kung (K'ung Hsiang-hsi). The example set at the highest level finally became notorious, and had its effect on those beneath. The Communists described this phenomenon as 'officialdom's capitalism' or 'bureaucratic capitalism' (*Kuan-liao tzu-pen chu-i*) and not unjustly regarded it as one of the cancers of Chinese public life.

Thus, in the decade prior to the outbreak of the Sino-Japanese War, in spite of many favourable factors which gave hope of a slow evolution and a stabilising of conditions in China there were already signs of the inadequacies and decadence on which the KMT régime was to founder in the subsequent upheaval. In contrast to the period after 1911 there had, in fact, been fundamental changes in the political structure. The social revolution, however, had been broken off before it could develop. Consequently it was to break out again with even greater force later.

The Alienation of the Intelligentsia from the KMT

The intelligentsia who rose to prominence in the intellectual revolution of the May 4th Movement were linked by general sympathy to the revolutionary camp as long as the KMT and the Communists presented a common front, even though only a comparatively small number actually became members of either party. After the establishment of the government in Nanking there were only a few people eminent in the cultural life on the side of the Communists, whereas the majority exhibited goodwill towards the new government. It was only when the trends we have discussed above gradually became dominant within the KMT and when the intellectual achievements of the May 4th Movement were cancelled out, that the liberal elements gradually turned away from the KMT. Of course, the turn towards restoration was not without its opponents even in the KMT; but this opposition was unable to gain the upper hand. Several were expelled from the party; others yielded to the conformist pressure that was applied. The government not only prohibited and if necessary confiscated publications of Communist revolutionary content; it also increasingly suppressed all liberal writings which opposed the policy of restoration. Even such a moderate liberal as Hu Shih was expelled in 1935 from the province of Kwangtung, the home of Sun Yat-sen and the revolution, and seriously threatened because he had spoken out openly against the restoration programme of indoctrination introduced by the KMT. Scholars and authors with more radical views often found themselves compelled to seek asylum in the International

Settlement at Shanghai or abroad, and sometimes even in Japan.

In the 1920s Marxism attracted a lot of attention in Japan and many Chinese first became more closely acquainted with it via Japan. Works of Marx and Engels and their followers were translated into Chinese from the Japanese editions. Reference has already been made to the fact that the agnostic, this-worldly approach of educated circles, which was part of the legacy of the Confucian tradition, made them particularly receptive to modern positivistic and materialistic theories. Historical materialism and Marxist theories on the origin and evolution of society have attracted quite a number of Chinese historians, archaeologists and sociologists since 1930. Many scholars who had no political connection with Communism at the time gave expression to Marxist ideas in their academic works. One of the most outstanding of such figures was Kuo Mo-jo, a gifted, versatile scholar taking an interest in many fields of knowledge. Originally a doctor, he became prominent as a writer; he translated Goethe's *Werther* and the first part of *Faust* into Chinese and wrote important books on the archaeology and sociology of China. In 1929 he published his almost sensational *Studies of Ancient Chinese Society*, in which he applied what is the officially accepted Marxist–Leninist theory of evolution in China today (primitive communism—slave society—feudalism) to ancient Chinese history. The book was reprinted in 1947 and 1951 with little modification. In the first decade of the Peoples' Republic Kuo Mo-jo occupied leading positions in education and science.

Among writers, dissatisfaction with the KMT régime continued to grow, as the government proceeded more sharply against publications and authors it did not approve of. Like the literary inquisitions of previous centuries the government in Nanking compiled lists of prohibited books; these included the names of Gorki, Lunacharski, Upton Sinclair, Strindberg and others, as well as many Chinese authors. In 1930 the 'League of Left-wing Writers' was formed in Shanghai to oppose the restoration-reactionary measures of the KMT government. It soon became the centre of the opposition. Although the organization was not actually Communist, government policy, which outlawed all leftist opposition as Communist, drove leftist-liberal writers increasingly on to the side of the Communists. Lu Hsün, China's most important

12—C.C.R.

modern writer (see above p. 111), openly entered the Communist camp after 1930 and up to his death in 1936 wrote for the Communist side. In the People's Republic, as a result, he was regarded as the most celebrated modern author in China, although most of his works are not expressions of Communist ideology. Other prominent members of the writers' league were Shen Yen-ping—known also in the West by his pseudonym, Mao Tun, because of his novel *Midnight*[1]—the first Minister of Education in the Chinese People's Republic, Pa Chin (really Li Fei-kan),[2] the authoress Ting Ling (Chiang Ping-chih),[3] etc. The 1930s reveal the beginning of the widespread readiness with which ten years later the majority of intellectuals accepted Communist rule.

THE REORGANIZATION OF THE COMMUNISTS

After the break with the KMT the Chinese Communists first tried to gain prominence in a number of geographically limited insurrections. In accordance with directions from Moscow these were usually undertaken in the larger cities, where there was an industrial proletariat. The most important weapon of the CCP was the reorganized 'red armies', which had emerged out of the Communist-inspired military units in the joint KMT–Communist armies during the Northern Campaign. The most famous of these armed actions was the insurrection which became known as the 'Canton Commune', in the capital of Kwangtung province at the end of 1927. None of these attempts, however, succeeded. They were all quickly suppressed by the local government troops and, far from enlisting new supporters for the Communist cause, resulted in heavy losses for the CCP. The Party leadership, which worked underground in Shanghai, was not in a position to affect the way events were developing, although it was extremely unfavourable for them. Communists were constantly being arrested

1. English translation by Hsu Meng-hsiung, Peking, 1957.
2. Wrote, e.g., *Living Amongst Heroes*, Peking, 1954.
3. Wrote, e.g., *The Sun Shines Over the Sangkan River*, translated by Yang Hsien-yi and Gladys Yang, Peking, 1954.

by the alert secret service of the Nanking government and were usually condemned to death. The CCP also visibly lost ground among the workers as a result of the suppression of all trade union activity by government agencies; moreover, the workers often gained the impression, not always unjustified, that although they were asked to devote themselves to the cause of the CCP the direct interest of the workers did not play a decisive role for the Party. The Chinese are habitually very realistic and cannot on the whole be won over to a cause which seems to offer no immediate personal advantage. Again and again the leaders of the CCP were held responsible for the failures they experienced and leader followed leader in quick succession. Ch'ü Ch'iu-pai was succeeded after a year by Li Li-san, who had studied in France and had become prominent as a capable organizer of workers; in 1930 he was displaced by a young theoretician, Ch'en Shao-yü (alias Wang Ming), who had just returned from studying in Moscow and who knew very little about the practical requirements of the revolution in China.

In view of the successes of the peasant movements during the years 1925–7 the Party leadership, despite its strict adherence to instructions from Moscow, could not close its eyes to the importance of the peasants for the revolution. But they regarded the leadership of the proletariat as a prerequisite of a successful agrarian revolution. This meant that revolutionary movements in country areas should be closely connected with parallel actions in the cities and dependent on them. This is clearly expressed in a circular of Li Li-san towards the end of 1928:

The Communist Party acknowledges that the peasantry is an ally of the revolution. At the same time, it recognizes that the peasantry is petty bourgeois and cannot have correct ideas regarding socialism, that its conservatism is particularly strong and that it lacks organizational ability. Only a proletarian mentality can lead us into the correct revolutionary road. Unless we are prepared to correct the dangers involved in this peasant mentality, it may lead to a complete destruction of the revolution and of the Party.[1]

1. From Benjamin Schwartz, *Chinese Communism and the Rise of Mao*, p. 137.

Despite this directive from the Party leadership in Moscow and Shanghai, individual Communist leaders, including in the first place Mao Tse-tung, continued their revolutionary activity among the peasants. By and large they proceeded in accordance with Mao's experiences in Hunan (see above pp. 139 f.). Separation from the KMT was followed by the decisive further step of dispossessing landlords who did not cultivate their own land, liquidating them for the most part and dividing the confiscated land among the landless peasants, in order to implement Sun Yat-sen's demand that the cultivator of the land should own it (see above p. 129). In many areas of central and southern China independent local soviets were formed. Their fight against the government and the existing order proceeded largely in the traditional manner of peasant revolutions described in the introduction (see above pp. 8 f.). The leading position among these local soviets was soon occupied by the one that Mao Tse-tung founded in central and southern Kiangsi. By allying with other leaders of the 'red armies', especially with Chu Te and P'eng Te-huai, who gladly accepted Mao's leading role, there began to develop a strong Communist power base with a well-organized, efficient army. In time it covered the greater part of south Kiangsi. The centre was always in remote mountain territory, at first west of Chi-an near the border of Hunan, later southeast of Chi-an not far from the border of Fukien. In spite of repeated 'campaigns of annihilation' which Chiang Kai-shek undertook with the help of German military advisers and a huge levy of troops, the 'red army', thanks to its excellent leadership and outstanding morale, was able to hold out for a long time. Mao Tse-tung's course of action was heavily criticized by the Shanghai CCP leaders—so much so, in fact, that there was an armed revolt in Mao's ranks at the end of 1930, probably on the instigation of Li Li-san. It was soon put down, however. Towards the end of the following year the 'Chinese Soviet Republic' with Mao Tse-tung at its head was formed in Kiangsi. At that time Communist territory embraced a population of more than fifty million altogether. Mao and his supporters were justified by the course of events. In the autumn of 1932 the Party leadership in Shanghai was no longer able to hold out against the pressure of the KMT government and at Mao's urging sought refuge in the area which he controlled. Thus, on the basis of his political and military successes Mao became the undisputed leader of the CCP and since that date his name has been inseparable from the fate of Communism in China. Moscow raised no objection to this development, although it had taken place without its aid, since this would have been tantamount to rejecting the CCP.

In the autumn of 1934 the increasing severity of the KMT offensive finally made the position of the Communists in Kiangsi untenable. By means of skilful manœuvres, however, the bulk of the 'Red Army' and their political leaders were able to escape encirclement and annihilation by the KMT. On the famous 'Long March' through the provinces of Hunan, Kweichow, Yunnan, Szechwan, Sikang and Kansu, the Communist army succeeded after great effort and heavy losses in escaping from the clutches of the government troops who were constantly in pursuit and harrying them. Ultimately at the end of the following year they reached the remote, poverty-stricken mountainous territory of north Shensi. Of the large numbers who left Kiangsi only about twenty thousand survived. The 'Long March' was a significant military achievement; it welded the survivors into a close community and developed into a legend among later Chinese Communists. During the 'Long March' no opportunity of publicising the revolution was left unexploited, wherever the Red Army came. Wherever the Communists appeared, officials and gentry took flight. The poor people, however, were normally well treated by the Red Army and this gave them a certain secret sympathy for the Communists. In north Shensi Mao Tse-tung and his followers established a new power base, which was to be the starting-point for the later conquest of the whole of China. In the first place they had peace to consolidate and reorganize. Then, as a result of increasing pressure from Japan, a new united front, this time directed against Japan, was soon formed between the CCP and the KMT. Although it did not lead to any close co-operation between the two parties and was always beset by mutual distrust, for a time it brought the conflicts between the two factions to an end.

CONFLICT WITH JAPAN

China and Japan before the Outbreak of War

There was bitter opposition to the KMT government from Japan as well as the Communists. Frequent reference has been made already to the way in which the island kingdom of Japan, by strengthening its political and economic position, was able to cast off the fetters initially imposed on it, as on China, by Western imperialism, until it was itself in a position to attempt colonial expansion on the opposite mainland. It was only natural, therefore, that Japanese policy should constantly oppose any consolidation of central power in China, in order to prevent a strong Chinese government acting vigorously on behalf of its national interests to the detriment of Japanese efforts to expand.

In 1928 the Japanese government, which had previously taken over all German rights in the province of Shantung—ostensibly to protect Japanese economic interests—sent a strong contingent of troops to Tsinan, in order to check Chiang Kai-shek's advance into northern China. It was unable to prevent this, however, since the revolutionary troops, despite having to circumvent Tsinan, continued to defeat the northern war-lords in battle. Japan's decisive action took place three years later, when the Japanese army, following the incident of Mukden on 18th September, 1931, separated Manchuria from China by force and in the following year set up the state of 'Manchoukuo' under its own protectorship, with the last Manchu Emperor of China, P'u-i, who had abdicated as a small child in 1912, at its head. The Chinese government at that time was not in a position to make any lasting resistance. But the Japanese action provoked a widespread boycott of Japanese goods in China as well as other anti-Japanese measures of protest. As a result there were minor clashes at the beginning of 1932 in Shanghai, where Japanese commercial interests were particularly strong, and where Japan, like all other Great Powers, maintained a garrison to protect these interests. The Japanese immediately despatched large numbers of reinforcements to Shanghai and serious fighting developed there, in which the KMT troops offered vigorous resistance for several weeks. As a result of the mediation of the Great Powers, who had equally important interests in

Shanghai, and who controlled the International Settlement in common with Japan, and particularly as a result of British efforts, the incident was finally settled. In Manchuria, however, in spite of the intervention of the League of Nations and its condemnation of Japan, to which Japan replied by leaving the League of Nations, Japan's position not only remained unimpaired but Japanese pressure on northern China and Inner Mongolia increased, until finally the incident at the Marco Polo Bridge, near Peking, on July 7th, 1937, became the prelude of the Second World War in the East.

The more active the Japanese in China became, the more decisive was the nationalistic anti-imperialist movement against Japan and the less violent the opposition to the West. Sun Yat-sen's description of China as a 'hypocolony', in which numerous colonial powers exercised equal rights (see above p. 124), was not without justice. The maintenance of equal rights and opportunities for all, known as the principle of 'the open door', was the basis of Western, and particularly American, policy in China against the Japanese. Although Chinese wishes and hopes for active intervention by the Western powers against the Japanese occupation of Manchuria were not fulfilled, the presence of Western troops and warships in China often acted as a limited local protection against Japanese encroachments. The Chinese were well aware that the Western colonial powers did not make common cause with China against Japan out of altruistic friendship for China, but only out of consideration for their own interests. But it is an old principle of Chinese politics 'to use barbarians to fight barbarians'; thus, under increasing Japanese pressure, the KMT government avoided taking any action which might have seriously upset the privileges and interests of the Western powers. The Japanese also increasingly regarded the Western Powers as their real enemies, who stood in the way of their aims on the mainland. Using the slogan 'Asia for the Asians' they developed a widespread propaganda campaign against Western imperialism, inciting the Asian nations to unite under Japanese leadership and to fight against Western imperialism until it was exterminated.

Chiang Kai-shek and the KMT government did not occupy an easy position between their principal opponents—Japan and the

Communists. As often in Chinese history, they saw themselves confronted with the difficult decision whether to give precedence to the fight against the internal or the external enemy. The policy of restoration followed by Chiang gave priority to the pacification of China and to the defeat of internal enemies. He was also convinced —probably rightly—that even if it were internally united China was not yet ready for a military conflict with Japan. It was clear in China, however, that such a conflict was inevitable in the long run, and the government, with useful assistance from German military advisers, made energetic efforts to build up an adequate striking force. The policy of the Chinese government was to avoid a collision on any wide scale with the Japanese for the time being, to negotiate discreetly and if necessary to yield a little. The choice of Nanking as capital can also be seen as a step in this direction.

Since about the 5th century A.D. a transfer of the capital to the region south of the Yangtze had always denoted the surrender of northern China to foreign, non-Chinese influences, whether Turks, Tungus, Mongols or Manchus. The Japanese were now pressing into northern China as these peoples had done earlier. After defeating the Mongols the Ming dynasty, whose example the KMT government followed, retained their residence at Nanking only during the reigns of their first two rulers, just fifty years. The third Ming Emperor, Yunglo, made Peking his capital and pursued a very active policy against the Mongols, who were seeking to recover their control over China. It is, of course, very doubtful whether the KMT government could have resisted the Japanese any more effectively from Peking. The fact is that from the very beginning they clearly did not feel strong enough to do so.

From 1932 onwards, after the Japanese attack on Manchuria and the incident in Shanghai, the Chinese Communists repeatedly declared their readiness to form a united front with all anti-Japanese groups in China. Their appeal did not find much response, however. It was only after the Comintern proclaimed in 1935 that a united anti-Fascist front was the right policy for Communists throughout the world that the efforts to form a Chinese united front gradually succeeded. When Chiang Kai-shek was overtaken and captured by a war-lord at the end of 1936 in Sian, near the new Communist base, the Communists secured his release. For they, too, regarded Chiang Kai-shek as the only possible leader of a united anti-Japanese front, which would include the KMT, the CCP and all smaller groups if possible. The roundabout way of a united front and a war against Japan seemed to the Communists the only way to gain power in China. The experiences of 1927, however, made them insist on retaining their own troops and their own power base. For the time being, therefore, all fighting between the KMT and the CCP ceased and gave way to friendly relations—at least on the surface. The Japanese observed this development with great concern. They feared that with this consolidation of the position in China, which was bound up with the unification of China, and with the swift growth of its war potential, Japanese efforts on the mainland would meet with stronger resistance from year to year and that a military conflict with China would become more and more costly for Japan. The incident at the Marco Polo Bridge was probably not deliberately provoked by the Japanese and at that time did not quite suit the intentions of Japanese policy. Nevertheless, after efforts to achieve a peaceful settlement had failed, the Japanese started a heavy offensive in northern China, and subsequently in Shanghai too. Chiang Kai-shek and many other members of the Nanking government would gladly have postponed the conflict and made concessions to the Japanese, but they felt compelled to resist because of the pressure of the united front. So began a war that was to prove equally fatal both for Japan and for the KMT.

The War, 1937–45

At the beginning of the war against Japan a wave of national enthusiasm and determination to resist the aggressors to the very end swept through China. The slogan of the united front overcame all internal Chinese conflicts at first. All prisoners of the KMT government who had been held because of Communist or leftist activity were released; others, who had gone into voluntary exile abroad, returned in order to put themselves at the nation's disposal. Reaction and restoration seemed to have given way to revolution once more. The war against Japan was widely felt to be a revival of the revolutionary struggle that had been broken off in 1927. Even Chiang Kai-shek spoke of the importance of the war for the national revolution in the sense of Sun Yat-sen. Hence, the resistance offered by the Chinese to the invading enemy surpassed all the expectations of the Japanese, who had hoped to be able to attain their objectives in a short successful campaign. Eastern China, of course, could not hold out permanently against the superior forces of the enemy. At the end of 1937 the government moved to Wuhan and in the following year to the well-protected Chungking in the rich province of Szechwan, which thus became the backbone of Chinese resistance. Government offices and administrative institutions along with industrial enterprises moved to the west, taking with them all movable equipment; similarly universities and research institutions. The intelligentsia left the old centres of culture in large numbers, after they were occupied by the Japanese. Schoolchildren and students made their way through the lines of fighting from the occupied areas into free China throughout the whole war period. There a new cultural and economic life began to flourish. The Chinese are unequalled when it comes to self-help and improvisation; this talent proved most useful when they settled in a part of China that was cut off from the rest of the country and had not been modernized and had an improvised capital. Communication with the outside world was possible by means of smaller ports on the coast of Chekiang, Fukien, and Kwangtung that had not yet been occupied by the Japanese, by means of what was then French Indo-China, and by means of the newly built Burma road. When the Japanese coastal blockade was tightened this last gradually became the only important route to and from China. The further into China the Japanese pressed, the more troops they had to send and the longer and the more precarious became their lines of communication. Chinese guerrilla units were active everywhere behind the Japanese lines; they destroyed the railway lines and greatly harassed Japanese communications. It has been said that 'space was China's weapon'. In the first two years of the war Chinese determination to resist was generally unbroken. The symbol of the resistance was Chiang Kai-shek.

As the war continued, however, the mood altered. Isolation—even the Burma road was cut by the Japanese advance into Burma and the air-lift 'over the hump' remained the only means of communication with the outside world—all sorts of deprivations and progressive inflation brought about a demoralization that even the air attacks, which were now being successfully warded off with the help of the US air force, had not been able to achieve previously. Corruption and cynicism began to undermine idealism and the will to resist. The united front was maintained until the end of the war, but as early as 1939 there were local clashes between KMT troops and Communist troops and afterwards there was no end to them. Before the start of the Pacific war on December 8th, 1941, China had to conduct the war more or less alone. It was this that had repeatedly bridged the internal differences of the Chinese and maintained the will to resist. But with the entry of the Allies into the war against Japan the Chinese increasingly thought that they could rely entirely on the United States to fight the war on China's behalf. In spite of the constantly worsening war situation both KMT and Communists no longer regarded resistance to the Japanese as their supreme objective—as they had at the beginning of the war. They began to think of ways of strengthening their position for the post-war period. Thus, Chiang Kai-shek kept many of his best troops back from the war against the Japanese, so that he could use them if necessary against the Communists. They, in their turn, sought to extend their influence as widely as possible behind and between the Japanese lines. The crucial difference between the two sides, however, lay in the fact that among the KMT leadership corruption and demoralization spread at an alarming rate, whereas the functionaries of the CCP, in contrast, were poor and honest and full of high ideals. The Communist troops were ill equipped, it is true, but they were well led and were characterized by an excellent fighting spirit. Consequently, the balance shifted every year, even from month to month in favour of the Communists, although it was not obvious on the surface. Chinese powers of resistance evaporated so quickly after the vigour and enthusiasm of the first years of the war that the Allies had to take great care to keep resistance alive and to prevent a separate peace treaty, which did not seem impossible, between the KMT government and Japan. The limited help which the Allies were able to put at China's disposal was always felt to be insufficient by the Chinese and there were tense moments in the relationship between China and the Allies, especially the United States. The final surrender of all rights and privileges resulting from the 'unequal treaties' by the United States, followed by England and France, was warmly welcomed as an objective of long standing, but it could hardly improve the general situation. The Americans, in fact, pointed out to the Chinese government the necessity of fundamental political and military reforms and offered to help, but with little result. Moreover, after apparent initial success, the attempt to persuade the KMT and the Communists to form a coalition government, or at least to coexist peacefully, finally failed. Ultimately the KMT had no serious intention of sharing the government with the Communists and was only prepared to negotiate because of fear of losing American goodwill and aid. The Communists were unwilling to place their own troops under a central command. The sudden capitulation of the Japanese in August, 1945, rather earlier than expected, faced the Chinese government with the problem of taking over at short notice large areas of eastern and northern China which had been occupied by the Japanese until then, together with the whole of Manchuria, and of setting up an administration and above all preventing the Communists from getting there first. The KMT régime was not adequate for such a difficult task; the role of a victor state was completely beyond it. Others had gained the victory; the whole of China was impoverished, starving, worn out and demoralized, torn by corruption and internal discord, ripe for a new stage of the revolution.

In areas that had been occupied by the Japanese—especially the main railway routes, the big cities and the seaports—the position was no better. The Japanese had established administrations favourable to themselves. The government in northern China was composed of second-rate, conservative politicians from the pre-1928 period, who were friendly towards Japan. The cult of Confucius and similar institutions from the past had been revived, and the ideas of the KMT and the revolution suppressed. In Nanking the government was organized by Wang Ching-wei and

composed of a group of old members of the KMT, who had originally belonged to the left wing but were bitter opponents of Chiang
Kai-shek and had left Chungking secretly to co-operate with the
Japanese. These administrations had little freedom of action and
little authority. The real rulers were the Japanese occupation
authorities, who despite all their efforts showed little skill in
winning over the Chinese to their objective of a 'Greater East
Asia' under Japanese leadership. Their propaganda about the
liberation of East Asia from the yoke of Western imperialism and
their publicly degrading treatment of Europeans and Americans
resident in China in front of the Chinese aroused little response. It
was not until several years later, when the Chinese Communists
acted similarly and used similar slogans against Westerners in
China, that the Japanese seed bore fruit. During the war the
Chinese noticed only that Western imperialism had been sup-
planted by brutal Japanese imperialism, which affected the
individual much more; and their sympathy lay largely with the West
that was allied to free China. Inflation and deprivation, the
arbitrary rule of the Japanese occupation forces and their Chinese
collaborators, corruption and embezzlement, produced progressive
demoralization in occupied China. The people waited longingly for
the day when they would be free from the Japanese oppressor.
Even if some reports of the sorry conditions in free China trickled
through, people put their faith in Chiang Kai-shek and the KMT
government to liberate them and had a correspondingly idealized
picture of them. Their consequent disillusionment was all the more
bitter, and this helped the Communists in their rapid climb. The
Japanese, by their short-sighted politics of violence against China,
brought about exactly the opposite of what they were aiming for.
Not only did they suffer a devastating defeat and have to resign
all claims to leadership in East Asia but they made a decisive
contribution to the collapse of the conservative KMT régime,
which probably could have been brought to co-operate with them
on reasonable terms. Hence they prepared the way for the real
unification of China under the powerful Communist government—
a development which was diametrically opposed to Japanese
intentions. An alliance of East Asian states is now conceivable
only under Chinese, not Japanese, leadership.

THE COMMUNIST VICTORY

The Extension of Communist Power

The existence of the united Chinese front against Japan and the subsequent war gave the Communists the opportunity to extend their influence on an unsuspected scale. The line followed by the CCP a of national bourgeois–democratic revolution taking account of China's special situation, as expressed in Mao Tse-tung's well-known writings *On the New Democracy* (1940) and *On Coalition Government* (1945), did away with the picture of extreme radicalism, which had been quite frightening to many people. Moderation in the social revolution, emphasis on readiness to co-operate with non-Communist groups and the idea of a national fight for freedom against the Japanese above all other aims attracted the best and most idealistic elements, especially among young people, to the Communist side. The stream of those who, disappointed or despairing of China's recovery, were leaving the areas ruled by the KMT or occupied by the Japanese for Yenan, the seat of the CCP leadership, or other centres of Communist resistance known as the 'Liberated Areas', in order to be able to support the national cause against Japan, continued to grow.

During the war years 1937–45 the membership of the CCP increased thirty-fold, from about 40,000 to 1,200,000. During the same period the number of regular Communist troops rose from 80,000 to 910,000—now called the 8th Route Army or the New 4th Army, no longer the 'Red Army'. The expanding area that came under Communist rule as the war continued was spread over the whole of the North and eastern China; most of it was behind Japanese lines, and it stretched as far as the gates of Peking, Tientsin, Nanking, Shanghai and other big cities. Because the railway lines and other routes of communication were under Japanese control the 'Liberated Areas' were divided into numerous segments that were mostly not directly connected with each other; methods of communication were extremely primitive. The normal way was by horse or donkey or simply on foot. Moreover, large parts of the 'Liberated Areas' were constantly threatened by the Japanese. In accordance with united front policies, the practice of establishing soviet districts was abandoned and only the National Government in Chungking was formally recognized as such. Thus, throughout the war there was no central government or administration for the 'Liberated Areas', but simply a number of higher and lower administrative bodies. The task of bringing the different areas together fell to the CCP, which since the beginning of the war had attracted the most heterogeneous elements. The numerous new Party members were mostly peasants; in addition there was quite a large number of intellectuals, but only a very few workers. During the rough and difficult war years the Communists in the 'Liberated Areas' established their material and ideological basis, so that afterwards they could rapidly and triumphantly unite the whole of China under their rule. A decisive feature of this was their widespread abstention from radical measures in the country areas. Often they left the question of land ownership untouched, simply reduced the rent, and put a stop to usury and similar local abuses. Apart from this they tried to support the peasants with advice and practical help in their most pressing, direct needs. In this way they were able to ensure the sympathy and active support of the rural population everywhere, which was indispensable in enabling them to apply guerrilla tactics successfully. 'The people are the water, the soldiers of the Eighth Route Army are the fish—the fish cannot live without water.' These words of a Communist commander describe the situation very aptly. In contrast to the luxuriant, rampant corruption and decadence affecting the areas ruled by the Japanese and the areas controlled by the KMT, there grew up in the 'Liberated Areas' a spirit of idealism, comradeship and self-sacrifice, which actually impressed every outsider who came into contact with it— even if he did not share the ideological presuppositions. In order to enforce a uniform manner of thinking and acting among Party members, who were the backbone of the 'Liberated Areas', Mao Tse-tung started his famous campaign to 'correct [unorthodox] tendencies', which was known as the *Cheng-feng* movement. Although this movement has been marked by self-criticism and confessions of guilt by leading Party members, in the course of which Ch'en Shao-yü (see above p. 169), a theoretician who was educated in Moscow, and his circle have been demoted from leading positions in favour of those with practical experience of the Chinese revolution, this was not actually a purge but an intensive indoctrination and education in the principles of Marxism–Leninism as interpreted by Mao Tse-tung. These principles, officially called 'The Thoughts of Mao Tse-tung', are 'a conglomerate of orthodox Stalinist tenets, but with a special point of emphasis. The use of Russian methods of organization and thought stamps Maoism as an import. But the adaptation of these methods to Chinese pro- blems—and the publication of an ideological handbook in Chinese written by Chinese—identifies Maoism as a Chinese possession. The Chinese Communists can interpret their own revolutionary pro- blems.'[1] The themes of the contributions to this ideological hand- book indicate its contents; for example, 'Correcting unorthodox tendencies in learning, the Party, and literature and art', 'Opposing party formalism', 'The Reform of our studies' by Mao Tse-tung, 'On the intra-Party struggle' by Liu Shao-ch'i etc. In this way the CCP was ideologically prepared for the coming conflict with the KMT. Russian help was limited to the ideological field. Chinese Communists at this time could not expect practical support from Russia. There is good evidence that Stalin did not take Mao Tse-tung and his Communism seriously at all.

The Collapse of the KMT

At the end of the war the relationship between the KMT and the CCP was extremely tense, despite American attempts at mediation. The resignation of Chiang Kai-shek at the height of his fame after the war might perhaps have made a settlement possible and created a climate of co-operation between Communists, the liberal wing of the KMT and other groups, and China could have been spared four more years of war. In any case Chiang Kai-shek would have retained throughout China the reputation and fame of having been commander-in-chief in the victorious war against Japan, and even the Communists could not have taken this from him. Chiang, however, was surrounded by a group of ambitious and avaricious Whampoa officers and reactionary KMT politicians, who had his complete confidence and succeeded in keeping from him all unwel- come news, so that in the years before the collapse of the KMT he may not have been accurately informed of the actual situation.

1. *Mao's China. Party Reform Documents, 1942–1944,* translation and introduction by Boyd Compton, Seattle, 1952, p. XLIV.

The KMT government tried to counteract the growing dissatisfaction by means of terrorist measures, directed not only against Communist activity but also against liberal and critical intellectuals. A particularly notorious case which lost the KMT government considerable sympathy not only in Chinese circles but also in the USA was the murder of the liberal Professor of Chinese Literary History, Wen I-to, in Kunming, which in spite of all official denials was attributed to the secret service of the KMT. As a result more and more intellectuals revolted inwardly against the KMT government and among young people at school and students the Communist underground movement grew stronger each day. The economic situation also contributed to the ease with which they turned to the Communist ideology. As a result of the disorders of the war many of those who nominally still owned land had been without land for ten or more years and had more or less written it off. This was particularly true of the younger generation, whose recollection of an economically secure, carefree existence of landownership and leasehold rents only extended to their earliest years, if at all. Consequently, the Communists and the revolutionary movement as a whole found a great part of their most enthusiastic champions and leaders among the former gentry, particularly among those who knew of their leased property almost only from hearsay, who no longer had any personal contact with it and who in practice had little or no property to lose.

Reference has already been made to the fact that at the end of the war in August, 1945, the government in Chungking was faced with the task of taking over from the Japanese extensive areas from northern Manchuria to Hainan in the South, and from Paotow in western Inner Mongolia to Formosa in the East. The government had to ensure their military security, disarm the Japanese and establish its own administration. The nearest government troops were often hundreds, sometimes thousands, of miles away from many of the places that were to be taken over; the lines of communication were broken and the intervening country occupied by the Communist forces, which refused to let any other troops through. The Communists claimed that the Japanese bases enclosed by the 'Liberated Areas' should be taken over by them. But the armistice conditions laid down that the Japanese should

13+C.C.R.

hand over the places they occupied to units appointed by the central government and they were responsible for law and order until such time. Hence, in many places, as, for example, in Peking, there was the absurd situation that a month after their capitulation Japanese soldiers were maintaining their positions fully armed and—so it was said at the time—'the defeated had to protect the victors from themselves'. Although a few small units of troops went over to the Communists, on the whole the Japanese undertook this thankless task with remarkable discipline. Never before had they and the Chinese officials whom they had appointed in the Japanese occupied areas co-operated so smoothly as in the days between capitulating and handing over. But the loyalty of the Japanese to the government of Chiang Kai-shek and the help given by the Americans was insufficient to establish his rule throughout northern China, let alone Manchuria. American aeroplanes transported Chinese troops from western China to the East and North to occupy important key positions. Many key places—such as Peking, Tientsin, Tsingtao—were even occupied by American troops in agreement with the Chinese government, in order to disarm the Japanese and repatriate them. Americans and Chinese Communists managed to avoid clashing; but there were frequent conflicts between the KMT and Communist troops and civil war on a grand scale seemed imminent. The United States government, therefore, at the end of 1945 decided to make a final energetic bid to establish peace, and with this in mind sent General Marshall, who had earned a high reputation as Chief of Staff, with special powers to China. After initial successes, however, all his efforts finally came to nothing because of the insuperable distrust and dislike separating the Communists and the KMT and because of the unwillingness of the radical elements on both sides to come to an understanding. In KMT circles it was thought that the Communists could be defeated in less than a year. Marshall warned Chiang Kai-shek against overestimating his power and gave him to understand that he would not be able to defeat the Communists by military measures. But the warning was unheeded. Even increased American aid could not preserve the KMT. American war material fell largely into the hands of the Communists because of treason and proved useful to the Communists rather than the KMT. In January, 1947, Marshall and the last American troops left China. Then, after a short pause in which both sides redeployed their forces, the final decisive phase of the struggle began.

The important key positions in Manchuria and northern China which were held by the KMT troops were increasingly isolated by the destruction of the railway lines, until finally they became islands which could only be reached by air. The military strength of the KMT, which had been many times superior to that of the Communists at the end of the war, decreased in same degree as that of the Communists increased. Losses from casualties, injuries and desertions decimated the ranks of the KMT forces. The strength of the Communists was multiplied by the incorporation of Chinese troops who had formerly co-operated with the Japanese in the occupied areas, of deserted KMT units and of new recruits. American war supplies, captured or even bought from the KMT, and former Japanese supplies, to which the Russians fed into the hands of the Communists when they withdrew from Manchuria, gave the Communists the armaments they needed for large-scale military action.

The military leadership of the KMT failed completely. Excellent, reliable commanders, who did not belong to the Whampoa clique, were given practically useless posts, while the Whampoa clique 'considering that it had won the war, was engaged in dividing the spoils'.[1]

In the Japanese occupied areas the population had no particular sympathy for the Communists at first and they welcomed the KMT troops enthusiastically as liberators from foreign occupation. This enthusiasm quickly cooled when people became aware of the general behaviour of the military and civil personnel appointed by the government to take over. The military leaders of the Whampoa clique set the example that was followed by those below them. Each one sought to acquire for himself as much property as possible, whether from the Japanese or from the Chinese authorities whom they had appointed or from actual or alleged Chinese collaborators, and even from foreigners quite irresponsibly and

1. F. F. Liu, *A Military History of Modern China: 1924–1949* (Princeton, 1956), p. 244.

without regard for the original Chinese owners. The population of the occupied areas saw to their surprise that their fellow country-men whom they had welcomed as liberators were on the whole just as corrupt and selfish and irresponsible as the administration appointed under Japanese rule. Conditions of life were no better, inflation advanced even more quickly than before, real law and order and the longed-for peace did not return. Disappointment and resentment at the complete failure of the KMT government became more and more widespread throughout China; general sympathy turned more and more to the Communists, not because their programme or theories were found to be better than those of the KMT, but because people saw in them a dynamic, healthy, uncorrupted force, that alone was capable of replacing the rotten, impotent régime of the KMT. The traditional idea of the concept of *Ko-ming* (see above p. 1), regarding the change of the heavenly mandate, also played a part in this. The KMT had forfeited its mandate; it had passed to the Communists. The Communist take-over was not essentially different from similar situations in the past, such as the overthrow of Mongol rule and the founding of the Ming dynasty (see above pp. 12ff). The revolutionary movement that stemmed from peasant revolts and was led by peasant leaders gradually gained in power and size with the help of the rural population and a growing number of intellectuals. The growth was slow at first, but increased rapidly later, until finally with the last big onslaught the weakened, hollow régime, despite its outward superior military strength, collapsed like a house of cards. Just as peasant movements and secret religious societies had often con-verged (see above p. 11) in the past, so now peasant unrest and Communism joined hands. The fact that superstitious belief in spirits, supernatural powers and supernatural revelations was replaced by superstitious belief in a utopian ideal made no essential difference. The fanaticism was the same, although it was inspired by religious doctrine in the one case and socio-economic doctrine in the other. In both cases there was a conviction that a new order was dawning.

In the last phase of the struggle the Communist armies, without any foreign help worth mentioning, marched nearly two thousand miles on foot within the space of a year, from November, 1948, to

November, 1949—a significant achievement in itself and one that made possible the complete collapse of the KMT and its leadership —in a unique triumphal march from Mukden to Canton and to Chengtu. The Japanese armaments that were relayed to the Communists in Manchuria by the Russians obviously helped them, but did not decisively influence the outcome of the struggle between the KMT and the Communists, as Chiang Kai-shek and his entourage later wished to make out.

The Communist Rule

The Communists took over in a very orderly manner everywhere. Their troops, in contrast to those of the KMT, were extremely well disciplined. The population had no need to fear for their lives or their property, and women and girls had nothing to fear from the Communist soldiers. The soldiers took nothing without paying for it. Peace and order soon returned everywhere. All privately and publicly owned industries were instructed to resume work. The Communists were reluctant and very cautious about intervening. Railway lines and other routes of communication were quickly repaired. In accordance with approved Chinese tradition the civil authority resumed its leading position, and military rule which had played such a fatal role since 1911 came to an end. There was peace at last and the tormented population was able to breathe again once more, before the decisive measures of the social revolution gradually followed. It is outside the scope of this book, however, to describe the events which followed.

After China proper had been pacified the outer regions of Sinkiang and Tibet, which had been largely independent of the KMT government, were firmly linked with the central government once more. Outer Mongolia, whose independence had been recognized by the KMT when the war ended, was the only territory the Communists had to surrender, for the sake of friendship with Russia. The return of the capital from Nanking to Peking revived the prominent position northern China had occupied since the beginning of the 15th century. It also indicated that the government felt strong enough to oppose any foreign influences that might threaten northern China. In 1955 the Russians withdrew from their last bases, Port Arthur and Dairen.

Reference has already been made to the fact that China gained recognition of her equal status in 1943 without any interference from the Communists. There was, of course, a certain amount of dependence on the USA in foreign and economic policy; in this China was no different from the great European powers. But the overbearing manner that had been displayed by foreigners to the Chinese still survived to some extent. Many foreigners continued to regard Chinese people as colonial natives who were beneath them and they behaved like colonial lords of fifty years before. Although all privileges that originated in the 'unequal treaties' had ceased, former humiliations were not forgotten and the behaviour of foreigners did not make it easy to forget them. Immediately after the war the KMT had occasionally practised some petty chicanery against foreigners in the way they had learnt from the Japanese. Now Communist slogans about the fight against imperialism fell on willing ears. Doors already open were, so to speak, smashed open again and those customary rights of foreigners in China that still existed were abolished once for all. The individual foreigner was now made to pay for the injustice that had been inflicted on China by the foreign powers in the previous century. Formerly foreigners had stood above the law. Now they were made to feel on every possible occasion that they were at best tolerated, but possessed no rights of any kind; they were, in fact, subjects of an inferior legal status in comparison with Chinese or citizens of other Asian nations. In the period since 1949 almost all Westerners who were resident in China have left, either voluntarily or under compulsion. The Communists have set themselves the task of transforming the old China, which they have described as semi-feudalistic and semi-colonial, into a modern socialist state, and they work for this end with great dedication. The social revolution that was now carried out was the beginning of the last stage of the revolutionary development of the preceding hundred years. Seen from the viewpoint of Chinese history as a whole, 1911 may represent a decisive point in that it marks the end of an epoch, in which Confucianism had been the controlling influence. Whether the Communist seizure of power in 1949 will achieve similar importance as the beginning of a new epoch, only the future will tell.

Select Bibliography

GENERAL

1. *Asia rekishi jiten*, 10 vols., Tōkyō, Heibonsha 1959–1962.
2. Balazs, E.: 'Tradition and Revolution in China', *Chinese Civilization and Bureaucracy*, New Haven and London 1964, pp. 150–170.
3. De Bary, Wm. Theodore: *Sources of Chinese Tradition*, New York 1960 (Chaps. XX–XXV).
4. Fairbank, J. K.: *The United States and China* (New ed.), Oxford and Cambridge, Mass. 1958.
5. Fairbank–Liu: *Modern China. A Bibliographical Guide to Chinese Works 1898–1937*, Cambridge, Mass. 1950.
6. Fairbank–Banno: *Japanese Studies of Modern China. A Bibliographical Guide to Historical and Social-Science Research on the 19th and 20th Centuries*, Rutland, Vermont 1955.
7. Fairbank, J. K., Edwin O. Reischauer, and Albert M. Craig: *East Asia: The Modern Transformation*, Cambridge, Mass. 1965.
8. Feuerwerker, Albert: *Modern China*, Englewood Cliffs, N.J. 1964.
9. Hu Hua: *Chung-kuo hsin-min-chu chu-i ko-ming shih*, Peking 1950.
10. Hua Kang: *Chung-kuo min-tsu chieh-fang yün-tung shih*, Peking 1951.
11. Levenson, Joseph R.: *Confucian China and its Modern Fate*, 3 vols., London, Berkeley and Los Angeles, Calif. 1958–1965.
12. Li Chien-nung: *The Political History of China 1840–1928*. Translated and edited by Ssu-yu Teng and Jeremy Ingalls, Princeton, New Jersey and Oxford 1956.
13. Teng–Fairbank: *China's Response to the West, a documentary survey 1839–1923*, Cambridge, Mass. 1954.

CHAPTER 1: GENERAL

14. Eberhard, Wolfram: *A History of China*, Rev. Ed., London and Berkeley 1960.

15. Franke, Otto: *Geschichte des Chinesischen Reiches*, 5 vols., Berlin 1930–1952.
16. Legge, James: *The Chinese Classics*, 8 vols., Hongkong 1861–1872 (Reprint Hongkong 1961).
17. Reischauer, Edwin B. and John K. Fairbank: *East Asia: The Great Tradition*, Boston 1960.

The Idea of Revolution in the Past

18. Franke, Otto: 'Der chinesische Staatsgedanke und seine Bedeutung für die abendländisch-chinesischen Beziehungen', *Ostasiatische Neubildungen*, Hamburg 1911, pp. 1–19.
19. Ojima, Y.: 'Confucianism and Revolutionary Ideas', *Shinagaku* II, Kyōto 1921, pp. 198–210 and 271–280 (in Japanese).

The Course of Revolutions in the Past

20. Balazs, E.: 'Landownership in China from the fourth to the fourteenth Century', *Chinese Civilization and Bureaucracy*, New Haven and London 1964, pp. 113–125.
21. Chang Chung-li: *The Chinese Gentry. Studies on their Role in Nineteenth-century Chinese Society*, Seattle, Washington 1955.
22. De Groot, J. J. M.: *Sectarianism and Religious Persecution in China*, 2 vols., Amsterdam 1903/04.
23. Eberhard, Wolfram: *Conquerors and Rulers. Social Forces in Medieval China*, Leiden 1952 (2nd ed. 1965).
24. Shih, Vincent Y. C.: 'Some Chinese Rebel Ideologies', *T'oung Pao* 44, Leiden 1956, pp. 150–226.
25. *Shui-hu Chuan*. English translations by J. H. Jackson, *Water Margin*, 2 vols., Shanghai 1937 (and reprints) and Pearl S. Buck, *All Men are Brothers*, London 1933 and New York 1957.

The Founding of the Ming Dynasty

26. Franke, Wolfgang: 'Neuere chinesische Arbeiten zur Geschichte der frühen Ming-Zeit', *Asiatica, Festschrift Friedrich Weller*, Leipzig 1954, pp. 131–141.
27. Taylor, Romeyn: 'Social Origins of the Ming Dynasty 1351–1360', *Monumenta Serica* 22, 1963, pp. 1–78.

CHAPTER 2: GENERAL

28. Fan Wen-lan: *Chung-kuo chin-tai shih*, Peking 1953. German translation: *Neue Geschichte Chinas*, Bd. 1 (1840–1901), Berlin 1959.
29. Hummel, Arthur W. (ed.): *Eminent Chinese of the Ch'ing Period (1644–1912)*, 2 vols., Washington, D.C., 1943.
30. Powell, Ralph L.: *The Rise of Chinese Military Power 1895–1912*, Princeton, New Jersey 1955.

The Taiping Revolution

31. Boardman, Eugene P.: *Christian Influence upon the Ideology of the T'ai-p'ing Rebellion, 1851–1864*, Madison, Wisc., 1952.
32. Chiang Siang-tseh: *The Nien Rebellion*, Seattle, Wash. 1954.
33. Hail, W. J.: *Tseng Kuo-fan and the Tai Ping Rebellion*, New Haven 1927.
34. Meadows, T. T. : *The Chinese and Their Rebellions*, London 1856 (Reprint Stanford 1953).
35. Michael, Franz: *The Taiping Rebellion:* Vol. I, *The History*, Seattle, Wash. 1965.
36. Shih, Vincent Y. C., *The Taiping Ideology: Its Source, Interpretation and Influences*, Seattle, Wash. 1967.
37. Schlegel, G.: *Thian Ti Hwui, the Hung League or Heaven-Earth-League*, Batavia 1866.
38. Teng Ssu-yu, *Historiography of the Taiping Rebellion*, Cambridge, Mass. 1962.
39. Teng Ssu-yu, *The Nien Army and their Guerilla Warfare*, The Hague 1961.
40. Torr, Dona: *Marx on China: Articles from the New York Daily Tribune, 1853–1860*, London 1951.
41. Wright, Mary C.: *The Last Stand of Chinese Conservatism. The T'ung-Chih Restoration, 1862–1874*, Stanford 1957.
42. Yap, P. M.: 'The Mental Illness of Hung Hsiu-ch'üan, Leader of the Taiping Rebellion', *Far Eastern Quarterly* 13, 1954, pp. 287–304.

The Reform Movement

43. Cameron, M. E.: *The Reform Movement in China, 1898–1912*, Stanford 1931.
44. Fairbank, John K.: *Trade and Diplomacy on the China Coast: The Opening of the Treaty Ports, 1842–1854*, 2 vols., Cambridge, Mass. 1953.
45. Fairbank, John K. (ed.): *The Chinese World Order*, Cambridge, Mass. and Oxford 1969.
46. Fitzgerald, C. P.: *The Chinese View of their Place in the World*, London 1964 and Oxford 1969.
47. Franke, Otto: *Ostasiatische Neubildungen. Beiträge zum Verständnis der politischen und kulturellen Entwicklungsvorgänge im Fernen Osten*, Hamburg 1911.
48. Franke, Wolfgang: *China and the West*, Oxford 1967.
49. Hsiao Kung-ch'üan: 'Weng T'ung-ho and the Reform Movement of 1898', *Tsing Hua Journal of Chinese Studies*, I, 1957, pp. 111–243.
50. Hsiao Kung-ch'üan: 'K'ang Yu-wei and Confucianism', *Monumenta Serica*, 18, 1959, pp. 96–212.

13*

51. Hsiao Kung-ch'üan: 'The philosophical thought of K'ang Yu-wei: an attempt at a new synthesis', *Monumenta Serica*, 21, 1962, pp. 129–193.

52. Langer, William: *The Diplomacy of Imperialism 1890–1902*, New York 1935, 2nd ed. 1960.

53. Lo Jung-pang: *K'ang Yu-wei. A Biography and a Symposium*, Tuscon, Arizona 1967.

54. Morse, H. B.: *The International Relations of the Chinese Empire*, 3 vols., Shanghai 1910–1918.

55. Oka Takahashi: 'The Philosophy of T'an Ssu-t'ung', *Papers on China* (vol. 9) from the East Asia Regional Studies Seminar, Harvard University 1955, pp. 1–47.

56. Schwartz, Benjamin: *In Search of Wealth and Power: Yen Fu and the West*, Cambridge, Mass. 1964.

The Boxer Uprising

57. Bland–Backhouse: *China under the Empress Dowager, Being the History of the Life and Times of Tz'u Hsi. Compiled from the State Papers and the Private Diary of the Comptroller of her Household*, London 1910, 3rd ed. Peking 1939.

58. Duyvendak, J. J. L.: 'The Diary of his Excellency Ching-shan being a Chinese Account of the Boxer Troubles', *Acta Orientalia* III, Leiden 1924.

59. Duyvendak, J. J. L.: 'Ching-shan's Diary—a Mystification', *T'oung Pao* 33, Leiden 1937, pp. 268–294.

60. Lewisohn, William: "Some Critical Notes on the so-called 'Diary of His Excellency Ching-shan'", *Monumenta Serica* 2, Peking 1936/37, pp. 191–202.

61. Purcell, Victor: *The Boxer Uprising: A Background Study*, Cambridge 1963.

62. Steiger, George N.: *China and the Occident: The Origin and Development of the Boxer Movement*, New Haven 1927.

63. Tan, Chester C.: *The Boxer Catastrophe*, New York 1955. Further: Nos. 28, 52, 54.

CHAPTER 3: GENERAL

64. Clubb, O. Edmund: *Twentieth Century China*, New York–London 1964.

65. Latourette, Kenneth Scott, *A History of Modern China*, London 1954.

66. Wright, Mary C. (ed.): *China in Revolution: The First Phase, 1900–1913*, New Haven and London 1968.

The Revolutionary Movement
67. Chen, Stephen and Robert Payne: *Sun Yat-sen, a Portrait*, New York 1934.
68. Favre, B.: *Les sociétés secrètes en Chine. Origine—rôle historique—situation actuelle*, Paris 1933.
69. Franke, Otto: 'Japans Asiatische Bestrebungen', *Ostasiatische Neubildungen*, Hamburg 1911, pp. 136–157.
70. Hsueh Chün-tu: *Huang Hsing and the Chinese Revolution*, Stanford 1961.
71. Jansen, Marius B.: *The Japanese and Sun Yat-sen*, Cambridge, Mass. 1954.
72. Linebarger, P.: *The Political Doctrines of Sun Yat-sen*, Baltimore 1937, 3rd printing 1963.
73. Linebarger, P.: *Sun Yat-sen and the Chinese Republic*, New York 1925.
74. Schiffrin, Harold Z.: *Sun Yat-sen and the Origins of the Chinese Revolution*, Berkeley, Calif. 1968.
75. Sharman, Lyon: *Sun Yat-sen. His Life and Its Meaning*, New York 1934; reprinted Hamden, Conn. 1965; Stanford, Calif. 1968.

The Outbreak of the Revolution
76. Ch'en, Jerome: *Yuan Shih-k'ai, 1859–1916*, London 1961.
77. Franke, Wolfgang: *The Reform and Abolition of the Traditional Chinese Examination System*, Cambridge, Mass. 1960.
78. E-tu Zen Sun: *Chinese Railways and British Interests, 1898–1911*, New York 1954.
79. Ichiko Chūzō: 'The Railway Protection Movement in Szechuan in 1911', *Memoirs of the Research Department of the Toyo Bunko* No. 14, Tōkyō 1955, pp. 47–69.
80. Maybon, Albert: *Le République Chinoise*, Paris 1914.
81. Teng, Ssu-yü: 'Chinese Influence on the Western Examination System', *Harvard Journal of Asiatic Studies* 7, 1943, pp. 267–312.
Further: Nos. 21, 67, 71, 72, 73, 75.

The Beginning of the Republic
82. Boorman, Howard L. (ed.): *Biographical Dictionary of Republican China*, 5 vols., New York 1967–
83. Ch'ien Tuan-sheng: *The Government and Politics of China*, Cambridge, Mass. 1950.
84. *China Year Book*, ed. by H. G. W. Woodhead, 20 vols., New York, Tientsin, Shanghai 1912–1939.
95. Putnam Weale, B. L.: *The Fight for the Republic in China*, London 1918.
Further: Nos. 76, 80.

CHAPTER 4: GENERAL

86. Chow Tse-tsung: *The May Fourth Movement: Intellectual Revolution in Modern China*, 2 vols., Cambridge, Mass. 1960–1963.

Political Development to 1919

87. Duyvendak, J. J. L.: 'De laatste dienaar der Mandsjoes', *China tegen de Westerkim*, Haarlem 1927, pp. 145–222.
88. Fifield, Russel H.: *Woodrow Wilson and the Far East: The Diplomacy of the Shantung Question*, New York 1952.
89. Li Tien-yi, *Woodrow Wilson's China Policy, 1913–1917*, New York 1952.
90. King Wunsz: *Woodrow Wilson, Wellington Koo and the China Question at the Paris Peace Conference*, Leiden 1959.
    Further: Nos. 71, 76.

Background to the May 4th Movement

91. Levy, Marion J.: *The Family Revolution in Modern China*, Cambridge, Mass. 1949.
92. Mao Tse-tung, *Selected Works of Mao Tse-tung*, 4 vols., Peking 1965.

Intellectual Background of the May 4th Movement

93. Brière, O.: *Fifty Years of Chinese Philosophy, 1898–1950*, London 1956.
94. De Francis, John: *Nationalism and Language Reform in China*, Princeton 1950.
95. Doré, H.: 'Le Confucéisme sous la République 1911–1922', *New China Review* 4, 1922, pp. 298–319.
96. Hsia, C. T.: *A History of Modern Chinese Fiction 1917–1957*, New Haven 1961.
97. Hsiao, K. C.: 'Li Chih, An Iconoclast of the Sixteenth Century', *T'ien Hsia Monthly*, 6, Shanghai 1938, pp. 317–341.
98. Hu Shih, *The Chinese Renaissance*, Chicago 1934, reprint 1964.
99. Huang Sung-k'ang, *Lu Hsün and the New Culture Movement of Modern China*, Amsterdam 1957.
100. Kiang, Wen-han, *The Ideological Background of the Chinese Student Movement*, New York 1948.
101. Kwok, D. Y., *Scientism in Chinese Thought 1900–1950*, New Haven 1965.
102. Löwenthal, Rudolf: *The Religious Periodical Press in China*, Peking 1940.
103. Průšek, Jaroslav (ed.): *Studies in Modern Chinese Literature*, Berlin (East) 1964.

104. Schwartz, Benjamin, *Chinese Communism and the Rise of Mao*, Cambridge, Mass. and Oxford 1951; new edition (paperback) London 1967.
105. Schwartz, Benjamin: 'Ch'en Tu-hsiu and the Acceptance of the Modern West', *Journal of the History of Ideas* 12, 1, 1951, pp. 61–72.

Marxism and Leninism
106. Huang Sung-k'ang, *Li Ta-chao and the Impact of Marxism on Modern Chinese Thinking*, The Hague 1965.
107. Meisner, Maurice, *Li Ta-chao and the Origins of Chinese Marxism*, Cambridge, Mass. and Oxford 1967.
108. Wilbur-How, *Documents on Communism, Nationalism, and Soviet Advisers in China 1918–1927, Papers Seized in the 1927 Peking Raid*, New York 1956.
     Further: Nos. 104, 105.

CHAPTER 5: GENERAL
109. Brandt–Schwartz–Fairbank: *A Documentary History of Chinese Communism*, Cambridge, Mass. and London 1952.
110. Brandt, Conrad, *Stalin's Failure in China 1924–1927*, Cambridge, Mass. and Oxford 1958.
111. Chesneaux, Jean, *The Chinese Labor Movement 1919–1927*, Stanford and Oxford 1968.
112. Ho Kan-chih, *A History of the Modern Chinese Revolution*, Peking 1959.
113. Payne, Robert, *Mao Tse-tung. Ruler of Red China*. New York 1950.
114. Roy, Manabendra Nath: *Revolution and Counterrevolution in China*, Calcutta 1946.
115. Snow, Edgard: *Red Star over China*, New York 1938; revised edition London 1969.
     Further: Nos. 64, 65, 67, 72, 73, 75, 82, 84, 104, 108.

The Revision of Sun Yat-Sen's Teaching
116. D'Elia, Pascal M.: *Le Triple Démisme de Suen Wen*, Shanghai 1930.
117. K'ang Yu-wei: *Ta T'ung Shu. The One World Philosophy of K'ang Yu-wei*. Translated by Laurence G. Thompson, London 1957.
118. Price, Frank W.: *San Min Chu I*, Shanghai 1927 and 1943.
119. Sun Yat-sen: *The International Development of China*, New York and London 1922.

Cooperation with the Communists
120. Eudin, Xenia J. and Robert C. North: *Soviet Russia and the East, 1920–1927*, Stanford 1957.

121. Liu, F. F.: *A Military History of Modern China, 1924–1949*, Princeton 1956.
122. North, Robert, *Moscow and the Chinese Communists*, Stanford and Oxford 1953, 2nd ed. 1963.
123. Whiting, Allen S.: *Soviet Policies in China, 1917–1924*, New York 1954; new ed. (hard and paperback), Stanford and Oxford 1968.

The Peasant Movement
124. Buck, John L.: *Chinese Farm Economy*, Chicago 1930.
125. Buck, John L.: *Land Utilization in China*, 3 vols., Chicago 1938.

The Split between the KMT and the CCP
126. Isaacs, Harold R.: *The Tragedy of the Chinese Revolution*, London 1938, rev. ed. Stanford 1951.
127. Latourette, K. S.: *A History of Christian Missions in China*, New York 1929.
128. North, Robert, and Xenia J. Eudin: *M. N. Roy's Mission to China: The Communist-Kuomintang Split of 1927*, Berkeley 1963.
129. Sheridan, James E.: *Chinese Warlord. The Career of Feng Yü-hsiang*, Stanford and Oxford 1966.
130. Tong, Hollington K.: *Chiang Kai-shek. Soldier and Statesman*, 2 vols., Shanghai 1937.
131. Tschang, H. H.: *Chiang Kai-shek. Asia's Man of Destiny*, 1943. Further: Nos. 48, 86.

CHAPTER 6: GENERAL
See: Nos. 64, 65, 82, 84, 112, 121.

The Unfinished Revolution
132. Chiang Kai-shek: *China's Destiny. Chinese Economic Theory.* With Notes and Commentary by Philip Jaffe, New York 1947.
133. Hsia Tsi-an: *Enigma of the Five Martyrs. A Study of the Leftist Literary Movement in Modern China*, Berkeley 1962.
134. Kirby E. Stuart: *Introduction to the Economic History of China*, London 1954.
135. Lang, Olga: *Pa Chin and His Writings*, Cambridge, Mass. and Oxford 1968.
136. Wright, Mary: 'From Revolution to Restoration: The Transformation of Kuomintang Ideology', *Far Eastern Quarterly* 14, 4, 1955, pp. 515–532.
Further: Nos. 23, 83, 96, 99, 101, 103.

Reorganisation of the Communists

137. Ch'en, Jerome: *Mao and the Chinese Revolution*, London 1965.
138. Hsiao Tso-liang: *Power Relations within the Chinese Communist Movement 1930–1934*, 2 vols., Seattle 1961 and 1967.
139. Johnson, Chalmers A.: *Peasant Nationalism and Communist Power: the Emergence of Revolutionary China 1937–1945*, Stanford 1962.
140. Rue, John E.: *Mao Tse-tung in Opposition 1927–1935*, Stanford 1966.
141. Schram, Stuart: *The Political Thought of Mao Tse-tung*, New York 1963.
142. Shanti, Swarup: *A Study of the Chinese Communist Movement, 1927–1934*, London 1966.
     Further: 92, 109, 113, 115.

Conflict with Japan

143. Borg, Dorothy: *The United States and the Far Eastern Crisis of 1933–1938*, Cambridge, Mass. 1963.
144. Feis, Herbert: *The China Tangle: The American Effort in China from Pearl Harbor to the Marshall Mission*, Princeton 1953.
145. Feis, Herbert: *The Road to Pearl Harbor*, Princeton 1950.
146. Jones, F. C.: *Japan's New Order in East Asia: Its Rise and Fall, 1937–1945*, London 1954.
147. Soong Mayling and Chiang Kai-shek: *Sian: a coup d'état*, Shanghai 1937.
148. Tsou Tang: *America's Failure in China 1941–1950*, Chicago 1963.
149. White, Th.–Jacoby, A.: *Thunder out of China*, New York 1946.

The Communist Victory

150. Bodde, Derk: *Peking Diary, a Year of Revolution*, New York 1950.
151. Chassin, Lionel Max: *The Communist Conquest of China: A History of the Civil War 1945–1949*, Cambridge, Mass. 1965, London 1966.
152. Compton, Boyd: *Mao's China, Party Reform Documents, 1942–1944*, Seattle, Wash. 1952.
153. Fitzgerald, Charles Patrick: *Revolution in China*, New York 1952.
154. Mende, Tibor: *The Chinese Revolution*, London 1961.
155. Yen, Maria: *The Umbrella Garden*, New York 1954.
     Further: Nos. 109, 113, 144, 148.

Index